SUNDARBAN FISHERMEN IN THE WORLD HERITAGE SETTING

A Community Striving in the Mystic Mangrove Ecosystem

SUNDARBAN FISHERMEN IN THE WORLD HERITAGE SETTING

A Community Striving in the Mystic Mangrove Ecosystem

R. M. Sarkar

SERIALS PUBLICATIONS
NEW DELHI

First Published - 2009

ISBN: 978-81-8387-179-2

Published by

SERIALS PUBLICATIONS
4830/24, Prahlad Street, Ansari Road
Darya Ganj, New Delhi-110002 (India)
Phone : 23245225 Fax : 91-11-23272135
E-mail: serials@satyam.net.in

Dedicated to

The Fisherfolk of Sundarban
from whom I learnt considerable
lessons on Fish, Fishing and Fish behaviour
in the Scenario of the Mangrove Ecosystem

CONTENTS

PREFACE

In the domain of mangrove ecosystem Sundarban tops the list in global perspective so far its diversity, gorgeousness and multiple nature are concerned. The fishermen working unabated in the ecosystem from the time immemorial present variegated patterns of activities in their efforts for fishing in the turbulent rivers and estuaries flourished paramountly in the midst of the network of mangrove forest with distinctive heterogeneous species of plants. This mangrove forest is characteristically inhabited by the variegated animals in land, water as well as in the air. All these animals have got specialised biological and behavioural features which are unprecedented elsewhere. The present study tries to explore the way of life and patterns of activities of the fisherfolk together with their psycho-philosophical adjustment with the adverse eco-environmental situations. The fishing community in this region has got its specific perspective which is characterized by the direct and indirect interactions of diversified biotic and abiotic factors. The study aims at exploring the multifarious modes of adjustment of the fishermen with the ferocious animals, violent rivers, hazardous nature as well as different detrimental human elements in their struggle for existence. On a close view to the way of life of these fishermen it would be seen that they have been really struggling very hard and many a time risking their life in the domain of multifaced uncertainties. In order to highlight the practical work-based life of the fisherfolk of Sundarban there demands a long-term, laborious and riskful close-set study, failing which the very intention of research would be futile.

The interest of this sort of work instilled in me during my stay in the heart of Sundarban region as a college teacher in the sixties of the last century. I had ample opportunities at that time to get a close view of the fishermen working in the tidal rivers, and not only so, I had so many chances to talk very intimately with those personalities closely associated with the incessant work in the network of vicious Sundarban rivers for having the fish crops to maintain their livelihood. Sundarban fishermen depict a discernible picture of formation of direct and indirect linkage with the natural and supernatural worlds and they are to bank on realistic as well as unviable ways and means to adjust themselves with the many-sided horror-stricken situations coming from nature, animals, plants, human as well as supernatural forces. Thus the work of fishing in this domain of mangrove ecosystem does not require only the technological abilities and inventive genius in fishing operations but also it demands the specific modus operendi to bring down all the incidental hazards and anxieties by coordinated struggle and earnest appeal for adjustment. It is to be noted that the indigenous knowledge of the tradition-bound fishing community has been taking the principal role in their adoption of technological devices and in the moulding of their behaviour-patterns to interact with the inimical forces.

The study is absolutely based on direct field investigation and for this I had to make arrangements for associating myself with the fishing groups while they were in the rivers and estuaries, on the shores, in the fish market as well as in their sweet homes. It was required to stay in the fishing villages for a considerable period to collect information on the working patterns of the fishing villages in their operations of fishing and in performing fish trade. The working procedures and thinking patterns of the Sundarban fishing personnel are heavily oriented with the supernatural beliefs and practices without which they feel themselves utterly helpless in the ultimate instability. Collection of information in this sphere essentially requires personal and timely visit to the places of occurrences which are spread over throughout the land and water of the region. During the field survey sufficient time was provided to look into the domain of supernaturalism which was not only a time consuming affair but also a very painful job. The gold mine of Sundarban fisheries is now in a rapid declining condition due to multiple reasons causing hazardous situation in the life of the fisherfolk as a whole. All the minor details in relation to that very stand have been elaborated in the present work through the close-set views based on participant observations for a long time. There is no denying of the fact that Sundarban mangrove ecosystem has been facing the unfortunate situation of ecological unstability which are aggravated by the evil practice of indiscriminate fishing in the rivers and estuaries here. For the maintenance of the ecological balance at this endangered ecological site the working patterns of the Sundarban Biosphere Reserve (started in 1989) are promising and it is to be hoped that its direct intervention into this calamitous situation would control the injurious effect on the mangrove ecosystem and thereby the fishermen directly connected with it would be benefited to a great extent. It pledges to resist the national loss connected with fish, fishing and fisherfolk in Sundarban. All the specific measures have been adopted here, in this work, to explore the trends of problems and prospect of this world heritage site exemplified by the Sundarban mangrove ecosystem.

The book is the outcome of the direct intervention of a large number of persons in the various capacities who extended full support and conspicuous help to conduct the field work in the inaccessible spots without which it would not have been possible for me to make the mission a success. At the very outset, I owe a deep debt of gratitude to all the fishermen concerned for their full-fledged cooperation in taking me in their midst, as well as the Research Investigators working with me, in their midst during their different fishing expeditions and the other various affairs connected with the organisational spheres of the fish trade. They did not show any sort of displeasure in the long discussions with them at the cost of their valuable time. Dr. Sankar Kumar Pramanik, a veteran researcher on the fishing communities of Sundaraban, always stood by my side during the whole period of field work. He was very kind enough in providing me with the different advantages in making the in-depth rapport fishing personnel as well as in getting the safe and comfortable shelters throughout the region of study. Dr. Dipak Kumar Barapanda and Sri Prasenjit Sinha devoted themselves whole-heartedly in the work of investigation. Both of them showed requisite potentialities in making the field work successful. Prasenjit helped me a lot at the various stages of post field work analysis of data. I consider it is my sacred duty to convey my sincere thanks to all of them. During my study at Gangasagar Island Sri Umapada Panigrahi took all possible care for my working tour throughout the island and also for my accommodation in their family setting. I shall be failing in my duty if I do not acknowledge with thanks the generosity extended to me by Sri Panigrahi and his family members for my work and stay over there. I am specifically grateful to Professor Amalesh Chowdhury, the distinguished marine biologist of world-wide reputation and the architect of S.D. Marine Biological Research Institute at Sagar Island, for his inspiration and suggestion forwarded to me from time to time. I do not forget the opportunity given to me by Sri R. Deb Roy, Divisional Forest Officer of the 24 Parganas (S) District and closely attached to the Sundarban Biosphere Reserve, for getting some close-view of the coastal villages by bestcwing me the responsibility to conduct micro-studies in a few villages through the application of the method of Participatory Research Appraisal, sponsored by the Department of Forest, Govt. of West Bengal. It was a thrilling experience to spend a few nights in the villages at the extreme south point. I take this occasion to extend my heart-felt thanks to him. I am grateful to the Indian Council of Social Science Research, New Delhi, for the financial assistance given to me to conduct this research-based work. The full-fledged cooperation of this organization is thankfully acknowledged. Special thanks are due to Mr. S.K. Jha, Director, Serials Publications, a prestigious publishing organisation of New Delhi, for the specific care and attention given by him to bring out this book in such a short-time and in a nice manner. I consider my endeavour would meet a profound success if requisite interest is developed among the readers to understand the specific spirit of the fisherfolk struggling continuously in the context of Sundarban mangrove ecosystem.

Mayurakshi **R. M. Sarkar**
15, Teachers' Housing Estate
Baghajatin Park,
Kolkata-700 094

1

INTRODUCTION

I

Fishing as a means of subsistence dates back to the hoary past. Right from the prehistoric stages of culture the profession of fishing has been continuing unabated. The gathering of aquatic animals constituted one of the essential factors for subsistence during the dawn of human existence. Along with this it was extensively supplemented with the practice of hunting of animals from the land. Both the spheres of economy were inter-related and the primitive people tried to adopt those two economic activities side by side. Despite this fishing in water became more conspicuous in the life of many human communities. The extensive water resources throughout the world provided these people ample opportunities to involve themselves in fishing pursuits all through the time. As because the fishes and other aquatic animals provided them a very good support in day to day life, so many communities started devoting their full time in fishing pursuits and ultimately the people belonging to those communities became identified as fisherfolk. But it took a long time and continued efforts conditioned by inquisitive mind and close-set observations on the behaviour-patterns of the fishes.

There is no denying of the fact that the early fishers had to face numerous hurdles in catching fishes from water and, at the very outset a large number of attempts were out and out unsuccessful. But those abortive effects could not stop them to proceed. As time went on they added much knowledge and considerable experience on the nature and extent of water and the fishes living in it. The fish-water attachment was carefully observed and analysed as well as the nature of movement of various species of fishes was understood to a great extent. At the very first stage, the fishing was done, no doubt, by bare hands and, of course, with much troubles. It was supplemented by the devise of various techniques adopted through a continuous process of trial and error. Gradually the attempt for contriving technical procedures for obstructing the fishes in running in water and confined them for ultimate catching was made. As the fishing pursuits are directly dependent on the nature and extent of the surrounding ecological settings so it is required that the people practising fishing must have developed the practical idea over the natural situations of their living and work. It is due to the differences in geological standpoint and ecological settings the technological equipments and related procedural activities differ according to the different regions. Thus there is a specific need for studying the fishing communities in the various regions of the country to understand the totalistic patterns of fishing economy.

In her 6500 km. stretched coastlines India is characterized by having a large number of fishing communities practising fishing from time immemorial. The people of these communities are to tackle with diversified ecological settings and multifarious local problems and thus they have developed characteristic patterns of life and work in the domain of fishing activities. Therefore, there is a specific need to take up the study on the different fishing communities at the various ecological setting to have an all-rounded idea on the life-ways and thought-ways of the fisherfolk. It is to be mentioned, in this connection, that the fisherfolk constitute an integral part of the Indian peasantry. Thus to get a practical and fullest idea on the peasant communities in India these fisherfolk must be given due importance.

Fishing pursuits are not only integrated with a deep-based technological procedures with the practical application of native science that have been developed through thousands of years of direct experience, but also these are processed through socio-ritual perspectives of everyday life and activities of the people concerned. Looking into that aspect of the situation it is categorically understood that the economic organisation of fishing is highly influenced by integrated interactional patterns of allied non-economic aspects of life.

Human interactions with the nature especially to ecological settings are highly effective in the total fishing pursuits. Success in fishing is practically dependent on the total understanding of the nature and extent of the ecological settings and effective processes of adjustment with the unfavourable situations. The fishermen, so to speak, represent the Indian peasantry, as has been noted earlier, and naturally they possess very little or no modern scientific knowledge on the various happenings of the vast and open ecological and related environmental factors against which they have been fighting for their existence from long time past. Being forced by the circumstantial perspectives the fishermen have to contrive diversified ways for making themselves adjusted with the situational context.

India is provided with immense marine and riverine resources. The estuaries of the different perennial rivers act as natural rearing ground for delicious fishes. A large number of heterogeneous communities living along the coastline and the estuaries have taken to the occupation of fishing and, in course of time, they have developed an inclination to this profession. These communities ultimately became known as the fisherfolk. The life and philosophy of these fisherfolk are intermingled with variegated ideas, beliefs, responses towards the surroundings; their activities are seen to be oriented with multiplex attempts for adjustment with bio-environmental and ecocultural perspectives. To understand the fisherfolk at the different regions of the country it is essential to highlight their activities and life-situation in the background of the particular regional surroundings.

Fishing is an age-old caste-based activity and the fishermen community has seen to be developed from heterogeneous caste groups. In spite of the fact that the fishing is regarded as one of the prosperous occupations the fishermen are characterized by economic backwardness and in the overall social setting they are ranked very low. Though some specific attempts have already been made to highlight the different facets of life of the fisherfolk yet there is a dearth of sufficient literature on this subject to get a full picture of the situation on an all-India level. Anthropologists in India have not yet shown the deep-based interest in the fullest exposition of the horizon of life-ways and thought-ways of the fisherfolk living and working in the long-stretched coastal line of India. There is no denying of the fact that fisheries play an essential role in the Indian national economy having its integrated resource potential that is still to be properly exploited. Fisheries in India have got two specially important aspects in their contributions to the national level. These constitute substantially to the national foods supply as well as these are linked to the sphere of national income and employment.

Fishing activities are shaped according to the ecological and bioclimatic surroundings. The birth and development as well as immigration of fishes of different varieties are dependent on the geo-physical and bioclimatic perspectives, and the fishermen practising fishing in any such territory must acquaint themselves fully with the different factors acting in the formation and functioning of the ecological zone concerned, at the same time they are required to make themselves expert in coping with the different factors to achieve success in fishing. It is for this reason the life-style as well as the methodological procedures of the fisherfolk vary with the community to community and region to region. Owing to this there is an inevitable requirement to study the ways and means of fishing activities as well as the life and thought of the fisherfolk in relation to various ecological zones separately. The results of such studies should then be processed categorically for having proper all-India picture in fishing as well as on the fish workers.

The fish workers are to fight continuously with the surroundings. Working in turbulent water is not an easy task and it necessarily needs joint endeavour of a large number of persons having close-set interest and mutual understanding. Thus fishing activity is not a solitary entity, rather it indicates a broad based aggregational pattern of living to fulfil the requisite purpose of fishing in great waters. Therefore, fisherfolk everywhere are to be seen in village settings that have been developed very close to the coastlines or in the places intermingled with the network of rivers, creeks, and estuaries. Sometimes these villages are exclusively inhabited by the fisherfolk and, many a time, these people are found to live within the village settings in association with other non-fishing groups of people having indirect relation with the profession of fishing. The fishing villages, it is to be noted, have got their own tradition and philosophy which have been developed through time and space, and these very naturally differ from the thinking patterns of the agriculture-based villages. As because fishing is centred round profound technicalities, so there is a specific necessity to inflict different methodological principles of fishing together with the conduction of fishing operations in turbulent water in the minds of the different personnel engaged in fishing activities. These are brought to effect, almost exclusively, through social norms and cultural traditions. The individual family plays the important role in propagating indigenous knowledge of fish and fishing in the minds of its members. In addition to this varieties of social groups take active part in the transmission of different concepts and ideas in connection with fishing techniques as well as fish-oriented behaviour-patterns that are to be maintained strictly while going out for fishing. In order to make the positive arrangements for the formation and transmission for these principles the fishing villages work as functional units. Various institutions as well as social observances and ritualistic festivals are all engaged to highlight the fishing techniques, their socio-economic implications, resisting of the problematic situations and the nature and extent of observance of various taboos and restrictions. Therefore, in order to get an overall idea on fishing economy and its multifarious dimensions there is an inevitable need to look into the structural patterns and functional perspectives of the fishing villages.

The way of life of the fisherfolk at the different parts of the world have attracted the attention of the anthropologists and sociologists from long time past. R.E. Coker, in the year 1908, made an attempt to focus the importance of fish and fisheries in some peoples of Peru. It was followed by B. Malinowski (1918) who highlighted the patterns and perspectives of fishing among Trobiand Islanders. Then in later years, A.M. Hocart (1937) and A.R. Radcliffe–Brown (1948) made specific studies on fishing in Edystone Island and Andaman Islands respectively. Though these are the basic attempts in the study of fish-based way of life of the people concerned yet these cannot be regarded as the integrated dimensions for focusing the fishing communities through broad-based sociological principles. Some specific patterns of studies have been made by a few other scholars like C.R. Edward (1960), M.F. Lebar (1964). In the perspective of studying the fishing activities with the scientific aim of exploring the socio-cultural settings of the human communities the name of Raymond Firth is conspicuous. He made the pioneering attempt in the focusing of the integrated life-situation of a particular community in the background of fishing activities. In his book of Malayan Fishermen (1946) Firth gave a new turn in the line of evaluating the different activity-orientations and life-situations centering round fishing economy practised by a particular community. The work in question by virtue of its mode of analysis and patterns of exposition in the background of all rounded life and activities readily became a specific marker in the sphere of study on fish-based economic life-ways and thought-ways. Here the peasant economy had been studied with the importance given to the totalistic life-activities centering round fishing and fish trade. Following that specific lead a good number of scholars engaged themselves in highlighting the holistic life of the fishing communities through their painstaking direct observations and requisite processing and analysis of the total situation surrounding fishing activity–oriented life. In consequence of this, several broad-based works on the nature and extent of fishing communities in different corners of the world have been resulted in due course giving a specific shape to the effort for highlighting the fish-based economic pattern in the background of the holistic life.

The profession of fishing in any part of the world is, no doubt, a very tremendous job and the fisherfolk are to face terrific risks and responsibilities during the different phases of work in the shallow and deep waters of the rivers and the seas. The fishermen are to face a lot of adversities in their daily mode of life as "fishing for living is a vigorous, thrusting and economically risky occupation which has few virtues and the single crowning disadvantage that it is hazardous in the extreme" (Dyson, 1977: 17). But the life and activities of these fishing communities deserve special attention because of the fact that their life-function focuses a broad horizon of continuous struggle of man's inventive genius with the unfavourable ecological setting. The people seem to have given a challenge to the hazardous natural condition which very often become furious and unmanageable. The tidal waves, cyclonic storms, dangerous cross-currents and similar other factors bring calamity to the life of the fisherfolk who have made the boats and launches floating over turbulent waters of rivers and sea as their second homes. While working on the Italian Community of fishermen B. Cattarinussi came to the same conclusion as regards the everyday life of fishing communities. He observed that the "living conditions were extremely hard. The fishermen sailed on Monday morning in the rowing-boats and came back on the following Saturday or Sunday. Earning were meagre; they placed the fishermen in a condition of static poverty"

(1973:31). What attracts the work on fishing people by Cattarinussi is that he has put forward a well knit study on the social system on the Italian fishermen who are engaged in deep sea fishing as well as in lagoon fishing. H.D. Smith is to be credited in highlighting the modes of development of fisheries and fishing communities in the Shetland Islands, along stretches of Coasts on both sides of the North Atlantic. He analysed the geographical factors in the development of fishing communities. In course of this study his prime attention was focused on the patterns of historical development of the various fishing communities in the said area in the perspective of particular geographical setting favourable for fishing and fish trade (1973:8).

In the perspective of the above trends and consequences the life and work as well as continuous struggling attitudes of the fishing communities in the Sundarban region have been taken up. It is to be noted with great concern that this particular part of the country is characterized by having bountiful natural resources in fragile environmental zones representing a delicate balance between man and nature. The ecological perspective of this region is conspicuously patterned by numerous creeks and islands, deltaic estuary system, mangrove forest covering together with the diversities of wild life. The tidal rivers and estuaries are characterized by conspicuous complications which many a time cause serious natural catastrophes. Fishing in such an environmental situation has got prospects as well as problems, and these problems are multifarious and highly complicated in nature that are conditioned by diversified ecological situations. In consequence of these Sundarban region in the world famous Bengal delta presents some specific characteristics of its own and the fishing communities living and working here very naturally present the distinctive features of adjustments with the surroundings which need proper record and analysis in the broader perspective of the total Indian situation. Thus there is always an inevitable requirement to bring this ecological zone with the characteristic fishing communities under the domain of the analytical study pattern in the total situational context of the country.

Deltaic Bengal is the comparatively recent landmass developed from the accumulation of silts from the Ganga and the Brahmaputra rivers. It is the largest delta of the world. This Ganga-Brahmaputra delta is famous throughout the globe by its estuarine system with the cluster of smaller deltas, a network of rivers and having a characteristic mangrove bio-diversity along its southern region. The southern part of this delta where the world's unique mangrove forests have developed is known as Sundarban. The Sundarban delta provides a wonderful natural drainage system which allows the incoming tidal waves from the Bay of Bengal. This situation enhances the coming of the fishes from the vast sea as well as their free movements throughout the network of rivulets and estuaries. The Sundarban delta is regarded as the most fertile site for fishing. From time immemorial the indigenous inhabitants as well as the migrant groups of settlers have been engaged in fishing practices through the adoption of native methodologies. The rivers and creeks of Sundarban have tidal saline water with the flushing of sweet water constitute an unique ecological niche for a rapid and large scale fish propagation. But these unique resources for fishing have never been utilized properly and still today most of the resources could not be brought under the active programme of utilization. There are 4,04,700 hectares of estuaries in the Gangetic delta but out of which only 20,000 hectares have been utilized for fisheries.

The fishermen in Sundarban delta belong to different scheduled caste groups. Most of these caste groups were originally connected with non-fishing professions and they had no inclination to fishing activities. The history of Sundarban reveals that the heterogeneous caste groups like Bagdi, Tiyor, Malos, Jele Kaibartas, Mahishyas etc. are all outsiders. In the remote past they immigrated to this landmass due to population pressure in their homeland and also for having been allured to get some easy means of livelihood in the reclaimed *abad* area of Sundarban. Though at the beginning of their coming over there these people engaged themselves in various agricultural activities in the fertile landmass formed of alluvial soil yet a considerable section of them were attracted to the network of rivers and creeks in considering their potentiality towards the supply of fish wealth. In course of time transformation of the agriculturists as well as agricultural labourers started– many people embraced the fishing profession through the adoption of various fishing methods. The heterogeneous caste groups became homogeneous in the perspective of fishing economy and with it joined various tribal people like the Oraons, the Mundas and the Santals, who also came here to reclaim the forest on a broad-based programme launched by the then British East India Company. Many people belonging to the Muslim community also took up the profession of fishing in the Sundarban rivers and in course of time they identified themselves as part and parcel of the fishing community in the Bengal delta. Thus the fishing community of the Bengal delta has been formed of diversified human groups with different, and sometimes, opposite thinking patterns and philosophy of life but all the barriers in between thoughts and ideas, principles and manners of living as well as conflicting attitudes have been lost owing to the troublesome and riskful fighting activities which made the people united on a common platform and to think and feel for each other. There are multiple occasions when the fishing groups constituted by heterogeneous castes and religious communities became united not only physically but also in the deeper recess of socio-cultural life and religious sentiments. In this way it is seen that fishing-oriented occupational pattern has done a great deal in cutting across the traditional norms and related social legislation based on caste philosophy and ritualistic thinking.

The present study pledges to bring out the distinctive traits of Sundarban fisherfolk who have been processed in a specific pattern owing to the integrated interactions with the mangrove ecosystem. In course of various discussions in this work it would be readily understandable how, in this particular area, the fishing occupation centering round that turbulent rivers and horrible forests especially on their unfavourable environmental-both abiotic and biotic-situation work to impose the mentality of integration of the people despite their traditional conspicuous social differences. The members of this integrated economic group readily lose their basic social identity while they work with common interest and to achieve common goal. The struggle for existence has brought them within a conspicuous occupational group irrespective of caste and community affiliations. The reciprocal relationship patterns amongst the members of the fishing units are the indicators of the particular concept.

Success in the fishing pursuits is not only dependent on the availability of fishes in a particular ecological setting but also it is explicitly related to the direct collective response of the fishermen of diversified situational context of the total ecosystem. The adaptive relationship with their ecosystem is established through the medium of culture which gives rise to cultural ecological processes. These help in the exploitation of their environment by means of the devise of indigenous technological equipments, cultivation of knowledge regarding the tidal rivers, the deep sea, their cross currents, weather conditions and the influence of celestial bodies as well as the formation of integrated fishing units with the establishment of close interpersonal relations, developing and nurturing of complicated supernatural beliefs and practices to save themselves from unknown mishaps that are very likely to happen in this world's largest mangrove ecosystem.

The main point of interest of this work is that it is designed to explain the adaptive processes of the fisherfolk to the mangrove ecological zone. It has been shown, in course of study of the total situation, how man-mangrove-fish interact with each other and how the fisherfolk struggle continuously to maintain the equilibrium in this interlaced eco-cultural perspective. Thus the study deviates from the earlier works in the Sundarban region especially due to their categorical limitations in exploring the total perspective of the fisherfolk in the line of their patterns of adjustment with mangrove ecosystem. Here ecology, economy and culture have been made intermingled to pin-point the basic nature of the fish-oriented life of the fisherfolk. In course of in-depth observations and relevant analysis of data it has been seen that the pattern of adaptation is the outcome of a long drawn process started since remote past. This specific ecosystem has been operating within the limit of natural ecosystem due to the fact that all material inputs entering into the human economic system are derived from the natural world. These material inputs and environmental situations can sustain human needs and survival provided they are harnessed and thereby extended in a manner that maintain the balance, integrity and stability of the ecosystems. Any sort of negligence towards this natural balancing situation would result in a disastrous happening both in the life of mankind and in the total biosphere zone. It has been observed through concrete study that continuous negligence and wanton destruction of the ecological balance Sundarban biosphere has had to meet with a perilous situation. This very state of affair has been categorically extended to the sphere of fishes, due to one reason or another, and the immediate result of which is that the traditional prosperous fish crops have been gradually dwindling.

There is another important perspective of the study and it is the outcome of present day circumstances. The traditional fishing community in Sundarban has always been caste-bound. The caste-based fishing groups are characterized by the integrated actions of various social legislations which each and every fisherman is obliged to follow. The fishermen violating the social norms and regulations are publicly prosecuted by the traditional caste panchayat or the gram sabha. There are distinct taboos in the catching time of different varieties of fishes, and not only so, there are strong regulations so that in no circumstances the ecological balance is lost. But the intruders in this sphere i.e. the fishermen having no fishing caste affiliation have been gradually penetrating into the economic system based on fish catching in Sundarban during the present period. The process, so to speak, had been started in the recent past. They are unquestionably non-traditional fishing personnel and are specifically business-oriented having least interest in the maintenance of ecological balance. With the help of better financial status and superior technology of modernistic type these newly introduced fishermen exploit the total ecological zone of Sundarban through devastating fishing operations. It has been seen through the analysis of various happenings that the caste-based fishing pursuit has faced an acute challenge, during the recent period, due to large-scale immigration of non-caste-based fishing people. The interactions between caste-based and non-caste-based fishing groups have resulted various unfortunate situations which have given a new turn in the fishing activities in Sundarban. All these patterns of interactions have been highlighted in various action-oriented behaviours of the fishing groups as well as through in-depth studies of the traditional and non-traditional fishing villages developed in the region.

The impact of mechanization on the overall fishing pursuits is a great concern in the fishing economy as a whole and, therefore, it has been focused from the different angles to highlight its patterns and perspectives. During the present period conditioned by the discoveries and inventions of various technological devices the manual practices in fishing activities must be replaced by mechanistic procedures. But the trend of mechanization in fishing has not been wide-spread here in comparison to the other states of India. Mechanization in fishing pursuits here, however limited it may be, has been proved to be an injurious one to the total ecological setting because of its improper utilization. This feature has been brought into thoughtful consideration in course of the various facets of this study.

Fishing is such an economic pursuit which not only need the close-set cooperation and integrated working of persons belonging to the different categories but also there is always an emergent necessity of harnessing variegated indigenous beliefs, ideas, experience, customs, traditions as well as ethics of the people concerned for having an all rounded control over the total situation. Through the micro-study of different fishing villages this particular domain has been explored; these also have helped in understanding the patterns of interactions of the fisherfolk amongst themselves as well as with the outsiders who are related to the fishing villages for economic matters. Therefore, in this study, specific stress has been laid on the direct observations of the behaviour-patterns developed within the fishing villages.

There are innumerable age-old problems in the domain of fishing in Sundarban rivers and estuaries, and in addition to these new problems are emerging in the present context. Owing to these, fishermen are always in great troubles-most of the time they are to face dangerous circumstances claiming their lives and properties. Despite multifarious problematic issues in the day to day fishing pursuits, there are a lot of prospects in the Sundarban mangrove dominated ecological zone which, if properly explored and then exploited in their proper perspectives, it would not only increase the amount of food supply to the nation but also it would bring a prosperity to the national economy and thereby open a broader field for employment of many people. These are the principal objectives of this study and in the course of analysis of the data in the different chapters these have been brought to light to understand the nature, integrated actions, their multifaceted influence as well as problems and prospects of fishing economy in the region flourished in the midst of mangrove ecosystem in Sundarban.

In this study the following hypotheses were categorically tested.

1. The age-old profession of fishing in Sundarban has been drawing many caste and community groups for a long time, and in coming over here all the diversified groups with different traditional occupations became fused together centering round

the profession of fishing. This historical process is to be regarded as a basic criterion in formation of Sundarban fisherfolk who ultimately developed a common fishing culture.

2. In spite of their heterogeneous life-situation based on different patterns of occupational linkage the people coming from outside, in the remote past period, readily became identified as a homogeneous fishing community having equal mental situation and similar modes of behaviour. In consequence of the fishing profession in a particular ecological setting through reciprocal understanding and the sharing of joys and sorrows the heterogeneity became transformed into homogeneity in course of time.
3. To cope with the requirements of occupation the fishermen have been proceeded for multi-dimensional adjustments which include socio-economic adjustments, technological adjustments, adjustments to changes in physical environment caused by different factors. These are needed to be explored systematically to highlight the patterns of interactions of the fishermen with eco-cultural, socio-economic and techno-economic spheres.
4. In consequence of time-long struggle and work the fisherfolk could have developed various ways and means, what are collectively known as native science, through a time-long direct interactions with the abiotic and biotic environmental situations. Various elements of this indigenous knowledge demand instant collection for their evaluation which may be helpful, to a considerable extent, in designing the programme relating to mangrove conservation and the maintenance of ecological balance based on the present day scientific concept.
5. Fishing economy is characterized by long-term and complicated process which embraces both fishing

and non-fishing people in a cycle of activities that starts right from the fishing operations and continues upto marketing of fishes. Thus the fishermen are subject to diversified interactions with the outside world and where they are tied up with various socio-economic regulations.

6. As a result of introduction of motor driven boats and trawlers in the Sundarbans considerable changes have been resulted in the internal relationship patterns amongst the people engaged in fishing occupation in different capacities. This state of affair has certainly broken down many traditional types of group formation, indigenous fishing procedures conditioned by the idea of conservation and at the same time it has developed many new trends in this connection.

II

Sundarban in the Indian side is seen to be distributed over two separate districts of lower Bengal. These are North 24-Parganas and South 24-Parganas. The region in the Southern part represents the active delta and it is unique of its kind because of the presence of the intricate coast line, estuarine system, innumerable islands that are criss-crossed by variegated distributories. It is due to these facts the total area has become characterized by a great diversity in the ecosystem. This region is identified by having a highly productive environment which has actively resulted in the emergence of varied economic activities related to fishing, agriculture and forestry. Amongst these fishing activities have become conspicuous, and it has a rich potential in this pattern of economy.

The fisherfolk working in the domain of the mangrove ecosystem of Sundarban region were studied principally in two distinct phases of their life and activities. Enquiries into their totalistic life had been made within the villages functioning through traditional as well as changed patterns of thinking. Their interactions with the non-fishing persons were recorded to understand their conflict and cooperation with them in daily mode of their life. Also they had been conspicuously investigated while their active workings on fishing practices were in the state of highest momentum. Thus during the period of study the investigators had always been alerted in looking into the affairs of the fisherfolk both inside and outside their habitats which required close-set time-bound direct observations within the village setting and thereby to note down the different facets of socio-religio-economic patterns of integration centering round the fishing activities. While investigating into the nature and extent of direct fishing performances the investigators were in a hurried tour through the region following the fishing units in their boats, launches as well as trawlers. The fishermen are by nature in a complicated interactions with the non-fishing persons in the sphere of marketing of the fishes. The different fish markets at various important sites had been regularly visited by the investigators to bring out the total working patterns of the market and the role of fishermen in these. It is to be noted that their different activities right from fishing in turbulent waters to the marketing of the catches are in a chain of complicated network of money and trade system which is specifically dominated and governed by the non-fishing people. In this state of affair a good deal of conspicuous interactions between fishing and non-fishing personalities had been brought to light. As because Sundarban fishermen are to work against varied adversities, so they are always in the all-rounded struggling atmosphere conditioned by various patterns of adjustment with the situational context. It is for this reason the work is pledged to highlight the adaptive processes of the fisherfolk to the mangrove ecological zone. Man-mangrove-fish interactions have, thus, become the most conspicuous issue in this sort of work. In course of discussion of the different facts and their related analyses in various chapters these trends of adjustment have been focused considerably drawing diversified data from the various domain of life and philosophy of the fisherfolk.

The fishing villages for micro-study have been selected from the three distinct zones– (1) Diamond Harbour Zone, (2) Kakdwip Zone and (3) Sagar Island Zone. Diamond Harbour is situated at the stable delta and it is regarded as the gateway to the Sundarban locality. The stable delta is comprised of slight higher elevations which is characterized by sluggish rivers and depressions. From this specific zone village *Nurpur* has been selected for micro-study. It is the oldest village in this region and has been developed by the side of the river *Ganga* (Hugli). Nurpur is a multi-ethnic village and the fishermen here belong to the tradition-oriented fishing castes. Kakdwip is flourished as a fishing-oriented zone at the junction between the stable and the active deltas. Being situated on the bank of *muriganga* it marks the entry point towards the vast Sundarban hinterland through the network of rivers and estuaries. Kakdwip is directly connected with the interior of Sundarban through a creek known as Kalnagini Khal. There are a number of fishing villages at the close vicinity of Kakdwip and from which the village *Dasherchwak* has been taken for integrated study for this purpose. So to speak, it is not a traditional village and comparatively it is of a recent origin. The village is principally populated by the fishing personnel together with a few other non-fishing castes having close linkage with fishing economic pursuits. Then comes the village *Beguakhali.* It is situated at the extreme south-west point of Sagar Island. It has been flourished not only on the active delta but also at the close vicinity of the Bay of Bengal. Principally dominated by the fishing communities this village has been developed for the purpose of instant settlement of the stray communities conducting their fishing as well as agricultural activities in the confluence of the Ganga and the Bay of Bengal, popularly known as *gangasagar.* It is at present more or less a homogeneous fishing village though some other non-fishing castes have made their entries into the village to serve the fishermen in their daily mode of life and activities.

During their struggle–oriented activities the fishermen are always on the move. Many a time they are to live on turbulent rivers for weeks together. When they come back to the shore after the catch they spend for sometime in their village homes. The period of staying in the village varies according to the season. Therefore, the fishermen had been investigated in these two specific situations, and naturally different methodologies were adopted to collect various informations on their way of life. In this connection, it is to be mentioned that the universe of this study is very large and it is extended over a vast geographical area. It was through a long-term integrated pilot survey over the larger part of the Sundarban region especially where the fishermen were engaged in fishing activities the principal concentrated zones in relation to these people were detected. These people were seen to be distributed in the South-western region of the South 24-Parganas district. It was for that reason all the endeavours were made to make direct and detailed investigation into the life and activities of the fisherfolk engaged in their fishing activities in the region concerned. This region is directly connected by roads from Kolkata. From Kolkata buses ply to the last point on the island i.e. Bakkhali. There are regular train services from Sealdah (Kolkata) to Diamond Harbour as well as to Kakdwip. These facilitate easy communication to the fish markets located at Kolkata. Different businessmen, traders and contractors can easily visit these places through motorable roadways which help maintaining a regular business link centering round fish. Thus in this region there is a good deal of interactions amongst the people belonging to fishing and fish trade related communities which forms the core of fishing economy.

Amongst the three fishing villages studied in a micro-level way in connection with the present project one comes from northern point of the deltaic region, the principal features of which include the following— (i) it is a very old and traditional fishing village having different castes and community orientation, (ii) due to the caste based fishing pursuits, all the norms and traditions are observed rigidly, (iii) a well-unit pattern of kin-based grouping works in the formation of fishing units, (iv) the fishermen are completely dependent on country boats and hand-made nets. Thus they cannot go beyond the mouth of the Ganga. The second village is situated further southward to the first village and its environment marks the conspicuousness of mangrove ecosystem. It is characterized by— (i) recent abrupt peopling due to population pressure resulted from large scale immigrants from the then East Pakistan (now Bangladesh), (ii) fishing pursuits are conducted through non-traditional activities as most of the fishermen have been transformed from non-fishing castes, (iii) exclusively based on mechanization and the whole fishing units are business-oriented, (iv) fishing is mostly done in the deep sea. Being developed at the furthest south in the Sagar Island the third village depicts the specific picture like, (i) exclusively fishing village despite the presence of a few non-fishing castes. All are fishing-oriented groups centering round both active fishing and fish-linked activities, (ii) fishing is exclusively done in the sea, (ii) fishing units are neighbour-oriented and caste barrier does not function here, (iv) the fishermen are identified here as sea faring group having the capacity of conducting sea fishing with native infrastructure.

The units of observation, in this study, were the villages inhabited by the fishermen engaged in fishing activities. Along with them there are other units like various non-fishing groups of people who are in direct association with the fishing communities centering round fishing and fish trade. While investigating into the interacting patterns between man and nature various natural resources and environmental factors in the totalistic ecosystem of the region have been taken up as units of observation. In order to collect the empirical data on the life-activities and the patterns of interactions with various adversities of the fisherfolk concerned in the village as well as in the actual field of fishing and fish trade various tools of research have very naturally been applied. In the integrated study of the village communities direct observations were the principal modes of collecting information. Day to day continuous observations on the various facets of the village life were made by staying with them in the villages concerned for a considerable period. Observations command an efficient method of getting information on the patterns and problems of life and thinking of the people working incessantly in the mangrove forest region. Firstly, most of the observations were of participant type. Through a continuous training and constant vigilance made by the Project Director the investigators themselves were made a part and parcel of the fishing communities. They were present in all the affairs of the fishing pursuits as active members to record everything from close quarters. In so doing, the investigators could discern the natural behaviours of the fishermen. At that time they got the opportunity to see and understand the multifarious activities like fishing pursuits, technological devices, exact manipulation, group formation and activities, worships and supernatural activities together with their interrelation with the non-fishing personnel. When situations demanded the patterns of observations were made in the non-participant way. While interacting with the non-fishing personnel coming from outside to serve some business purposes the manner of investigation was always of a non-participant type.

Because of its broad-based nature of study some controlling factors were put to the technique of observation. At the very outset, a particular plan of observation was framed up so that the observation would not be haphazard. Specific observational schedules were designed to keep the observations within the control of the investigators. Sociometric scales were freely used to make observations perfect and effectual. Individual observations were also supplemented by team observation. Steps were taken to observe the varied phenomena of the social settings by the trained observers having different background of study and discipline but with the same *focus* of attention for getting the all-rounded view of the individual phenomenon. It was essential in the sense that fishing profession and trade depicted a complicated perspective which needed multifaceted investigation. Thus there was always a specific trend to highlight the total situation through interdisciplinary understandings.

To cover the different domains of life, various perspectives of work and fisherfolk's direct interactions with the surroundings different structured questions were incorporated as per specific requirements in addition to various blank tables. The structured questions had helped the investigating personnel to ask the relevant questions to the respondents and with the help of these questions the interview conducted by the different investigators remained in the standardized condition. It helped in the recording of easily comparable data.

To get the pin-pointed answers to a number of enquiries various types of schedules had been framed up which were used as per necessity. The schedules were applied in drawing the data on the topics like the working patterns of the caste-based fishing groups, their interactions with non caste-based business oriented groups; their reactional view-points on the impact of Sundarban ecology on their life and work; role of supernaturalism in fishing pursuits; impact of native science in day-to-day activities–its importance during the present period. The questions in the structured schedules were framed in such a way that illiterate and busy fishermen could answer readily and without wasting much of their precious time. There were arrangements for transforming qualitative data into quantitative terms.

To bring out the historical perspective of the profession of fishing and its pattern of coming down through generations to highlight the changing spheres both in the technological development and in evaluating the caste-based nature genealogical method had been proved highly effective. A large mass of data of genealogical nature had been gathered devoting much time and through a long-term contact as well as making close intimacy with the people. It was specifically understood that in the kin-oriented and caste-based profession genealogical method did a great deal in highlighting many dark events which had so far been out of our sight. The genealogical method was used broadly to trace the nature and extent of occupational patterns through generations. Migration of people especially of the different fishing families was successfully determined through this method of study. It was also convenient to bring out the impact of modernization on the traditional fishing devices as well as age-old taboos and many other restrictions based on traditional norms. Their changes through generations could only be profitably assessed through the genealogical method. Needless to say, the application of the method in question during field study was done after formation of a very good rapport with the people and through the gathering of all-sided firsthand information on the people and their work. For throwing discernible light on the historical background of the fishing pursuits and the fishermen's involvement in these affairs both the types like structured and unstructured interviews were conducted. The senior sections of the community were very naturally selected as respondents for such interviews. While gossiping with the respondents, of course in a planned scientific way, the investigators found ample opportunities to understand the psychological settings of those senior fishermen and with those the investigators concerned could have been able to collect some new thinking patterns and behavioural activities which helped them remoulding the work plan as per necessity. Fishing does not depict an isolated means of livelihood—it not only brings together the persons from different categories but also diversified ways and means are adopted to make the fishing successful. Thus it had been the duty of the investigators to collect first-hand data on the total process of fishing and the allied perspectives–both human and natural events-through a close-set interview with the fishermen in their work as well as in leisure. From the very beginning the interviewers had tried to gain confidence of the interviewees who might have been in the different mental set up.

The fishermen were all along very much busy during their fishing operation when they had to cope with various adverse situations, and therefore, arrangements were made to conduct the interview without taking much of their busy time. The questions in the schedules were very specific as well as direct type and the investigators were all along trained up to that line of action. They were made alert in observing the total situation of work and the behaviour-patterns of the fishermen with the coworkers as well as with the people of other communities so that the area of investigation through interviews would be more elaborate. As because the fishermen had been in a continuous patterns of interaction with the surroundings, so the relevant data in relation to those were collected through the adoption of focused interview. The interviewer concerned focused his attention to a specific points of adjustment with the natural element related to fishing and through a series of participant questions he was able to get into the deeper level of the situational context. Repetitive interview was very often used to examine the modes and patterns of a particular situation. It was, no doubt, helpful in studying the change in continued sequence.

To make visual observations perfectly reliable photographic method had been deliberately used for the collection of relevant data. As a specific technique for 'lifeful' reproduction of the objects and achievements photographic principles were applied to get the detailed view of the total context of research. Photographic technique in exploring human life and activities or in other words visual anthropology was proved very much effectual during the work of investigation on the fishing communities as it gave the full view of the work and struggle of the fishermen on water as well as on land which were not possible in simple eye observation. Specific reliance on photographic technique was adopted as it helped in recording accurately the full details of an event or happening which might have escaped the simple observation through the eyes. In the work in question the action-oriented and exploration-based life of the fisherfolk was expected to be properly drawn up by means of the different stages of photography conducted through the following of scientific principles.

Through a number of relevant action photography the diversified aspects of exploitation of the natural resources by the fishermen as well as their continuous struggle to face the unfavourable circumstances in land and water were explored to have a perfect view of the situation which could not be done in any other method of study. Care had always been taken to see that the photographs on the different aspects of their life would present the lifeful representation of the theme of study.

Along with the collection of visual information in systematic and broad-based pattern the case study method was utilised extensively for serving the specific purpose of intensive study on the persons who were thought as useful and inevitable factor in the sphere of work on which the research activities were centralised. For the purpose of deep-based and detailed study in that regard the life-histories of a few key persons/families that represented the various "actors" in the village economy had been gathered. The life-histories were collected maintaining all the required formalities of field methods and those were necessarily gathered through long-term and close-set interviews with the selected informants.

The data thus collected through the adoption of different conventional sociological methods were processed through careful sorting and analysis. The editing of the descriptive data was done in a very careful way to avoid distraction from the principal angle of vision of the study concerned. The coding of the various entries had been made to facilitate the work of classification, tabulation and other statistical treatment during the time of data analysis. The tabulation of data was done to present the total information systematically and of course within a meaningful perspective. From the data so far collected both general purpose and summary tables had been prepared illustrating simple and complex patterns of information.

III

Overview of Literature

Fishing economy in India dates back to the remote past from 3000 B.C. The people of Mohenjodaro used fish extensively but in Vedic period (2500 B.C. – 1000 B.C.) it was not definitely known if fish was in vogue at that time. But in the Rig-Veda and other religious texts like the Atharva-Veda, the Smritis, the Upanisads etc. there are definite mention about *Jala* (net) and Yayur-Veda is provided with the reference of *sutra* (thread) and hook. In Kautilya's Arthashastra (between 321 B.C. and 300 B.C.) references are met with the fishing industry, fish processing and fish eating. In Bengal, fish production came to be known during the region of Pala Dynasty from the copper inscription of Devapal ranging from 810 A.D. to 850 A.D. In her multitude of rivers, creeks, estuaries and wide open seas, the different communities have been maintaining their life through the systematic catching of fishes. These communities, in course of time, have developed requisite talented devices for fishing as well as pisciculture.

It was W.W. Hunter who put forward the fishing castes–their nature of economy and fishing procedures in his *A Statistical Account of Bengal* in 1875. Then in 1908, K.G. Gupta published a report of study on the fisheries of Bengal and the related personnel. J.H. Hutton, in his book *Caste in India,* published, in 1931, categorically mentioned some fishing caste groups. Some reference of marine fishing groups had been highlighted by L.S.S. O'Malley in his *Eastern Bengal District Gazetteers* brought out in 1908. James Howell, in his two articles entitled "The Boats of the Ganges" and "The Fishing Methods of the Ganges", published in the Memoirs of the Asiatic Society of Bengal, between 1922 and 1924, discussed the fishing communities and their methods of fishing as well as the utilisation of fishing gear in the Ganges.

In 1929 S.T. Mosses published a paper in *Man In India* in which he discussed the life and fishing activities of the Valayens of Pamban living in the coastline of Tamil Nadu.

In 1931 and 1932 T.C. Das in his illuminating articles published in *Man In India* tried very efficiently the various beliefs and practices developed round fish. His article was entitled "Cultural Significance of Fish in Bengal", and brought out in the two different issues of the said journal. It was a broad-based study on the various belief-patterns on fish and fishing. The role of fish in different social ceremonies as well as its ritualistic background have been discussed in great details. Fish as symbols of magical beliefs has been highlighted through concrete examples. While discussing the fish-based culture in Bengal the author traced various illustrations right from the Vedic period to understand the background situation of the present day happening. While making a comparative study between Ugerian and Indian fishing implements Biren Bonnerjee's attempt to evaluate the two specific cultures centering round fish put forward a new trend of approach. According to him, fishing is not only a means of subsistence but also the total process is intermingled with the different facets of life-situation giving rise to distinguished culture traits. He traced the parallel patterns of thinking and activity orientation in the devising of material equipments for fishing practices throughout the different population groups. In a broad-based paper entitled, "Ugerian Fishing Implements and Some Indian Parallels", Sri Bonnerjee depicted that particular view-point. It was published in *Man In India,* in 1938. M.N. Basu's work, published in the *Calcutta Review,* in 1946, provides some basic information on fish, fishing and fishermen in a Bengal village where he showed the economic adjustment in the area of fishing and thereby he put forward some suggestions in that regard. In the same year, S.N. Mitra presented an interesting study on the estuarine and foreshore fishing in the Sundarbans in which he highlighted the patterns and principles of fishing by the fishermen. S.L. Hora, in his six different papers, written between 1940 and 1954, and published in the *Journal of the Asiatic Society of Bengal,* principally focused the matter relating to the perception of the ancient Hindus on fish and fisheries. He also highlighted various proverbs and popular saying on fish as prevalent amongst the people of ancient India. J.M. Datta threw discernible light on the fishing practices and related usages of the fishermen in the district of 24-Parganas especially in Panihati-Sukchar region. It was published in *Man In India* in the year 1959. In the same year, V.B. Punekar published a detailed account on the way of life of the Son Kolis–a fishing community of Bombay Coast. The study is principally based on empirical findings. It shows how this fishing community has not been distracted from its traditional culture despite the close impact of urbanisation. In this connection, two interesting works on the fishing villages under the specific programme of Village Survey Monograph, Census of India, 1961, must be mentioned. In 1966, M. Ahmed presented the monographic study on Nuegolabandh village inhabited by the fishermen. Then R.K. Trivedi's work on Sutrapada fishing hamlet was published in 1967. Both the works show the nature and traditions of the fishing villages in India, and these successfully put forward the systematic way of life of the fishermen concerned. A. Mukhopadhyay gave a brief as well as superficial information on the life of the Sundarban fishermen, but it is helpful to get first hand knowledge on these people. It is published in *Frontier* in 1968. In the same year C.T. Samuel presented the nature, problems and prospects of marine fisheries in India. It was published from the Oceanographic Laboratory of the University of Kerala. By way of discussion it highlighted the life of the fishermen engaged in marine fishing. A.M. Klausen, in the year 1968, made a detailed study on the techno-economic help forwarded towards the fishermen in Kerala belonging to two different religious sects and with their habitation in two different villages. He examined the pattern of social behaviour of fishermen as a continuous process of choice. The study was based on Indo-Norwegian Pilot Project which started as back as 1955 in two fishing villages in Kerala. B. Mukherjee deserves the credit for presenting a systematic discussion on the Noliya of Puri. Their fishing organisation was analytically discussed. It was published, in 1969, in the *Bulletin of the Anthropological Survey of India*. Then in 1970 he attempted at the comparative study amongst the fisherfolk living in coastal West Bengal and Orissa. It is a very useful study made through detailed analysis of the life-situations published under the auspices of the Anthropological Survey of India. In this connection, D. Hazra's work on the marine fishermen of Gujarat, published in 1970, under the auspices of the same institute, should be mentioned. K.A. Razaq's account on marine fisherfolk of Andhra appeared in the same volume which was centred round the exploration of life and activities of the fishermen of Andhra Pradesh. B. Roychaudhuri gave an interesting account on the methods of fishing in the background of the total ecosystem of Chilka lake which was appeared in the *Journal of the Indian Anthropological Society* in 1977.

M. Suryanarayan published a paper on the political organisation among the fisherfolk of Andhra Pradesh in the *Bulletin of the Anthropological Survey of India,* in 1971, where he put forward the roles of the social and religious heads of the community. Beside this the activities of the political heads had been brought to the limelight to point out the specific importance of these in the organisation of fishing groups and related working patterns. In 1977, he published a monograph under the auspices of the Anthropological Survey of India where the marine fisherfolk of North East Coastal Andhra Pradesh had been brought under consideration. In 1971, S.N. Pandey published a paper in *Man In India* where he discussed the perspectives of economy and society among the fishermen of coastal Orissa. It gave a broad-based idea on the organised work of the fisherfolk in the background of caste unity, cohesion and solidarity. The nature and extent of cooperatives of fishermen in Manipur had been focused in a paper by M.C. Goswami and C.H. Singh published in 1973. This small paper reflected different attempts of the fishermen at Thanga in Manipur in the sphere of Cooperative system to meet the various crises of life. C. Selvaraj's (1975) work on the small fishermen of Tamil Nadu presented before us some specific ideas on the tradition and culture of the fisherfolk. K.L. Norr, in his article published in 1975, has highlighted the nature of coastal fishing in Tamil Nadu and the structure of its total organisation has been framed up and analysed with the help of empirical data collected through field survey. R.K. Gupta published an interesting paper in *The Indian Anthropologist* (1975) in which he very skilfully presented the various instances of mutual aid in the production system of hilsa fishing in West Bengal. He analysed the organisational set up of 56 fishing families living near Kolaghat in the district of Midnapur, West Bengal. Besides economic features a large number of socio-ritualistic performance had been brought forward to understand the actual perspective of the whole system. P.R.G. Mathur, in the year 1978, put forward a systematic account on the interrelatedness of habitat, technology, economy, society and culture among the Mappila Fisherfolk of Kerala. It is evidenced by a close study on the different patterns of behaviours of the fishing community in the background of fish oriented occupation. He has shown efficiently how the economy of the fishermen is interwoeven with the socio-cultural milieu. B. Roy Choudhury (1980) has presented an authentic field based study on the transient fishing community who assemble during winter months at Jambudwip–an island in the Bay of Bengal, 10 km. from the shore. In the background of his vast amount of empirical data he has examined the socio-cultural background of the fisherfolk and how the fishing unit works in the network of compromise and cooperation as well as conflict and dissociation. The study pin-points the technological and environmental knowledge of these people and he has shown the way how these run down through traditions. He has also highlighted the process of the development of supernatural beliefs in the background of the great risk of uncertainty in fishing pursuits. In 1980, S.N. Dwivedi has focused some concrete problems faced by the fishermen. His work entitled, *Socioeconomic problems of Fishermen,* published under the auspices of Central Institute of Fisheries Education, Bombay, is a landmark of direct field investigation amongst the female fish workers in the West Coast of India. Leela Gulati, in a series of working papers under the auspices of the Centre for Development Studies, from 1981 to 1984, has highlighted the role of the women in fishing pursuits, their work participation and technological changes amongst the fisherfolk in Kerala fishing villages. The author has pinpointed her observations on the day to day life and work of the women and thereby she has attempted to analyse their status in the perspective of total fishing economy. S. Bhakathavatsala Bharathi has contributed his observations on the spirit possession and healing practices in a fishing community in coromondel region. A number of deities and spirits which constitute the basic belief patterns of the fisherfolk have been analysed and their roles have been evaluated in the life and activities of the fisherfolk. It has been published in *Man In India* in 1993. In his *Fishermen Community of Coastal village in West Bengal*, published in 1993, S.K. Pramanik has given a beautiful and analytical account of the life and work of the fisherfolk in a few villages situated close to Diamond Horbour, at the confluence of the Ganges with the Bay of Bengal. He has shown how the fishing occupation is linked up in the complicated perspective of social, ritual, administrative as well as perfect knowledge over the surrounding ecological setting. In two separate papers, published in *Man In India* in 1994 and 1996, he has thrown specific light on the work participation of fisherwomen and on the life-situation and adaptive strategy of the women dry fish workers in Sundarban.

Of late, various mechanization processes have been incorporated into the fishing activities. Introduction of motor driven boats, motor launches, trawlers, and machine-made nets etc. has resulted a lot of changes in the traditional pattern of fishing technologies based on indigenous knowledge running down through generations. Though a very limited stray works have been conducted on this issue yet these are worth-mentioning as regards their line of approaches to the specific event. In 1983, L. Gulati worked on three fishing villages in Kerala, under the auspices of Centre of Development Studies, Trivandrum, and pointed out the effects of mechanization on the fishing activities. A lot of improvement has been effected in the various fishing procedures as well as different uncertainties have been minimized to a considerable extent. With the application of new scientific innovations to the ways of fishing the fisherfolk's continuous strain for hard struggle with the unfavourable ecological circumstances has been lessened. Mechanization on fishing activities, on the other hand, has brought changing situations in the traditional economic dealings amongst themselves as well as with the outsiders. The former pattern of group formation based on mutual socio-cultural relation has been replaced by categorical economic situation. In a similar paper on the effects of mechanization on the fishermen's work in South 24-Parganas, written by S.K. Pramanik, and published in *Socialist Perspective* (1992), it has been shown that mechanized boats, trawlers and machine-made nets have done a great deal in lessening the hazards and anxieties of ecological perspective but these have snatched away the time-long net making and mending activities of the elderly persons and womenfolk in the fishing villages. The fishing parties with mechanization system do not bother for any traditional norm, rather they are always thinking in terms of increasing the daily catch by any means to cope with the heavy expenditures incurred for mechanization of the process. It has transformed most of the social norms into the categorical economic dealings.

From the review of literatures centering round fishing communities and their activities throughout India it is seen that most of the works have been conducted with a view to highlight the socioeconomic conditions of the fishing communities. These studies are based on different regions. It is true that in Southern part of India especially in Tamil Nadu, Andhra Pradesh and Kerala there are worth mentioning evidences of analytical work based on long-term and systematic field investigation where the fishing pursuits have been discussed in the background of other dimensions of life. But it is completely lacking in eastern region especially where the world's largest delta is found with its characteristic landforms, flora and fauna. No broad based work has been done here to highlight the Sundarban fishing communities, their activities, problems and prospects in the background of the mangrove ecosystem. It is for this reason the present study principles have been framed to find out the trends of man-nature relation in the total perspective of fishing pursuits conducted by the fisherfolk through the ages. The study pledges to examine the nature and extent of the approaches made by the fisherfolk to balance and harmonize the various enterprises in land and water to make themselves successful in fishing as well as to protect themselves from the horrible surroundings of the Sundarban ecosystem. It is a double-headed struggle and one sphere has been fused with the other. So there is a specific need for an integrated study to search out the forces of interactions between man and environment which is expected to contribute valuable information on the patterns of human adjustment with the surroundings. For any sort of development programme in relation to the Sundarban fishing communities and thereby to increase the fish based wealth these data would be very much effective to proceed through the right path of progress.

Wide Open Sundarban Rivers Lined by Mangrove Forest

A Sundarban Village in the Midst of Vegetative Growth

A Jetty Leading to the River Water

Bamboo Structure to Prevent Erosion

A Boatman Sailing Through the River

Ferry Boat Engaged in Ferrying Passengers

2

SUNDARBAN ECOLOGY AND HUMAN POPULATION

I

Sundarban, etymologically means the beautiful forest, is really beautiful in the strict sense of the term. The forest is traditionally characterised by the celestial calmness; it is gorgeous and at the same time it has got an alarming appeal. It is said that nature is specifically distinctive by her exclusive elucidations which are so depth-oriented and widespread that it becomes almost impossible to have a totalistic view of the situational context conditioned by the diversified interaction patterns of living and non-living elements reigning over here from the remote past. The emergence of Sundarban raises a lot of questions and in answering these the scholars from the different spheres of scientific knowledge have contributed the results of their research-based activities and long-term thinking perspectives. Sundarban is regarded to have been formed by the combined effect of fluvial marine activities. From the different observations it has been assessed that the Sundarban landmass might have been developed, to a great extent, through the continuous upheaval and subsidence of the gneissic hills together with the gradual deposition of alluvial silts carried by the Ganga and Bhrahmaputra rivers from the Himalayan regions. The effectual emergence of the region is explicitly rooted to the diversified geomorphological, climatological as well as biotic factors which by way of interactional activities for a long period have made the actual possibilities in favour of land formation.

Opinions differ regarding the origin of the name Sundarban applied to the dense forest exuberantly developed throughout the vast region by the side bordering the Bay of Bengal. There is very likeness that the name Sundarban has been derived from the characteristic Sundari tree (*Heritiera minor*) having abundant growth over the region concerned. Some say that due to the sea side setting of the forest it was originally named as Samudra vana (a Sanskrit word) meaning sea-faced forest, which later on got corrupted into Sundarban. According to the other scholars, the name Sundarban ows its origin to the name Sundha–a river in Backarganj. Once Backarganj had a popularity in having its identity as the river-side of the Sundha. The forest attached to the river-side was called Sundarban which in course of time corrupted into Sundarban. There is also a suggestion regarding the fact that owing to the crescent shape of the shore area where the luxuriant forest was developed the adjacent forest became known as Chandraban. But the foreigners especially the French people failed to spell it properly. It was misspelled as Chandarban which during the British regime became converted to Sundarban. Some are interested in attaching the derivation of the name Sundarban from Chandradwip–a Kingdom of Backarganj (in Bangladesh, previously in Barishal district of Bengal). The forest attached to that kingdom was popularly termed as Chandradwipban ultimately giving rise to the term Sundarban. In this way a lot of conjectural views are put forward to answer the question as regards the naming pattern of Sundarban. However, it is most probable that the name Sundarban is closely related to the Sundari tree the multitude of which contributed the spectacular view of the forest as a whole.

There is no denying of the fact that a series of events like upheaval and subsidence of the genissic hills together with the slow deposition of alluvial silts carried by the Ganga and Brahmaputra rivers are the root cause of the development of the greatest delta of the world. Various geological evidences as put forward by the different scholars in this domain of study are to be worth-noting in this connection. According to Hooker and Theobald, the total area of the Lower Bengal was practically an estuary. Various geological factors indicate the extension of the tidal swamp upto the Rajmahal Hills. As per different authorities during the late phase of the Tertiary Period it was filled up by the Himalayan drainage from the north side. In the year 1863, Fergusson, opined that during the Early Pleistocene this part of Bengal Basin was filled up by shallow marine water but in the Late Pleistocene the sea completely receded from the area in question. Older sediment started covering with thick river borne alluvium. All these studies were made in the middle of the 19th Century. Then Oldham, in 1893, came forward with the opinion that the whole area including Sundarban, stretched between Hugli river in the west and Meghna in the east, was the specific delta created by the deposition of debris regularly carried down by the Ganga and Brahmaputra rivers together with their tributories. It was also stated by Oldham that the Gangetic plains in question got their formation through the sinking of the crust due to the weight of the alluvium brought down by the Himalayan rivers.

The geologic history of the area indicates the phenomenon of subsidence of the region followed by deposition during the recent period. From the different excavations made during the implementation of various developmental projects in the urban centres lately established on the alluvium plains in question it has been seen that there is no trace of marine deposits supporting the fact that the underground region comprises of alluvial brackish water deposits. This deposition is conditioned by obvious factors. The geography of the coastal part and the two flanks of Sundarban are suggestive of the view that in the remote past period the main flank of the water having its origin from central and eastern Himalayas started flowing towards sea through small channel. The tremendous velocity of water started flooding the coastal region resulted in the formation of large and shallow continental shelf of the Bay of Bengal. In that continental shelf the rate of deposition of alluvial strata was accelerated because of subsequent depression of geneissic hills, which helped in the deposition of the enormous silt burden of the rivers.

The innumerable creeks and channels of the Sundarban region were formed due to splitting up of the main channel from the Himalayas. Those were characterized by having low depth in comparison to the width. As a natural consequence it restricted the capacity for carrying the water load. On coming to the plains of Lower Bengal after travelling a long way the current of Ganga became slow and naturally profuse silt load in the water began the process of sedimentation resulting in the formation of a large number of islands which in course of time created the condition for the development of unique natural biosphere. The formation of various small islands in Sundarban region is characterized by the specific phenomenon in which it is seen that the deposits of the Ganga alluvium that are forced to the sea are turned back, due to the influence of the tides, and redeposited in the estuarine region. Owing to this reason the low-lying Sundarban area is still in the formative stage.

According to many experts, repeated occurrences of various subsidence and earthquakes are principally responsible for conspicuous instability of Sundarban. In addition to these inherent climatic hazards in the form of violent thunderstorm and consequent tidal wave play the great role in the physiographic change in the area. Despite its closeness to the Tropic of Cancer the Sundarban region does not experience extreme climatic condition mainly because of its proximity of the sea and the continuous flushing of a large number of tidal creeks and rivers. Thus, the climate of Sundarban is salubrious in nature. The total area is highly influenced by Nor'wester locally known as *Kalbaisakhi*. The occurrence of cyclonic storms or tropical cyclones in the Bay of Bengal affects the total region causing tidal bores and storm surges.

The soil in Sundarban region is characterized by silt brought down from the Himalays through the rivers like Ganga, Brahmaputra and their tributories. This silt plays the essential role in the formation of the characteristic deltaic alluvium. The soil of Sundarban is divided into three major categories—(1) Fine Silt Clay in the northern portion of the region, (2) Peaty deposits in the middle portion, and (3) Swampy areas in the sea faced portion alongwith sandy clay and sand dunes. The profile of Sundarban soil highlights the fact that the upper layer is grey to greyish black in colour. In the sub-soil greyish clay with trace of sand together with varied types of silt are met with. Medium to fine sand characterized by grey to bluish-grey colour in seen in certain depths. According to the local people, the Sundarban soil can be categorized into four different types based on their colour and texture. These are (1) *Dhal* or lowest land soil, reddish in colour, (2) *Dhap* or *Chura,* whitish in colour, (3) *Matial* or loose type with whitish in colour, and (4) *Baliara or Dorasa,* reddish in colour. This type remains moist for a long time. The surface soil of the region is characteristically saline and this salinity changes to a great extent which is governed by the quantity of fresh water flow through the connecting rivers. During monsoon times the torrential rains cause a great deal in decreasing or washing out the salinity of the surface soil.

The eco-geography of the region is totally dependent on the tidal effect of the drainage system. Most of the physiographic area of Sundarban is actively influenced by water bodies. The rivers of the region are mostly the distributories of the Ganga. The main rivers of the area are Ganga (Hugli), Muriganga, Piyali-Bidyadhari, Thakuran, Saptamukhi, Matla, Gosaba and Hanribhanga. All these rivers are estuaries in nature. Being formed by the union of smaller rivers these estuarine rivers have found southwardly course towards the sea. These are seen to be separated from each other by innumerable islands. In these island perspectives, the Sagar Island, between the Ganga and the Channel creek, is the largest of all. The other large types of islands are Lothian Island, Halliday Island, Bulcherry Island etc. The *Khals* or smaller channels are the characteristic features of Sundarban physiography. The innumerable streams and water courses formed between the large estuaries and rivers constitute the perfect network of waterways all through the region. There are a few khals which connect two larger rivers and hence tide flows into these through both the ends. These types of khals are called by the term *doaniya*.

Thus, it is seen that Sundarban is a tidal dominated autochthonous coast which has been formed by transported sediments. The tidal currents are responsible for the dispersion of sediments carried to the coast by rivers. These sediments form elongated sand bodies in the shore zone. In this region all the river mouths are wide and funnel shaped. These are regularly fed by tidal creeks. The estuaries, inlets and tidal creeks are seen to be broadly separated by tidal flood plain. The wide river mouths at Southern region bordering the open sea are composed of marine sands a due to marine transgression these sands are reworking landward.

At present the Sundarban region is demarcated on the north by the Dampier-Hodges line, the Bay of Bengal on the South, the river Hugli on the west, and on the east it is marked by Ichhamati–Kalindi–Raimangal rivers. As back as 1831, William Dampier and Lt. Capt. Hodges in the capacities of the Commissioner and Surveyor respectively during the British regime conducted the work of demarcation of the total forest area from the rest of the 24-Parganas District. Dampier-Hodges line, known after the name of the said workers, runs a slightly zig-zug course from the vicinity of Barasat in the North-East to the Hugli near Kulpi in the South-East. Since then this line has been indicating the northern boundary of the forest area constituting the south-western part of the 24-Parganas district (now South 24-Parganas).

Looking into the past period it would be readily understood that the forest area was extended more and more than the present situation as noted above. It was spread upto Calcutta and its surrounding areas. It is evidenced by the fact that while excavating an area in Sealdah region in the heart of the present day Calcutta stumps of Sundari trees (*Heriteria minor*) had been found 30 feet below the present ground level. In the Keoratala region remains of Keora tree (*Sonneratia apetala*) were found underground while there was a digging operation during the construction work of the famous Keoratala burning ghat/complex. There are many references in the old journals and newspapers that Chowringhee and Kalighat areas were covered with dense forest. The forest region under reference was impenetrable, so to speak, and many ferocious animals became permanent inhabitants of the area. The growth of saline-infested shrubs and trees became so lavish and extensive that human penetration became almost impossible. Nobody could dare to face that horrific site which automatically became secluded. But the history does not accept the fact that the region concerned was all along cut off from human influence, rather the different locations of that vast area were pulsated with human civilizations. During the present period various chance findings of the different artifacts designed by man indicate the existence of flourishing human life in this landmass. Various archaeological excavations made at different places have added considerable informations to the old historical days here like Maurya, Sunga, Gupta and Pala periods of the ancient Indian history. The findings of the remote prehistoric times like various stone tools exemplified by the different types of microliths, neolithic celts, stone and shell beads in Kakdwip, Mandirtala, Patharpratima, Deulpota and other adjoining places support the antiquity of human culture and civilization here. But the human civilization did never face any sort of continuity rather it had to meet interruptions for some unknown reasons probably for subsidence of the bed of the delta or the direct impact of some natural calamities in the form of devastating floods and widespread cyclones. These unfortunate situations buried underground various human civilizations with relics of art and culture establishing the evidences of the signs of destructions throughout the region. In course of time the rapid growth of bushes and jungles with tall trees covered the entire area which ultimately became converted into the excessively dense forest. In this way human civilizations grew and fell here through the times but keeping some concrete indications of these underneath. Thus, the history of Sundarban region is characterized by the disappearance of civilization followed by its reappearance. From the study of the eminent historians we could understand that there were evidences of continuous civilizations in the western part of the Sundarban region from 5th-6th Century A.D. upto 12th-13th Century A.D. and after that the total area was completely abandoned caused by certain unknown problems. The area thereafter became deserted for several centuries and ultimately it was totally engulfed by the dense forest which ultimately became impassable.

The British colonial Government took the initiative in the reclamation of the Sundarban forest. It was such a hazardous and dangerous job that nobody could think of going to the thickest jungle for cutting down trees for land reclamation. But the colonial Government not only started to think for reclamation rather the administration was directly set to do the needful. It was a pressing need for the then colonial Government to procure more land for the purpose of cultivation in order to open up new sources of revenue as well as for the provision for more human settlements. The first official attempt to reclaim the forested land was made in the year 1770 by the Collector-General of the 24-Parganas District, Claude Russell. But the administration had to proceed with conspicuous obstacles to perform the task of reclamation. The trees in the forest were so closely set and in many places the trees were so large and extensively spread through the profuse branchings that it was almost impossible for the human being to conduct the job perfectly. Moreover, there were ferocious and poisonous animals at every step, there was dearth of drinking water in that saline based landmass and with these utter unwillingness of the workers for jungle-cutting activities added more and more problems in the line of implementation of the policy for reclamation. Years after years were rolled down, the colonial administration devised various ways and means from the experiences through times and ultimately it could win over the success *i.e.* the greater parts of the devastating forest areas were brought under cultivation and, to some extent, for the establishment of human settlements. This Sundarban has become attractive by the exuberant growth of mangrove forest occupying the mouth of the Ganga–Brahmaputra river system of the Lower Bengal estuarine landscape. The Sundarban delta is the largest mangrove forest belt in the world. It has been estimated that out of 50 different and most important mangrove species of the world altogether 35 species are found in Sundarban region.

It is for this reason Sundarban is credited in having the largest mangrove reserve on the globe. But due to various ecological disbalanced conditions principally caused by environmental pollution together with indiscriminate felling of trees and killing of the different faunal species the richest mangrove resources have faced dwindling in a rapid pace. The situation has aroused, very naturally, an alarm not only in the country but also it has created a condition of anxiety in the global contemplation devoted to conserve the nature-oriented resources having multi-dimensional effects on the humans, animals and plants. Also the land concerned is deeply inter-linked with the intermingling factors arising out of these effectual circumstances. It ultimately has stirred the personnel committed to the cause of safeguarding the traditional bountiful nature and to rejuvinate the same for the interest of the world as a whole. Being the world's largest and diversity-oriented cherished mangrove forest set-up Sundarban has very naturally received the requisite attention of the Man and Biosphere Programme (MAB) sponsored by UNESCO with an International Co-ordinating Council (ICC). This programme is specifically meant for devising various ways and means to keep a constant watch over the natural resources of specific importance and thereby to help these tide over the crises. Considering Sundarban as the largest propagating delta in the world and its harbouring of the largest chunk of mangrove vegetation it has been given the status of world heritage site.

Mangrove is not only a specific type of plant species growing wild in the salt influenced environment but it is to be regarded as a whole the symbol of reciprocal existence in relation to humans, animals, plants as well as land which are seen to be tied together forming an interlinked bondage of continuation. If in case any injury is caused to that life-line all the associated participants will have to face disastrous situation. The mangrove-dominated atmosphere is highly characterized by specific fragility and thus any sort of interference would lead to the extinction of the different components creating conspicuous wreckage of the total ecosystem. Thus, the mangrove situation is needed to be deciphered properly to develop an overall conception on Sundarban in its perfect perspective on the one hand, and to create a consciousness over the inevitable necessity to conserve the world famous mangrove phenomenon on the other. Mangrove is a term which has been derived from two separate words, *Mangaue* (Portuguese) and *Grove* (English), the meaning of this is salt-loving or salt-tolerant halophytic plants growing in tidal swampy lands. Mangrove is defined as a community of trees and shrubs which grow abundantly in the particular inter-tidal ecosystem of the tropics. They may also be described as a self-maintaining coastal, inter-tidal estuarine component which flourish under constant interactions with terrestrial and marine ecosystem. Mangrove species are characterized by glacy, leathery and evergreen leaves which are provided with deeply embedded stomata together with aqueous tissue. These help the trees to lessen the rate of transpiration. Roots of these trees have a large number of lenticels as well as stilt roots and pneumatophores. The speciality of mangrove is that they are adapted to the special type of ecological niche. The mangrove is not only the specific features of Sundarban but also it can be regarded as a symbol to this deltaic landmass. The mangrove complex of Sundarban has been divided into three categories— (i) Fresh water mangrove forest (ii) Moderately salt-water mangrove forest (iii) Salt-water mangrove forest. Based on the tidal level, mangroves have also been divided into four groups, viz.— (i) High tide mangrove (ii) Above general tidal level mangrove, (iii) Frequently inundated by salt-water mangrove, and (iv) Below tidal level mangrove. Mangroves are important both for providing requisite nutrients to support estuarine and coastal marine life forms and for providing a peaceful sheltered habitat in which certain varieties of fishes lay their eggs, and where the development of juvenile fishes takes place. A good number of fishes of commercial importance spend part of their lives in the mangrove wetlands and mangrove lined estuaries. Thus the mangroves have a beneficial role in the care and development of fishes in Sundarban. It is for this reason mangrove ecosystem is directly linked with the fishes *vis-a-vis* the fisherfolk.

It is to be noted that mangrove comprises a very specialized forest ecosystem found at the land-sea interface of the tropical and sub-tropical regions of the world that are bordering the sea coasts and estuaries. Mangrove forest systems are exposed to high and low tides twice in every 24 hours of the day and night. Mangrove soil is fine, clayey; it may semi-fluid or ill-consolidated. In the tropical hot humid climate, the river-borne fresh-water silts that are mixed with saline and brackish-water estuarine debris ultimately result in the formation of complex environment of water, air, soil that are linked with flora and fauna, create the mangrove ecosystem. Therefore, mangrove forest should be called as mangrove ecosystem because here man is seen to live in close association and harmony with nature. In this specific environment men, animals and different vegetative species live together in an atmosphere of co-existence.

Sundarban mangrove ecosystem is heavily important for the ideal and effective habitat of the fauna of the region. This ecosystem supports substantially a wide assemblage of animal communities. It has been gathered through prolonged observation that some of the animals are the permanent dwellers in the mangrove forests while others are casual visitors to the region. They come to the mangrove forested zone during the breeding times and also for the search of food. There are other animals who use mangrove forests for taking shelter or roosting. The estuaries of Sundarban are the fertile fields for birth, growth and development of many varieties of sea fish. There are many commercially important species like shrimps, prawns, crabs etc. here and for these the mangrove swamps constitute important nursery grounds. It has been reported that the brackish-water fish culture is exclusively dependent on mangrove ecosystem. From the reports of the fishery personnel, it has been found out that there are 133 different species of fish getting direct support from the mangrove ecosystem in Sundarban. The mudflats of Sundarban set up the magnificent homes for the mangrove flora and fauna. These mudflats are characteristically vegetated by mangroves protecting them by their intricate root system. Economic significance of mangrove ecosystem is diverse. Mangrove forest products supply a great many materials of commercial importance which range from firewood, different varieties of timber to crocodile skins, snake skins, honey, wax, alcohol, leather-colouring and fisheries. Owing to the high caloric value of the mangrove trees these are highly effective for fuel and charcoal making purposes. These plants stabilize the coastal shore-line by arresting the bank-erosion which in the long-run help in the formation of new islands. Mangrove plantations protect the inhabitants of the islands by reducing the possibilities of the outbreak of storms and cyclones. These also guard the landmass against tidal surges, cyclonic storms and high winds. Through the providing of nutritional imputs to the shallow channels and bays these constitute the basic habitat of the different varieties of aquatic species having commercial importance. Both in-shore and off-shore types of fishery are specially dependent on a common resource that is sustained by the estuarine mangrove ecosystem spreading over the large areas of back-waters and lagoons is known as the world's highly potential nursery. In addition to these mangrove plants have got various medicinal properties and these are extensively used in the traditional medicine system practised by the indigenous people of the region. Mangrove tress are rich in tannin content. The tannin is collected by the professional collectors in the Sundarban region and these are sold to the market especially in Kolkata. The different tanneries here are the principal purchasers. It is also used for the manufacture of plywood; tannin is also very much useful in joining of the pieces of wood.

The mangrove forest has offered an ideal home to the variegated animal species and these live in a chain of inter-relationship. Most of the fauna here have developed an amphibious nature. The fauna found in the mangrove ecosystem-their species diversity, their seasonal and diurnal abundance or fluctuation relating to salinity and other factors like temperature, humidity, tidal fluctuation etc. present tremendous importance of study. Mangrove flora and fauna, it is to be noted, have become the centre of focus for ecologists, naturalists, biologists, social scientists, tourists and nature lovers. All the animals living in this ecological zone have fruitfully adapted themselves to the surrounding environmental situation. It has been seen that the tigers here have become salt-water consumers and they have developed the power of swimming in the heavy currents of water. Deers prefer dry land but in Sundarban ecological setting their adaptation to swampy humid atmosphere is noteworthy. Almost all the aquatic animals here have developed a beautiful conception about the timing of rhythmic cycles of tides and thus they adjust all their activities according to that specific idea. Examining all the features of activities it can very well be maintained that all the organisms have got the ability to develop a kind of biological clock for accomplishing the rhythm of life in this particular biosphere.

Sundarban mangrove ecosystem is the ideal habitat of the majestic species of tiger popularly known as Royal Bengal Tiger. Sundarban tiger is believed to be the highly mysterious amongst all other animals found in this area. The Sundari and Hental forests play a great role in the formation of popular tiger habitat because of the fact that these stand on high ground and, therefore, these are saved from inundation excepting during the very high tides. The dense forested region created by the heavily grown genwa plants is the befitting habitat of the Sundarban tigers. The yellow-green colour of the leaves of the genwa plants are very much like the coat colour of the tigers and thus it helps the tigers to camouflage easily. The food chain in Sundarban explores the situation that the tiger is at the apex of the hierarchy of terrestrial as well as aquatic animals. The tiger's prey-animals include pigs, deers, monkeys, monitors lizards, birds, fishes, crabs and a number of other animals. Sundarban tigers have become man-eaters and very often they prey upon human beings. Their man-eating habits has been resulted due to various circumstantial consequences. It is due to this terrible habit of the tigers the people who enter the forest for fishing, crab catching, honey collecting, wood cutting and similar other purposes are to face dangerous situations. The human workers in the interior of Sundarban are always in a panic striken condition because of the fact that the horror of death may suddenly appear at any moment. But despite the danger of death the forest centred people cannot sit idle at home. They are to enter into the interior of the forest for their livelihood. Here life and death walk hand in hand. The fishers, wood cutters, honey collectors conquor the tremendous fear of being killed by the tiger through the infliction of spiritual power by way of paying of respectful homage to the tiger-god–Dakshin Roy. Sundarban tigers are very cunning and strategist. They have got the specific skill to jump upon the prey with the twinkle of an eye. Most of the time their principal aim is directed to working human group in the land and water of Sundarban. This situation causes such a panic in the minds of these working people in the interior of Sundarban that they enter the forest with the full risk of life. Despite this risk of life the traditional profession of these people cannot be abandoned. Thus these people are always faced with challenging attitude. This situation has been continuing from time immemorial which ultimately has done a great deal in framing a specific contextual mentality to fight with the hazardous condition not physically but by the application of supernatural forces. The tiger, the symbol of unlimited power, is believed to be overpowered through the proper understanding of some suprasensuous energy for which there are some experts who are known in this rural society as *gunins, fakirs* or *bauleys*. Numerous myths and legends have been developed surrounding that terror-oriented animal which in course of time has been raised to the level of god. The *gunins* through the chanting of *mantras* invoke the tiger-god and makes such a supernatural atmosphere which neutralizes the activities of that dreadful animal. Estuarine crocodiles are also regarded as the factors for panic-striken consequences. These aquatic animals are man-eaters and more often they cause great casualty to human beings with their heavily strong and tremendous sharp jaws. Thus in Sundarban the working people, in addition to many other dangerous situations, are to struggle with the tiger in land and the crocodile in water. There is a popular local saying "Jale Kumir, dangay bagh" (Crocodile in water, tiger on land) which is always given proper importance by the forest-based and water-centred workers in this mangrove ecosystem. It has become the philosophy of their life; life is full of acute adversities and there is no alternative but to move on to draw the sustenance of life through the bypassing of all the hazards and anxieties.

Thus it is seen that mangroves are important for diversified ways and as regards the land and people of Sundarban alongwith its variegated species of animals the mangroves have a beneficial role. It is because of this situation Sundarban Biosphere Reserve was established, in 1989, through a notification of Ministry of Environment and Forest, Govt. of India; as a part of the National MAB Programme. The said programme was specifically meant to establish a formal mechanism for coordinating and integrating varied research work. It was also directed to look into the conservation and training in national and international level for activating the harmonious existence of the people with their environment. The Sundarban Biosphere Reserve covers 9,630 sq. km., being the total areas of the Indian part of Sundarban. It includes 6 Blocks of North 24-Parganas District and 13 Blocks of South 24-Parganas District. There are 3 Wild Life Sanctuaries, within it, which are located at Sajnekhali, Lothian Island and Halliday Island. There is one National Park which covers the area of 1330 sq.km. The aims of the Biosphere Reserve are improvement of socio-economic status of the people, protection and conservation of flora and fauna, eco-restoration, scientific soil conservation activities, joint forest management and eco-development of people in and around Sundarban. The entire area lies to the South of Dampier-Hodges line of the mangrove forest. In other words, the Dampier-Hodges forms the northern boundary of the Sundarban Biosphere Reserve.

II

It is very difficult to look into the nature and growth of population in this part of Lower Bengal constituting Sundarban region because of its unsettled physiography which does not allow much to trace out the old relics forming the essential elements of history of the area. The geological, archaeological and anthropological evidences so far met with are very insignificant in comparison to the vastness of the problem. The matter of peopling of Sundarban region especially the Lower Bengal can never be properly highlighted without getting any hard evidence. But due to the large scale disturbance related to the total landmass caused by complicated events of natural disasters everything had been wiped out and these took resort in the abyss of oblivion. The specific references of the region of study are to be found in the different ancient literatures, religious texts as well as epics. But at that time the region was not known as Sundarban– the name came into existence during the recent past. There is a reference in the Ramayana regarding the region in question–it is indicated here as *patal* or *rasatal* (Nether world of infernal region). In the historical perspective we find that the region was referred in the travellers' accounts of Megasthenes, Deodorus etc. Tolleny, in his map, showed all the islands in Lower Bengal as belonging to Gangaridi kingdom. It was also shown that the capital of that kingdom was situated in the largest island of the region presently known as Gangasagar, and in close association of which there developed a prosperous harbour named Gange. Huen Sung referred the region as under the jurisdiction of Samatat. During the Pala and Sena Dynasties the region in question was included within the administrative sphere of Baghratati. Long after this, at the time of Muslim rulers of the country it was known as Bhatidesh. In this way this coastal part of Lower Bengal was named differently during the different periods of history. During the early part of the British Colonial administration the region concerned did not receive the name of Sundarban. The name Sundarban came later on. There are a number of legends depicting the origin of the name of Sundarban. According one legend, the name Sundarban was derived from the Sundari trees (*Heritiera fomes*) which were present in abundance in that region. Some say that the forest or *ban* adjoining the sea or *samudra* became popularly known as *Samudraban* amongst the local people which was then corrupted to form Sundarban. As per another legend, the vast tract of land on the coast of sea was under the jurisdiction of an ancient kingdom known as Chandradwip which was popularly called Chandraban. The forest surrounded Chandraban gradually converted into Sundarban. But the multitudes of Sundari trees throughout the whole region might have been the most important issue in the naming pattern of the region.

There are lots of evidence regarding the existence of well-developed human settlements with prosperous life and activities in the present Sundarban region. Through the analysis of several environmental and geological events occurred during different times it can easily be assessed that many a time human civilization faced overall destruction in consequences of sudden flow of water which inundated everything of human existence. The land formation of this region was such that there were frequent happenings of subsidence. Many experts are of opinion that the repeated subsidence of some parts of Sundarban caused vanishing great chunk of forest land as well as busy ports and prosperous settlements. According to the geologists, the bottom soil of the sea slowly gets eroded which results in the creation of vacuum in the lower layers of the sea. This sort of vacuum formation is scientifically called "Swatch of No Ground". When this sort of cavity is formed, the layers of the soil in the surrounding areas becomes depressed which causes vibration in the earth's surface. It is followed by the subsidence of the whole region. As soon as the land subsides, the salt-water of the sea immediately engulfs the total area. In this way the time-long effort and perseverance of the human communities for the creation of a particular life-way were forced to take watery grave within a moment. At the time of any sort of excavation relating to tank or well a large number of evidences of subsidence of the area are still coming out. When various types of large-scale excavation works were being conducted at Canning during the first phase of the British regime a large number of stout trunks belonging to Sundari trees were seen in the deepest layers of the earth in planted condition. These were the proofs of subsidence of the areas with the total forest cover. In course of time that subsided area became filled up gradually with the slow deposition of silt. As per natural cause that specific area became covered with vegetative growth and ultimately there developed a dense forest. From the underground regions of different places within the Sundarban region *e.g.* Pathar Pratima, Pakurtala, Rakshaskhali, Deulpota, Raidighi, Kankandighi, Mandirtala and many others a large number of stone and terracotta materials for daily use were discovered. The Sagar Island furnishes many proofs of ancient human settlements, buried under water in different periods of its past history. During the early forties of the last century two-mile long ruins of a city on the sea coast in Sagar Island was discovered by Mr. G. S. Dutta, and at that time a number of prehistoric and historic materials of daily use of the people concerned were brought to light. All these happenings support in the existence of age-old human civilization in this part of Sundarban. The famous *ashram* (hermitage) of Purana-fame Kapil *muni* was established at the Coastal region of the Bay of Bengal near the confluence of the Ganga river and the sea–an age-old holy site well-known and deeply adored by the people throughout India. The original hermitage popularly identified as "Kapilmunir ashram" witnessed a watery burial at the Bay of Bengal in consequence of the greatest earthquake in 1897. The present ashram had been built afterwards at a place far north from the previous site. The Sagar Island *vis-a-vis* the Sundarban region has become famous throughout India because of the presence of the hermitage of *Kapilmuni.* It is regarded as the celebrated spot of Hindu pilgrimage. A festival is held every year on the day of *makar sankranti* when the sun enters capricorn. It is tallied with the last day of the Bengali month of *Pous* (corresponding to 14th or 15th of January). A large fair is held at the coast of the Bay of Bengal in front of the present temple of *Kapilmuni*. The principal attraction of this assemblage is to take a holy dip in the confluence of the Ganga and the sea. The fair is attended by the pilgrims coming from the different parts of India. It is for this reason the coastal region of this part of the Bay of Bengal takes the form of a miniature India for a few days. This is one of the so many specialties in Sundarban region which requires integrated analysis in highlighting the life and culture of the locality in question.

Thus the history of the land and people of Sundarban is shrouded in mystery; but the different relics so far discovered and other evidences of a continued life-situation, of course with repeated breaks, indicate that the region saw the development of well-knit civilization from the remote past periods. Early settlement of the Sundarban surface was probably washed out and destroyed by transgressive sea waters due to local subsidence and auto compaction of deltaic sediments and then by catastrophic floods of Ganga river system in this area. The Sub-surface geology and sedimentary facies of some area of the lower delta proves this idea. Mild erosion is taking place and sea transgressing slowly over the subaerial part of the subdelta with a veneer of marine sediments at present. Thus many past remains of sediments may found along the river banks and island shores of the region.

Sundarban was extended far inland in the historical past and by natural situation the land has been sufficiently raised than the present one. The naturally raised land successively encroached by settlement after reclamation in the near past. Relics of the past settlement are also found all along the banks of Adi Ganga course. These areas were the parts of Sundarbans in the 14th and 15th centuries but probably by the end of 16th Century settlements might have advanced into these areas (Mukherjee, 1983). Land reclamation and settlement in the Sundarban progressed each year as the wetlands proved to be generally fertile and productive. In 1793, Cornwalis, the British Governor-General of Bengal for the East India Company, imposed a new rule of landed property for Bengal under the terms of the "Permanent Settlement". The Sundarbans, alongwith other lands lying outside the area of cultivation and settlement fell under state ownership. It was not until 1816, however, that the Bengal Government appointed a civil officer as Commissioner of the Sundarbans. This Officer was charged with demarcating and managing the water-logged forests and swamps of the lower delta. He was to regulate and encourage extraction of timber and fuel wood for growing needs of Kolkata (Calcutta) and other towns and cities in Bengal. However, the Commissioner was above all to ensure that private landowners cleared, settled, and reclaimed Sundarban forests and swamps for rice cultivation. A protracted survey operation completed in 1830 demarcated boundaries and offered security of tenure to improving landowners in this difficult terrain.

Affronted by the sight of so much culturable waste land lying unused, Bengal Officials adjusted their land policy to encourage smaller peasant farmers to engage in land reclamation on their own behalf. By the early years of the 20th century over 5000 km. of the Sundarbans was under cultivation and in the course of the 20th century, clearance and cultivation continued to cut into the Sundarban forest as pioneer settlers approached the coastal tidal islands. Under different reclamation phases settlement progressed in the Sundarban since 1770. Earliest reclamation in Sagar Island took place in 1811 with the intention of befiting the navigation of the river Hugli. Under the Saugor Island Society the land reclamation progressed upto 1849 in the island for salt manufacture and rive cultivation, but repeated storms of 1842, 1848 and 1852 damaged the land and earthen embankments. The cyclone wave of 1864 swept over the island with full force and wrought a great havoc. Considering all those ill-fated situations the then Presidency Commissioner of Bengal, Mr. Chapman, urged some protective measures to secure human life after 1867 in the largest island of Sundarban. Thus many storm refuges and protective fresh water tanks with high embankments were constructed within 1877 in the island. Some of storm refuges and protective tanks in damaged condition are still found in different parts of the island.

Thus reclamation of the forest area covering the estuarine Ganga-Brahmaputra deltaic Lower Bengal was an affair of the colonial Government in India.

Considering the urgency of human habitation and agriculture the colonial government initiated the policy of clearing the forest from the later part of the 18th Century.

The lease holders of the forested land took all possible steps to clear the jungle. But it was not an easy task. At that time Sundarban was a terrific locality–at each step there was the direct clutch of death. Different types of ferocious animals, both on land and in water, made the life of the people working there miserable. Many workers fled away–there were practically no worker with whom the lease holders could proceed with the work of deforestation. There was acute scarcity of drinking water which made the workers puzzled. There was conspicuous want of a sufficient number of raiyats who could be induced to migrate and settle down. Finding no other alternative the lease holders started bringing migrant labours from the tribal concentrated regions of Chotanagpur, Orissa and the adjoining regions. These people had the direct experience in tackling with forested regions–they knew how to adjust with the forested surroundings. They belonged to the different tribal groups like the Munda, Oraon, Santal, Bhumij, Ho etc. On reaching the new land with different ecological settings and surrounding atmosphere these tribal people tried their level best to find out the positive ways to shoulder the heavy burden. The tribal people with their sincere workmanship associated with hard labour and the courage to face the various adversities in the dense forest could win over the success. They really established themselves as efficient forest clearance workers. There was an allurement for them in addition to the payment of wages. It was decided that they would be allotted some plots of lands on individual basis after the reclamation work and when those plots would be transformed into agricultural lands. It was, no doubt, a great attraction to them and that factor very naturally enhanced their spirit of work. After the transformation of the forested land into agricultural fields there were the possibilities of growing of abundant crops. At that specific stage many people from the neighbouring districts like Midnapur, Howrah etc. migrated to the Sundarban region with the hope of changing their fate. In this way a large number of *joteders* reached here especially from Midnapur district to engage themselves in the work of cultivation in that virgin land. Some sections of the local people also joined their hands in that programme of activities. This situation ultimately attracted many common people belonging to the different caste groups to come to the newly created agricultural fields at Sundarban region for working as farm labourers. At the formative stage these workers including *joteders* used to stay in the Sundarban region during the period of cultivation of paddy and when the season was over they went back to their original homelands. But with the gradual development of the region when the possibilities of agriculture in the reclaimed land were proved to be prosperous, they started staying here permanently and gradually became the permanent settlers of the region. Thus the present inhabitants of the reclaimed lands in the Lower Bengal are mostly the descendents of the migrant groups of people from the far and near places.

Sundarban is such a tract of land which is principally populated by a large number of lower caste groups. In comparison to these people there are lesser number of higher caste groups which live side by side with the former groups. Among the low caste Hindus, the Pods or Paundra Kshatriya in the western side of the region and the Namasudras in the eastern side are numerous. The Paundra Kshatriya constitute the major scheduled caste population in Sundarban region. Numerically Namasudras come to the next. Besides these two principal castes there are others like Rajbanshi, Bagdi, Keora, Tiyor, Chamar, Dhopa, Jelia Kaibarta and Malos. Amongst the general caste groups Mahishyas are preponderant. Then there are Brahmins, Kayasthas, Goala, Napit, Kamar, Teli, Chutor as well as Muslim Communities. All these groups had migrated to the new land mostly from the northern part of the 24-Parganas District, and also from Midnapur, Howrah and Nadia districts. Thus the majority of the earlier settlers of Sundarban were composed of migrant low caste and tribal population in addition to a smaller number of resident aborigines of the remote past period. All of them, irrespective of their traditional occupations, faced a conversion in their economic habits to a certain extent. The people belonging to different caste and community groups accepted the different occupational activities in the newly settled areas and those were agriculture, fishing, wood cutting, honey collecting. Though cultivation and fishing were traditional occupations of most of the caste groups migrated to the region but the total ecological and environmental set-up was such that they had to adopt a different mode of approach in the performance of those common occupations. Nature was always unfavourable to conduct those activities in a regular manner. The influence of salt-water, high tidal waves, occasional cyclonic affairs, land slides and large scale erosion were the basic problems in addition to many other circumstantial mishaps. Thus the people had to fight constantly, and in that there was an urgent necessity to make united efforts to resist the adversities. The close-set cooperation and mutual understanding which developed amongst the dispersed group of migrant labourers from the adjoining districts and other far off places to meet the inevitable necessity for survival gave rise to permanent settlements in the different spots which ultimately led to the development of villages. In this difficult terrain due to heavy risk and uncertainty in earning livelihood, people belonging to the same social group started staying together so that they could help each other at the time of need. Among the Muslims the converted Sheikh Community is in great majority here. A large number of low caste Hindus was converted to Islam due to many socio-political reasons. These people have been living alongwith the different Hindu caste groups without any sort of difficulty despite their different religious philosophy.

The principal migrant tribal groups like the Munda, Oraon, Santal, Ho, Bhumij, Mahali, Kora and Mal Paharia who took the sole responsibility in the reclamation work of Sundarban forested region despite a lot of troubles and uncertainties gradually started staying at Sundarban locality on getting a portion of reclaimed agricultural lands as per contract with the lease holders. At the very outset of the reclamation work the local wood-cutters and other concerned labourers failed to do any large scale work and ultimately it became impossible for them to continue. The tribal people who were brought from the neighbouring states, having close association with forest, to Sundarban region through the medium of some agents appointed by the lease holders could make the impossible events possible by dint of their tremendous physical strength, mental preparation and sincere approach for conducting the work in question. But the forests of Chotanagpur in Bihar (now Jharkhand) and of Mayurbhanj in Orissa, from where the large chunk of labourers came, were completely different in character and composition as well as in the nature of flora and fauna. Thus the forest-oriented tribal people of Bihar and Orissa did not find the work of jungle cutting and staying, though temporarily, in Sundarban so easy as they thought. But these people did not think for a moment to retreat from the face of the hazards and anxieties. The strong tribal sentiment was rightly utilized by the lease holders and the concerned administration. They were given the hope of permanent settlement in the newly reclaimed locality by becoming the land holders. Ultimately lands were allotted to those tribal people who became very much energetic to set-up tribal settlements centering round their only agricultural lands. Thus these tribal groups were the primary settled residents of the reclaimed Sundarban. The total situation made the migrant labourers from Bihar and Orissa forests the actual sons of the soil and that status was acquired by them through their whole-hearted dedication to the cause of reclamation work in Sundarban. But the total context started changing rapidly. With the increased prosperity of the region there was a large-scale migration of different people to the reclaimed locality and ultimately it took the shape of a complex population pattern. The late comers were highly motivated–they were after getting some concrete things through tricy ways. These fortune seekers belonged to the different categories of people–from day labourers to zamindars. The tribal landholders became easy prey to those people. The simple-minded tribal people having deep faith in human values fell in complicated traps of the unscrupulous people and thus the tribal people started losing their lands and whatever materials they had in their possession. There were occasions when the tribal people were intoxicated by offering free *hanria* (rice beer) to them to get their thumb impressions in favour of selling their lands to those people. The tremendous exploitation of the *mahajans* (money lenders) in the name of helping them during the time of need ultimately resulted the tribal people in becoming full destitute. As that specific process of exploitation went on unabated all the tribal people in course of time came down from the status of land holders to the condition of wage labourers.

The agriculture-oriented life of the tribal people became converted to various other occupations in Sundarban like fishing, crab-hunting, honey-collecting, earth-cutting, wood-cutting and min-collecting. The speciality of the Sundarban tribals lies in the fact that in the new ecological set up and changed condition of life the different tribal communities show no differentiation amongst them. Being detached from the original stock in the parental land, both physically and mentally, the tribal people here have developed a specific culture, a philosophy of life designed to fit with the present circumstances. It may be called a regional tribal culture where the different tribal sentiments have been mingled to form a holistic pattern. To the local non-tribal communities these tribal people are not identified according to their specific tribal affiliation. The tribal people as a whole have taken shelter in the secluded spots as they prefer to live away from the so-called advanced people. The life-philosophies of the different tribal groups have been mingled to form a concerted consciousness because of their similar mode of approach to fight with the different surroundings. These tribal communities could not maintain their social connection with the original stalks at the parental villages in Bihar and Orissa owing to great distance as well as financial stringencies. Thus the adverse situation instigates these communities to think and stay jointly after breaking down the barriers of social distinctions. To the non-tribal people of the region these tribal people are not known according to their tribal names like Munda, Santal, Oraon, Ho etc. but altogether they are recognised as *buno* i.e. the inhabitants of forests. The *buno* is the amalgamated identity arisen from the specific situational context. Despite their living in separate places as well as their fellow-feeling attitude the tribal people as a whole frequently come close to the non-tribal lower caste groups in various economic arenas to work hand in hand and thereby to fight jointly against the adversities. Thus after living together of centuries and facing the similar problematic situations in life all these people, irrespective of castes, classes and tribes, in course of time evolved a specific life-philosophy which became the characteristic feature of the Sundarban regional culture. This cultural tradition is unique in itself and it cuts across all the social and religious barriers which are highly functional and rigidly maintained in other places. This is the direct consequences of the holistic ecological set up of Sundarban on the human population.

Sundarban region's varied resources in forest and in salt water rivers and estuaries have been attracting many people of the neighbouring areas and this specific phenomenon is still going on unabated. Thus there has always been an effective trend of migration to the Sundarban region and in course of time the migrant people make themselves permanent residents of the locality. In this way the peopling of Sundarban is in process. The waves of migrants to this landmass reached in the wake of partition of India in 1947 and the Bangladesh Liberation Struggle in 1971. Many such migrants who were in search of refuge from atrocities and harassments found the place suitable for settlement. In this way of large number of people from the neighbouring country started their march towards the Indian Sundarban region and after conspicuous troubles and tremendous distress they managed to reach here and thus constituted the region's permanent population. Those alien migrant groups of people after reaching the region in question following the partition of India started settling in small and homogeneous fishing villages and thereby making these heterogeneous and complex ones. Sometimes the migrant groups selected the open fields near the rivers and estuaries to start new village settlements. In this way in Sundarban region different instant villages developed with heterogeneous people after the partition of India. Of late, large-scale migration of people from Bangladesh, during different times, has brought a significant change in the content and character of population in the region in question.

A View of the Mangrove Forest

A Typical Forest Office

The Havoc of Erosion in Sundarban Region

Way to the famous Kapilmuni Temple

A Gathering in Front of the Kapilmuni Temple

The Image of Kapilmuni and the Traditional Priest

A Holy Dip at Ganga Sagar

A Pious Activity with the Cow–the Mother

A Poor Fisherman's House Type at the River Side

A House Type at Sagar Island–adjustment to Ecology

3

FISHING VILLAGES AND THEIR ECO-CULTURAL SETTINGS

Villages in India are by nature the concerted units wherein we find the interactions of the people not only amongst themselves in respect of variegated necessities of life but also these interactions are seen to be extended towards the geophysical, biospheric and ecological systems to cope with the entire environmental surroundings for the sake of biological as well as ecological existence. These double-headed purposes are very well illustrative in the fishing villages. Fishermen, as per their professional characteristics do not continuously stay in the villages meant for their living–they are to build their second homes on water as without staying on water and moving about here and there their economic purpose will not be fulfilled. Fishing in turbulent water far away from home specifically needs group mentality based on close cooperation and mental understanding. Thus the fishermen have always been in an urgent necessity to settle down in the villages having the characteristic features of the basic philosophy of rural setting. The social structure of the villages is in a well-knit comprehension with the economic perspective and both are intimately tied together to form an integrated whole. Mention may be made that the fishing villages have got their specific patterns–here the economic trend is seen to be focused on the work of fishing and fish-oriented trade and other activities. There may be conspicuous caste groups of non-fishing tradition but despite their non-fishing activities they, as a rule, have clung to the fish-related way of life. It is seen that many non-fishing caste groups through their continuous living with the fishing castes and fish workers have, in course of time, been transformed into the fishing groups though they have got uninterrupted affiliation with the traditional caste name. There is a regular clash between the traditional and non-traditional fishing strategies. The latter groups are the possessors of mechanized fish gears and with the help of these they dominate the indigenous people having country made fishing appliances. It is due to the conflicts between these two groups some sorts of conflicts and tensions have been resulted in the total village atmosphere. Recently the phenomenon like class structure has been raising its head in the non-traditional fishing villages. With the help of better economic support and modernized fishing gears the higher classes of fishermen practically dominate the traditional group with indigenous fishing procedures. This structural pattern of class formation and its functional dimensions are to be seen to exert their influences on the fishing villages. In the traditional homogeneous fishing villages these sorts of conflicting behaviour are not in existence. The forms and functions of the three types of fishing villages having different contexts and philosophy would help in understanding the impact of fishing economy on the people irrespective of castes, classes and religion, and thereby to clarify and explain the pattern of interactions through time and space.

Village Nurpur

Nurpur is a traditional fishing village developed long ago on the east bank of the river Ganga, 42 km. West of Diamond Harbour–the gateway to the Sundarban deltaic region. The river Ganga flows southward and ultimately in travels furthest south to meet with the Bay of Bengal. Nurpur falls within the jurisdiction of South Twenty Four Parganas district which has flourished throughout the eastern and south-eastern banks of the Ganga. On the other side of the river i.e. at the western side the district of Howrah has developed. At the southern border of Howrah district river Rupnarayan flows down to Ganga, and it marks the northern boundary of the district of Midnapur. This district then runs parallel to the South Twenty Four Parganas district; the Ganga throughout its course divides the two districts mentioned. Village Nurpur is situated at a very distinct landmass. Coming directly straight from north the Ganga suddenly takes a short curve in its course and then flows in the south-eastern direction. Nurpur is found to be developed on this point of curvature. The village is bounded by Srifalberia village in the north, Diamond-Harbour-Nurpur Road in the south, the Ganga in the west and Sukdevpur village in the east. The selection of site for Nurpur village was an ideal one. The Ganga in the olden days was highly navigable and it was the principal waterway to Calcutta port from the Bay of Bengal. Because of the existence of the confluence of the Rupnarayan with the Ganga it was always fed by sufficient water. Owing to unsilted river bed there were always conspicuous tidal waves in the Ganga which were highly suitable for the incoming of fishes from the sea. Thus the total situation as regards fish based occupation was highly productive and naturally Nurpur developed as a conspicuous fishing village in this region. Table 1 gives the

Table 1
Distribution of Families
According to Castes and Community in Nurpur

Sl. No.	*Castes / Community*	*Total number of families*	*Percentage*
1.	Bagdi	80	28.07
2.	Jele Kaibarta	77	27.02
3.	Mahishya	16	6.61
4.	Goala	25	8.77
5.	Gandhabanik	11	3.86
6.	Kamar	11	3.86
7.	Kumhar	9	3.16
8.	Malakar	5	1.75
9.	Keora	6	2.11
10.	Muslim	45	15.79
	Total	285	100.00

sex-wise number of persons and their relevant percentages. There are altogether 285 families and Table 2 has been employed to show the caste-wise number of families. The Bagdi caste possesses the largest number of families and then comes the Jele Kaibarta. Muslims come at the third position. So far as the family size is concerned Table 3 depicts the caste/community wise distribution of the total population of the village. Medium-sized families are commonly seen here which are followed by small-sized families. Large-sized families run parallel to the small-sized families. The number of very large-sized family is very limited. These are found among the Bagdi, Jele Kaibarta and Gandhabanik caste groups.

Table 2
Castes/Community-wise Distribution of Population in Nurpur

Castes / Community	*Total population*	%	*Male*	%	*Female*	%
Bagdi	442	30.01	223	29.97	219	30.04
Jele Kaibarta	396	26.88	186	25.0	210	28.80
Mahishya	85	5.77	55	7.39	30	4.12
Goala	107	7.26	55	7.39	52	7.13
Gandhabanik	70	4.76	40	5.38	30	4.12
Kamar	54	3.67	25	3.36	29	3.98
Kumhar	49	3.33	26	2.49	23	3.16
Malakar	22	1.49	13	1.76	9	1.23
Keora	37	2.51	17	2.28	20	2.74
Muslim	211	14.32	104	13.98	107	14.68
Total	1473	100.00	744	100.00	729	100.00

Among the fisherfolk in Nurpur, like in other fishing communities, the family acts as the essential primary economic unit in the strict sense of the term. In these families the total behaviour patterns of the different members are specifically conditioned by the fishing activities as a whole. The family of the fishermen still today works as the effective training centre for the boys and girls to propagate the knowledge of fishing technicalities, net weaving, net mending, fish sorting and other related affairs. Within the family, there is a remarkable division of labour between the

Table 3
Distribution of Family Size on Castes/Community Basis in Nurpur

Castes / Community	Various Family Size: Small-sized family (upto 3 members)		Medium-sized family (from 4 to 6 members)		Large-sized family (from 7 to 9 members)		Very large-size family (upto 10 members)		Total	
	No.	%	No.	%	No.	%	No.	%	No.	%
Bagdi	13	19.40	44	31.21	17	26.15	6	50.00	80	28.07
Jele Kaibarta	20	29.85	35	24.82	18	27.69	4	33.33	77	27.02
Mahishya	2	2.99	10	7.09	4	6.15	–	–	16	5.61
Goala	7	10.45	15	10.64	3	4.62	–	–	25	8.77
Gandhabanik	3	4.48	2	1.42	4	6.16	2	16.67	11	3.86
Kamar	1	1.49	8	5.67	2	3.08	–	–	11	3.86
Kumhar	1	1.49	5	3.55	3	4.62	–	–	9	3.16
Malakar	1	1.49	4	2.84	–	–	–	–	5	1.75
Keora	1	1.49	1	0.70	4	6.15	–	–	6	2.11
Muslim	18	26.87	17	12.06	10	15.38	–	–	45	15.79
Total	67	100.0	141	100.00	65	100.00	12	100.00	285	100.00

sexes. The adult males take active part in the fishing operations and related laborious activities while the women keep themselves engaged in indoor works like cooking, child rearing and the like. But among the fisherfolk the women are not totally confined within the household. The fisherwomen are to mend nets at the landing ghats, participate in fish trade, as well as to keep outside contact when the male members are out for fishing. During the absence of the male members for weeks together the women are to take full responsibilities of maintaining the family, looking after the children as well as performing the essential family duty like the socialisation of the young ones. As the male persons frequently go out for fishing expedition and also for seliing the catch through auction at the distant market place, it is almost impossible for them to look after the children to help them socialise according to social norms and traditions. Amongst the fisherfolk it has perfectly become the feminine duty. Most of the time the fisherwomen are to stay at home with profuse anxiety and tension due to the long absence of the male persons. Their anxiety reaches the maximum point during cyclonic weather. Sometimes they are to take many decisions themselves in the running of the family. So unlike other women the fisherwomen are to take comparatively heavy responsibility in the running of their respective families. The families of the fisherfolk are completely patrilineal and the males are always dominated here. They are the decision makers in all sorts of familial affairs; the women in the family may be consulted but it is not obligatory. Even after the shouldering of the heavy responsibility and passing of their days with anxieties and tensions the women among the fisherfolk do not get high status.

In Nurpur the fishing activities are conducted by the fishing castes and this tradition has never been deviated here. Table 4 shows that the Bagdis and the Jele Kaibartas are the two principal caste groups in whose hands the fishing operations are maintained. Out of other caste groups three from Mahishyas and three from Goala castes have taken up direct fishing activities and they accompany the fishing groups belonging to the Bagdis and the Jele Kaibartas. The inclusion of these six persons (vide Table 4) belonging to the non-fishing castes is due to the fact that they have developed a special inclination towards fishing and in addition to this they are all characterized by desperateness in riskful journey in the turbulent rivers. None from other five castes has ever accompanied or is allowed to join the fishing team. But the Muslims of this village depicts a different picture. They came to Nurpur about 80 years ago. The grandfather of Taimur Bux migrated to Nurpur from Midnapur district and at that time Nurpur was a small hamlet having only a few Bagdi and Jele Kaibarta families practising fishing in the Ganga. Some other castes like Kumhar, Kamar and Gandhabanik were there but they were in a very negligible percentage. After coming to the new settlement Jiaul Bux, grandfather of Taimur Bux, attracted to the profession of fishing and its prospects. Mr. Bux was a moneyed man and thus he wanted to extend monetary help to the fishermen out of sympathy. He had sufficient cultivable lands at his ancestral place in the district of Midnapur. The fishermen were highly obliged for his support and ultimately that Muslim gentleman became a prominent figure in the village of Nurpur as by nature he came forward to help the distressed persons. He was once approached by the obliged fishermen to invest money directly in the development of fishing operational technology. It was accepted by him and he gradually started accompanying the fishing troops for having direct knowledge over the situation. His overall interest in the fishing operation gradually brought him direct to the fishing activities. He became directly involved in active fishing with the attempt for exploring new horizons in this line. In course of time he could make himself not only a successful fisherman but also an efficient boatman with practical knowledge on fish behaviour as well as on river and ocean currents. His prosperity in the different spheres of occupation attracted many of his neighbouring relatives at Midnapur district who gradually migrated to Nurpur and settled there permanently. At present the Muslims of Nurpur are prosperous fishermen and one of them have got the capacity of keeping one motor launch for fishing in deep sea. He has got his own fishing unit in which the fishermen and the helpers work on monthly salary basis. At present the Muslims in Nurpur dominate in the fishing operations as a whole and all other fishermen belonged to Bagdi and Jele Kaibarta castes are obliged to take suggestions from them and ask their help in solving any problem.

The Bagdis are the original settlers of the village. They were originally cultivating caste and used to engage in diversified agricultural activities organised by the higher caste groups in addition to their inclination for fishing in ponds and ditches with small nets and traps. But on reaching the reclaimed Sundarban region during the 18th century the Bagdis (who migrated in large numbers) were allured by the circumstances to change their traditional occupation. On reaching the new land they came across the high prosperity of fishing in the rivers, creeks and estuaries in

Table 4
Standard of Literacy in Nurpur According to Caste/Community

Different educational standards	*Different sexes*	*Bagdi*	*%*	*Jele-Kaibarta*	*%*	*Mahishya*	*%*	*Goala*	*%*	*Gandha-banik*	*%*	*Kamar*	*%*	*Kumhar*	*%*	*Malakar*	*%*	*Keora*	*%*	*Muslim*	*%*
	M	101	45.29	93	50.0	12	21.82	11	20.00	2	5.0	2	8.0	9	34.62	2	15.38	7	41.18	23	22.11
Illiterate	F	108	49.32	127	60.48	10	33.33	21	40.38	2	6.67	5	17.24	9	39.13	3	33.33	15	75.0	47	43.93
	T	209	47.29	220	55.55	22	25.88	32	29.9	4	5.48	7	12.96	18	36.73	5	22.73	22	59.46	70	33.18
Can sing only	M	32	14.35	31	16.67	2	3.64	3	5.45	1	2.5	0	0	0	0	0	0	2	11.76	11	10.58
	F	34	15.53	11	5.24	1	3.33	1	1.92	0	0	1	3.45	2	8.7	2	22.22	0	0	4	3.74
	T	66	14.93	42	10.61	3	3.53	4	3.74	1	1.37	1	1.85	2	4.08	2	9.09	2	5.41	15	7.11
Primary	M	56	25.11	38	20.43	10	18.18	11	20	9	22.5	4	16.0	7	26.92	2	15.38	7	41.18	34	32.69
up to	F	60	27.4	43	20.48	10	33.33	12	23.08	9	30	6	20.69	7	30.43	3	33.33	5	25.0	37	34.58
Class IV	T	116	26.24	81	20.45	20	23.53	23	21.5	18	24.66	10	18.52	14	28.57	5	22.73	12	32.43	71	33.65
Secondary	M	32	14.35	19	10.22	22	40.0	26	47.27	20	50.0	17	68.0	10	38.46	8	61.54	1	5.88	35	33.65
up to	F	17	7.76	28	13.33	8	26.67	16	30.77	17	56.67	16	55.17	5	21.74	1	11.11	0	0	19	17.76
Class X	T	49	9.73	47	11.87	30	35.29	42	38.32	37	50.68	33	61.11	15	30.61	9	40.99	1	2.70	54	25.59
Higher	M	1	0.45	3	1.61	3	5.45	3	5.45	5	12.5	0	0			1	7.69				
Secondary	F	0	0	1	0.48	0	0	2	3.85	2	6.67	1	3.45			0	0				
up to Class XII	T	1	0.23	4	1.01	3	3.53	5	4.67	7	9.59	1	1.85			1	4.55				
Graduation	M	1	0.45	2	1.08	6	10.91	2	3.64	3	7.5	2	8							1	0.96
	F	0	0	0	0	1	3.33	0	0	0	0	0	0							0	0
	T	1	0.23	2	0.50	7	8.24	2	1.87	3	4.11	2	3.70							1	0.47
Total	M	223		186		55		55		40		25		26		13		17		104	
	F	219		210		30		52		30		29		23		9		20		107	
	T	442		396		85		107		70		54		49		22		37		211	

that locality and gradually they started fishing with full devotion. The practice of fishing gave them a good return as the abundance of fishes in the virgin locality went to the extreme all through the time. Ultimately they turned themselves into full-fledged fishing groups, and became identified as fisherfolk. The Jele Kaibartas are the second caste group who reached Nurpur to settle down. This caste group is a derivative of the Chasi Kaibarta whose occupation is centred round agriculture and its allied activities. A section of them took fishing as the principal concern of their way of life and ultimately identified as Jele Kaibartas. This caste group reached the Sundarban delta during the same period as did by the Bagdis, and it could avail itself of the favourable circumstances of fishing in the southern deltaic landmass. In course of time they could turn themselves as the efficient fishermen in Sundarban delta. Thus these two traditional fishing castes are the architect of Nurpur fishing village which could attract many persons from the neighbouring region on assessing its prosperity in the olden days.

Nurpur fishing village developed completely centering round the river Ganga. At the time of inception of the village Ganga was a highly prosperous river with its conspicuous tidal waves. It was perfectly navigable and the water of which was highly suitable for the breeding, growth and development as well as migration of the different species of fish. The fisherfolk did never think of going any other site beyond the course of the Ganga as it fulfilled all their requirements in fishing. Thus the life of the fisherfolk at Nurpur village was interwoven with the Ganga–the holy river in the earth. The Ganga is called as Divine Mother, and thus the river is believed to be animated with life-force who is always kind and sympathetic to the people of all concerned. And the fisherfolk of Nurpur deeply believe that the Ganga is the manifestation of bringing good luck to the fish-workers–not only so, she keeps constant watch over their activities and saves them in times of danger. Thus they have developed a specific reverence for the Ganga–

respectfully called as Holy Mother. On this ground it is seen that the fisherfolk, irrespective of castes and communities, have developed a pattern of "sacred complex" with the Ganga. Fishing operation in Nurpur is not only an integrated economic affair but it depicts a pattern of synthesis amongst the economic pursuits, social life and ritualistic performances. The philosophy of village life in Nurpur is thus attuned with these modes of behaviour.

The settlement pattern in Nurpur is a compact one. The village is connected with the metalled road from Diamond Harbour by a brick-lined narrow road. Buses ply from Calcutta and Diamond Harbour regularly and these terminate their journey at the ferry ghat of the Ganga. After alighting from the bus at Dewantala stoppage one can reach the village through the brick-lined road by walking at least for half on hour. Cycle vans can also be hired from Dewantala to reach Nurpur. The brick-lined road leads through the paddy fields and at the vicinity of the village the road is seen to be traversed through the green canopy made by the leafy growth of numerous trees. The houses are mostly made of mud walls and thatched by straw, and in some cases with corrugated iron sheets. The houses are not properly arranged, rather these are constructed haphazardly. There are narrow muddy paths in between the houses which run in a zigzag manner. There are a few brick-built houses that have been constructed recently by the comparatively well-to-do fishermen but the number can be counted on fingers.

The central point of the village is hatkhola, which is situated at the river bank. From a very early period their was a regular fish market-named hatkhola–which held on every Wednesday and Saturday. Other commodities for daily life were also sold here, and thus Nurpur developed as a business centre of the whole locality and the hatkhola became famous all through the time. But during the present period the hatkhola has lost all its glamour and economic appeal due to the large-scale erosion at the bank of the Ganga. The erosion has washed away the highly raised land with a large number of big trees. The destruction occurred gradually year after year before the eyes of the inhabitants. Now at the western point of the village a specific remnant of the glorious hatkhola is seen in a very dilapidated condition with an old banyan tree which is on the verge of falling down due to loosening of the earth at its root system. Hatkhola is still regarded as a place of importance and the fishermen during their leisure time gossip here as well as the important social assemblages also are held here. Many villagers pass their lazy hours here under the banyan tree; especially during the summer months it becomes a pleasant spot for cooling down the body and mind.

The village is divided into four wards–Jelepara, Bagdipara, Moyrapara and Kamarpara. Jelepara is situated along the bank of the Ganga and just at the eastern side of it Bagdipara has been flourished. The hatkhola is situated at the extreme northern end of Jelepara. There is a narrow canal at the northern boundary of the village and near hatkhola it falls on the Ganga. After Bagdipara on the eastern side there is a brick-lined path stretching from north to south and after which Kamarpara and Moyrapara have developed. Though the wards are named after the castes, yet these are not exclusively meant for the castes only after which these are named. There are evidence that Moyrapara accommodates Kumhar and Gandhabanik castes as well as the Muslims. In Bagdipara, some Kamar families are seen. Thus the physical boundaries of the different wards are not well-marked. Similarly, there is no conspicuous social distance among the villagers belonging to the different castes and community groups. The village works as a perfect socio-economic unit. This has become possible due to the centralised common economy based on fishing and its allied activities. The people belonging to the non-fishing castes like Mahishya, Kumhar, Kamar, Malakar, Gandhbanik, Goala perform activities related to their professional callings or other non-fishing activities but they are all indirectly dependent on the fishermen's work centred round fishing. Therefore, on economic sphere all the caste groups as well as the Muslim community are seen to be functioning in a well-knit reciprocal understanding.

There are three free primary schools in the village and the children can find the opportunity for getting themselves educated upto Class IV. But after this one is to go outside the village for the continuation of education. For Higher Secondary and Collegiate education a few students from this village regularly go to Diamond Harbour. Educational standard in the village is not unsatisfactory in spite of the lack of proper opportunities. Table 4 shows that a considerable number of villagers have got inclination towards formal education. Amongst most of the castes it is seen that a good number of persons are educated upto secondary level. There are 17 graduates in the village and they are distributed among 6 castes and 1 community groups (see Table 4). There is no Post Office here and the people do not feel any discomfort for it. There is one Shiva temple and one Sitala temple at Bagdipara. A few types of folk deities like Manasa, Banabibi, Barathakur which are spread here and there in the shrines raised at the foot of the trees. There are altogether 7 grocer's shops at the different corners of the village. The number of tea stalls are four. At hatkhola there is one stationery shop and two tea stalls. There is only one working tube-well near hatkhola which is now the only source of drinking water for the whole village. There is another tube-well that has been sunk at the landing ghat but it has gone out of order for long. After the dilapidation of hatkhola the bi-weekly market has been shifted to Dewantala–a neighbouring village by the side of the metalled road. The people of Nurpur are to visit this market for getting their necessary commodities.

The village was formerly administered by the traditional panchayat. The member of such panchayat were always selected on the basis of ability and influence on personal level. Most of the members used to come from the two dominant fishing castes as well as from the Muslim community especially when the Muslims started to develop themselves in the domain of fish-based economy. Members from other castes were also drawn to make the panchayat an all-village affair. But in all the discussions the dominant caste and community groups used to exert influence. Still, it is an ideal one for solving various intra-village problems. In times of any hazards in the village life or in the event of any familial calamity the traditional panchayat readily tries to find out the instant relief from the distress. But with the introduction of the statutory panchayat the function of the traditional panchayat has become limited though it has not been abolished. Both the systems are functioning parallelly but the statutory panchayat has become the most valued and effective organisation in the political structure of the village. The caste-based panchayat is still there and these are acting fruitfully amongst the fishing caste groups. In order to maintain various normative and traditional fishing regulations the caste-based panachayat is essential. The traditional caste-oriented fishermen are always alert in the strict following of the social legislation that have been imposed on the fishing operations and allied activities. If anybody disobeys or violates the regulations the cases are referred to the caste panchayat which takes up the matter seriously and if the accused is found guilty he is punished as per panchayat regulations. Strict observances of fishing regulations are always compulsory for the personnel joining the fishing group or performing individual fishing to maintain the discipline in the multifaceted operational understandings.

The overall fishing operations in Nurpur is conducted through group fishing organisations. Group fishing is a compulsory affairs during fishing in the estuaries as it needs the joint action of a number of persons. The group is generally comprised of 10-25 persons. Participation in a group is voluntary but it is obligatory that a person should serve the same group during a particular season. Group fishing personnel in Nurpur are generally recruited from within the villagers but sometimes persons from the different neighbouring villages may be taken up to form the group. Planning for group formation is made at least a month before the date of starting for fishing. The leader of the party, generally from the Jele Kaibarta or Bagdi castes, holds a formal meeting at any convenient place. Most of the time it is held at the hatkhola or at any place by the river side. This group fishing is continued for 15-20 days but it varies according to the availability of fish as well as the weather condition. In this type of group fishing the earnings are distributed on the basis of boats and nets and the number of persons involved. All the persons get equal shares excepting the leader of the party and the *manjhi* or the principal crew who receive two shares. Payments are generally made in cash after selling out the fishes or sometimes fresh fishes are also given as shares.

At times fishing groups are formed with the persons coming from the extended families of the group leader. It is commonly done for the serving three-fold purposes: (i) if the fishing group is formed by the members from the extended kin groups, there is minimum chance of any misunderstanding and thus the difficulty in conducting the group becomes nil, (ii) the group becomes less expensive and naturally the risk would be minimum, and (iii) the young members of the kin groups, if selected, would be automatically trained up in the work.

The third from of group fishing is conducted through the categorical fishing units. In Nurpur there are six active fishermen who are the owners of such fishing units. The workers here are selected from both the fishing and non-fishing castes. Those who have got the ability of fishing and knowledge of boating are selected in the formation of such fishing units. These units are the professional fishing bodies and they all work on share basis or get monthly salary as per nature of work. In this professional fishing groups persons from distant villages may join. The owners of these units most of the time like to form permanent groups for getting better results.

Fisherman in Nurpur very often goes out with smaller boats and nets individually. In this case, the fisherman concerned is assisted by two or three workers who mostly belong to his own family or the neighbour's family. In this individual fishing practice the helpers are paid in fresh fish.

This sort of fishing is held for a day. At the very early morning the boat starts fishing on the Ganga and on day break it returns to the landing ghat of the village. Most of the fishermen in Nurpur are involved in this sort of individual fishing to meet the daily expenses when they are not engaged in the organised group fishing.

The fishing operation does not end with the catching of fishes, and until and unless these are sold against reasonable price the fishing enterprise would not be meaningful. Generally the boats land fishes at the shore of the Ganga from where fish merchants collect fishes for final transmission to the fish markets at Diamond Harbour or Calcutta. The fishes are generally auctioned amongst the merchants present. Sometimes women venders purchase smaller fishes directly from the landing ghat for reselling these in the neighbouring villages or in the markets. But during the present period most of the group leaders are in economic stringency and thus they take advance payments (*dadan*) from the godown owners or *aratdars* to meet the expenses in group fishing. So they are always obliged to deposit the total catch to the *aratdar* concerned for auction. Here the fishermen concerned are to wait for sale and which is done through a very complicated process. Various stages of that process demands payments from the fishermen which are deducted from the total price of the catch. In this way the fishermen fall prey in the hands of the *aratdar*. The study of Nurpur reveals that about 88% of the fishermen are indebted and the circumstances have fallen them in such an unfortunate situation. The group leaders are to take loans from the moneylenders to meet the expenses for boat repairing, net repairing and other allied necessities. Also the fishermen joining the group are to arrange for day-to-day family expenses when they go out for fishing for weeks together. Thus they are also dependent on the moneylenders. Fishing devices are always full of uncertainties. If the catch is poor, the fishermen fail to repay the loans taken from the *aratdars* or *mahajans*. In this way the fishermen are always in the clutches of complicated debt.

Despite all such adversities the fishing operation amongst Nurpur fishermen is continuing unabated. It is their life-philosophy–it is inextricably interwoven with their very existence. The Table 5 indicates that there are 211 active fishermen in Nurpur who are involved in direct fishing in turbulent water. Out of them 20 are from non-fishing castes of the village. All the villagers are directly or indirectly, attached to the fishing operations through their close cooperation. The Table 5 also shows that the non-fishing castes are conducted fish-related activities like boat repairing, fish trading, fish-oriented jobs, van pulling etc. Even the service holders (59 in number) keep touch with the profession of fishing. Irrespective of castes and services the villagers unitedly think for this profession and they become happy with the prosperity of fishing devices, and suffer from affliction when these face calamity. The multifarious uncertainties in fishing profession are not only fought with by the contriving of various technological devices but also these are resisted through some supernatural mechanisms which are effected by the conduction of ritualistic performances. Those are regarded as village-level ceremonial occasions in which all the villagers participate with the appeal for requisite prosperity of the fishing operations in which all are intimately linked.

This struggle is specifically ritual oriented and characterized by supernaturalism. At every step of their fishing expedition there is ritualistic performance. The owner of the fishing units calls in a priest to perform a worship in the house just before the starting of fishing operation. The priest finds out an auspicious date and time after consulting the almanac. It is followed by the ceremony of data puja. It is the ceremonial tying of the first two pieces of a net. It can be done by the majhi (the head of the crew) or by any one of the unit members after taking a purificatory bath in the river. After tying the two pieces of the net on the ground the worship starts in honour of the specific power. Then turmeric paste and vermilion are applied to the net, and water of the Ganga is sprinkled over these.

Table 5
Different Occupational Patterns Among the Various Caste/Community Groups

Castes / Community groups	*Working people*				*Active fishing*				*Fish oriented jobs*			
	M	*%*	*F*	*%*	*M*	*%*	*F*	*%*	*M*	*%*	*F*	*%*
Bagdi	147	30.43	55	31.43	88	41.70	–	–	9	18.37	14	53.85
Jele Kalibarta	133	27.34	46	26.29	103	48.82	–	–	11	22.45	5	19.23
Mahishya	31	6.22	20	11.43	3	1.42	–	–	4	8.16	3	11.54
Goala	37	7.67	17	9.70	3	1.42	–	–	5	10.20	4	15.38
Gandhabanik	19	3.93	9	5.14	–	–	–	–	–	–	–	–
Kamar	19	3.93	6	3.43	–	–	–	–	–	–	–	–
Kumhar	16	3.30	9	5.14	–	–	–	–	2	4.09	–	–
Malakar	7	1.45	4	2.29	–	–	–	–	–	–	–	–
Keora	8	1.66	5	2.86	–	–	–	–	–	–	–	–
Muslim	66	14.07	4	2.29	14	6.64	–	–	18	36.73	–	–
Total	483	100.00	175	100.00	211	100.00	–	–	49	100.00	26	100.00

Table 5 (I)
Different Occupational Patterns Among the Various Caste/Community Groups

Castes / Community groups	*Agricultural activities*				*Fish trade*				*Other business*			
	M	*%*	*F*	*%*	*M*	*%*	*F*	*%*	*M*	*%*	*F*	*%*
Bagdi	12	26.67	16	30.19	–	–	4	26.67	8	25.0	–	–
Jele Kalibarta	2	4.44	13	24.53	1	9.09	6	40.0	3	9.38	1	25.0
Mahishya	8	17.78	11	20.75	1	9.09	2	13.33	2	6.25	–	–
Goala	4	8.89	5	9.44	–	–	–	–	2	6.25	–	–
Gandhabanik	2	4.44	3	5.66	–	–	2	13.33	7	21.88	1	25.0
Kamar	3	6.67	2	3.77	–	–	–	–	–	–	–	–
Kumhar	1	2.22	2	3.77	–	–	–	–	1	3.12	–	–
Malakar	–	–	–	–	–	–	–	–	1	3.12	–	–
Keora	3	6.67	–	–	–	–	–	–	1	3.12	2	50.00
Muslim	10	22.22	1	1.89	9	81.82	1	6.67	7	21.88	–	–
Total	45	100.00	53	100.00	11	100.00	15	100.00	32	100.00	4	100.00

Table 5 (II)
Different Occupational Patterns Among the Various Caste/Community Groups

Castes / Community groups	*Daily labour*				*Handicrafts*				*Van pulling*				*Boat making / repairing*			
	M	*%*	*F*	*%*	*M*	*%*	*F*	*%*	*M*	*%*	*F*	*%*	*M*	*%*	*F*	*%*
Bagdi	14	50.0	11	30.56	–	–	–	–	–	–	–	–	12	70.57	–	–
Jele Kalibarta	4	14.29	10	27.78	–	–	–	–	–	–	–	–	–	–	–	–
Mahishya	–	–	3	8.33	1	4.76	–	–	1	14.28	–	–	–	–	–	–
Goala	6	21.43	3	8.33	–	–	–	–	3	4.86	–	–	–	–	–	–
Gandhabanik	1	3.57	2	5.56	–	–	–	–	–	–	–	–	–	–	–	–
Kamar	2	7.14	3	8.33	7	33.33	–	–	–	–	–	–	2	11.77	–	–
Kumhar	1	3.57	2	5.56	7	33.33	5	55.56	–	–	–	–	–	–	–	–
Malakar	–	–	–	–	6	28.58	4	44.44	–	–	–	–	–	–	–	–
Keora	–	–	–	–	–	–	–	–	3	42.86	–	–	–	–	–	–
Muslim	–	–	2	5.55	–	–	–	–	–	–	–	–	3	17.66	–	–
Total	28	100.00	36	100.00	21	100.00	9	100.00	7	100.00	–	–	17	100.00	–	–

Table 5 (III)
Different Occupational Patterns Among the Various Caste/Community Groups

Castes / Community groups	*Dairying*				*Service*				*Maid servant*				*Tuition*			
	M	*%*	*F*	*%*	*M*	*%*	*F*	*%*	*M*	*%*	*F*	*%*	*M*	*%*	*F*	*%*
Bagdi	–	–	–	–	3	5.56	2	33.40	–	–	8	38.10	1	20.0	–	–
Jele Kalibarta	–	–	–	–	8	15 09	3	50.00	–	–	8	38.10	1	20.0	–	–
Mahishya	–	–	–	–	9	16 98	–	–	–	–	1	4.75	2	40.0	–	–
Goala	4	100.00	5	100.00	10	18.87	–	–	–	–	–	–	–	–	–	–
Gandhabanik	–	–	–	–	8	15.09	1	16.60	–	–	–	–	1	20.0	–	–
Kamar	–	–	–	–	5	9.43	–	–	–	–	1	4.75	–	–	–	–
Kumhar	–	–	–	–	4	7.56	–	–	–	–	–	–	–	–	–	–
Malakar	–	–	–	–	–	–	–	–	–	–	–	–	–	–	–	–
Keora	–	–	–	–	1	1.89	–	–	–	–	3	14.30	–	–	–	–
Muslim	–	–	–	–	5	9.43	–	–	–	–	–	–	–	–	–	–
Total	4	100.00	5	100.00	53	100.00	6	100.00	–	–	21	100.00	5	100.00	–	–

The boats, nets and other fishing appliances are not only indispensable parts of the fishing expedition but these are regarded as animated. These are not mere inanimate objects–rather they are pulsated with life. Thus they are required to be worshipped properly. People attached to fishing or fish-based economy must pay proper respect to these. Boat worship is a regular phenomenon amongst the fisherfolk. In the early morning of the day of starting for fishing expedition the two ends of the boat concerned are smeared with mustard oil and some water of the Ganga are poured on these. It symbolizes the bathing ceremony of the goddess Kastha Devi–the presiding deity of the boat. Boat worship is a matter of greatest importance not only in the way of life of the fisherfolk but also the whole village take active part in it.

The relationship amongst the fishing caste groups and the different non-fishing castes and community in Nurpur is based on reciprocal understanding. Various activities of the caste groups rotates round the fishing-oriented existence. The fishing communities everywhere are seen to occupy the low position in the caste hierarchy. There is no Brahmin caste in the village but his service is always required by the fisherfolk during various ritualistic performances especially which are done through the following of shastric tradition. The Brahmins from the neighbouring villages are called in for serving these purposes. The Mahishyas are the cultivating caste and they supply agricultural products to the fishermen during the time of their need. Sometimes they are seen to supply rice to the fishing parties on the condition that the price will be paid after their return from fishing. As herdsmen the Goalas of the village provide milk and milk products for the fishermen families. They regularly supply milk for the ritualistic performances arranged by the fishermen. The Gandhabaniks are traders by profession and they are the owners of grocer's shops in the village. The fishermen take the delivery of different commodities from the Gandhabanik grocers on the eve of their going out for fishing. The payment for these articles are made when their fishing operation is over and come back home. Besides this the fishermen make arrangements with the Gandhabanik grocers to supply different articles from their shops to the respective families without immediate payment. These are paid after the return of the fishermen. Kamar caste people are professional boat repairers and boat painters. Thus they are always at the service of the fishermen. They are paid in cash by the fishermen. Sometimes fresh fishes are also given as presentation. Kumhars are the makers of earthen ware vessels which are regularly utilised by the fishermen in their day-to-day family requirements. Moreover, they need large types of earthen vessels for keeping drinking water in the boats. These are specially prepared for the use of the fishermen. The Malakars are the artisan castes and they supply various artistic materials for the decoration of the boats during boat worship. They also supply dress of tinsel to the earthen idol of the goddess Ganga during her worship by the fisherfolk. In return the Malakars receive payments both in cash and in fresh fish. Keoras are the lowly ranked caste, and they serve the fishermen by pulling cycle vans (vide Table 4). The fishes after their landing are sent to the local market and to the neighbouring villages for sale by these cycle vans–the only conveyance in the village. Sometimes passengers are also carried by these vans. The Keoras are always dependent on the fishermen for their subsistence whereas the fishermen get the opportunity for sending their catches outside the village for sale by vans run by the Keoras. A few Muslim of the village are moneyed man and some others have got their expertise in fishing activities. Fishermen very often take loans from the well-to-do Muslims on reasonable interest. Moreover, as the co-villagers the Muslims extend their co-operation to the fishermen who in turn are very much obliged for that and show proper respect to them. Also fishermen take the help of Muslim experts in the problematic situations relating to fishing. Thus in Nurpur caste and community relations are specifically conditioned by the various activity patterns with regard to fishing practices organised by the dominant fishing castes–the Bagdis and the Jele Kaibartas. The Bagdis and the Jele Kaibartas took every possible steps to develop a flourishing fish-based settlement in the distant past on the bank of the Ganga with the idea of utilising the multi-dimensional resources of the traditional river. In order to make the settlement a full-fledged habitational unit with the close co-operation of the occupational caste groups they allowed such caste groups to come over here and settle down. Ultimately a developed village unit resulted and Nurpur became a famous settlement in the whole region with its thriving fishing economy. The hatkhola of Nurpur became the conspicuous centre of fish trade where fishes with numbers of varieties and ample qualities were regularly brought by the fishermen concerned as a result of their estuary fishing. But the present day situation becomes completely different owing to some conspicuous geophysical changes connected with the Ganga which has resulted in the abrupt alteration in the overall ecosystem. The Ganga has been in a rapid process of silting during the present time and the heavy siltation at the mouth of the Ganga prevent the fishes from the deep sea to make an entry into the flow of the Ganga. When the flood level becomes five to eight metres high the fishes migrate upstream to breed in fresh water. A moderate current in the river helps the spawns in drifting down. All the factors were highly effective in the Ganga of the olden days. But the recent circumstances give a different picture–rapid upraising of the river bed due to siltation resists the inflow of sufficient water and thus the spawning grounds become disturbed. Therefore, the fishes are facing environmental hazards and their number is decreasing day by day. Besides this, industrial affluents from the large scale industrial units developed on both sides of the Ganga bring injurious effect to the fishes and also these kill different aquatic micro-organism on which the fishes feed. What is now needed in the Ganga is high flushing of water throughout the year, but the diversion of water load to Bangladesh has minimised the water contents in the river. The silt load from the river bed cannot be removed by mere heavy discharge during the monsoon times. These changes in the ecosystem have caused the disappearance of various species of fish in the Ganga. The rise in the river bed at the estuary has blockened the way of fish migration.

The virtual ruin of the riverine ecology has posed a great problem to the fisherfolk in Nurpur. The river has become so polluted that a good catch is almost impossible at the present time. The fishermen of Nurpur practise estuary fishing with their small country boats alongwith indigenous technological equipments. It is not possible for them to go beyond the estuary region to conduct deep sea fishing because of the fact that they are devoid of any mechanical device to cope with the situation as well as they have got no such training to work in the deep water of the sea. Therefore, most of the time the fishing units are to come back empty handed. This specific situation has brought a dead blow to the fishing economy in Nurpur. One fisherman from the Jele Kaibarta caste, Bhagyadhar Barik, has purchased a trawler after a long fight with many adverse situations. It is completely a personal enterprise and the trawler organisation is conducted by the fishermen coming from outside. It regularly visits the sea and conducts fishing operations which is still a dream to many others. One Muslim gentleman, Anwar Bux, purchased a motor launch a few years ago for carrying passengers to Sagar Island and other such places. But it could not be continued. The motor launch is now engaged in sea fishing activities. Besides these two there are no other mechanical devices to facilitate fishing beyond the estuary. The traditional fishermen of Nurpur with their age-old setting conditioned by fish-oriented norms and philosophy are at present in the state of dwindling caused by environmental hazards and disbalanced ecosystem.

Village Dasherchawk

The village Dasherchawk has grown up and developed into a fullfledged fishing village on the deltaic South Bengal having the direct influence of Sundarban mangrove ecosystem. The villagers are composed mainly of fisherfolk and partly of non-fishing groups but having indirect relation with fish-based economic sphere. The village settlement pattern and the economic organisation are shaped and processed according to the total ecological set up.

Dasherchawk is inhabited by 250 families belonging to eight caste groups which comprise the total population of 1360 having 722 males and 638 females. Table 1 and 2 give the details of the number of families and total population patterns of the village according to caste groups. The highest number of families belongs to the Kaibarta caste and the Mahishya comes to the secondary importance in this regard. Table 2 gives the details of the number of families distributed according to eight caste groups of the village. These families are of different sizes which have been classified according to the number of persons constituting the families. Table 3 depicts the distribution pattern of the different-sized families amongst the different caste groups. In the village it is seen that medium-sized family dominates among all the caste groups which is followed by large-sized family. The small-sized family is not discouraged here but to the fishing personnel the families with a good number of persons are preferable as these are helpful in fishing operational activities. During large-scale fishing in deep sea when the fishermen are to spend weeks together on water in the far off sea the families of the concerned fishermen are to face a lot of troubles owing to the absence of the male members. But if there are a number of male members in the family they would very easily look after the family by turn. In this case the responsibilities would very naturally be divided which is out and out impossible in the three membered families. The Kaibarta caste, the dominant fishing community of the village, has got large number of medium-sized families. Amongst them all the other types of families are also seen. After them comes the Mahishya caste group. In this caste medium-sized families are common. These people are also in favour of small-sized families. But other two types of families are comparatively limited in number.

The Paundra Kshatriya constitutes the third important group of the village. Amongst them medium sized families are seen in great numbers. Side by side with these they possess small-sized and large-sized family types also. Amongst the other five caste groups like Jaladas, Dhopa, Brahmin, Kayastha and Namasudra mostly three types of families–small-sized, medium-sized and large-sized–are seen. But amongst the Brahmins and Kayasthas there is no evidence of small sized family. Like all the fishing villages the families of Dasharchawk takes specific responsibility to train up the young ones in the sphere of fishing. The children are specialised according to the fish-based traditions which still prevail in the social setting of the fishing villages. The male members are always on the move–they are to stay out of the village for a longer period. The absence of the head or the important members of the household very naturally create a critical situation in the family and the vacuum created by them becomes conspicuous. Amongst the fisherfolk as well as the people who mainly live on fishing in distant rivers and sea the elderly female members of the families are to come forward to shoulder the responsibility of all the affairs of the families concerned. Thus it is the duty of the head of the family engaged in fishing activities to make a compromise with the diversified adverse situations during his absence and mention is to be made that the womenfolk in the family are the only and the last hope for him to bring the situations in his favour. The specific circumstances make the women in the families all rounders; they not only work sincerely inside the family boundaries but also they unhesitatingly take part in all sorts of outdoor activities that are exclusively masculine as per tradition. There are instances that the emergent meetings of the village are attended by the women as the male persons of the families concerned are out for fishing. Thus the women in the fishing families always take the double roles in their day to day living. It is to be noted that these women have got no formal educational qualifications and they seldom go far away from their native village, still they prove themselves efficient enough to manage the multifarious affairs they are to face during the absence of their male counterparts. Therefore the role of women in the family as well as in the total village perspective is worth mentioned and it is indispensable for the maintenance of the fish-based economy. In each and every family of the fisherfolk a very common scene is to be noted. On the specific cloudy days or at the advent of rains the womenfolk in the families are passing their days with tremendous anxieties most of them carefully listen to the AIR News Bulletin as their male partners have gone out for fishing expedition. These are the days of their maximum tension. But despite all these the fisherwomen do not find any suitable status in the family. It is the common picture in all the fishing villages. From the close study into the families it has been found out that

Table 6
Distribution of Families
According to Caste Groups in Dasherchawk

Sl. No.	*Different caste groups*	*Total number of families*	*Percentage*
1.	Kaibarta	163	65.20
2.	Mahishya	49	19.60
3.	Paundra Kshatriya	15	6.00
4.	Jaladas	5	2.00
5.	Dhopa	6	2.40
6.	Brahmin	5	2.00
7.	Kayastha	4	1.60
8.	Namasudra	3	1.20
	Total	250	100

Table 7
Caste Groups-wise Distribution of Population in Dasherchawk

Sl. No.	*Different caste groups*	*Total Population*	*%*	*Male*	*%*	*Female*	*%*
1.	Kaibarta	926	68.09	496	68.70	430	67.40
2.	Mahishya	233	17.13	117	16.20	116	18.18
3.	Paundra Kshatriya	75	5.51	41	5.68	34	5.33
4.	Jaladas	30	2.21	15	2.08	15	2.35
5.	Dhopa	30	2.21	20	2.77	10	1.57
6.	Brahmin	29	2.13	15	2.08	14	2.19
7.	Kayastha	24	1.76	9	1.25	15	2.35
8.	Namasudra	13	0.96	9	1.25	4	0.63
	Total	1360	100	722	100	638	100

the women concerned do not feel anything for not getting the requisite status in the overall village society despite their conspicuous sacrifice. They have got no complaint regarding this or they do not show any sort of dissatisfaction rather they take consolation by accepting the situation that it is the traditional pattern of the fisherfolk social system. The trend of socialization of the girls in the fisherfolk families is such that they from their very tender ages are processed through the traditional modes of behaviour relating to the hazards and anxieties of the fishing families. It is done through customs and folkways in such a manner that the fisherwomen find no opportunity to think for a while that they are maltreated. The situational context does a great deal in thinking their misfortune as destined and thus they never think these as hazardous affairs but a continuous struggle to conduct the work of fishing in a realistic way. Their male counterparts are fishing tremendously outside against the turbulent water of rivers and sea to maintain their living, similarly they are also struggling indoor for the fulfilment of the same purpose. Thus struggle, whatever and wherever may be its area of action, is at the focal point in solving the common problem i.e. existence.

Table 8
Distribution of Family Size on the Basis of Caste Groups in Dasherchawk

Different Caste Groups	*Small-sized family (upto 3 members)*		*Medium-sized family (from 4 to 6 members)*		*Large-sized family (from 7 to 9 members)*		*Very large-sized family (10 members and above)*		*Total*	
	No.	*%*	*No.*	*%*	*No.*	*%*	*No.*	*%*	*No.*	*%*
Kaibarta	26	57.78	91	65.94	37	64.91	9	90.00	163	65.2
Mahishya	12	26.67	27	19.56	9	15.79	1	10.00	49	19.6
Paundra Kshatriya	3	6.67	8	5.80	4	7.02	–	–	15	6.0
Jaladas	1	2.22	2	1.45	2	3.51	–	–	5	2.00
Dhopa	2	4.44	2	1.45	2	3.51	–	–	6	2.4
Brahmin	–	–	4	2.90	1	1.75	–	–	5	2.0
Kayastha	–	–	2	1.45	2	3.51	–	–	4	1.6
Namasudra	1	2.22	2	1.45	–	–	–	–	3	1.2
Total	45	100	138	100	57	100	10	100	250	100

In the village studied there is no worth-mentioned educational institutions excepting one Free Primary School. But due to the closeness of Kakdwip township the inhabitants of Dasherchawk get ample opportunities for receiving education at various levels. There are a large number of educational institutions in Kakdwip including a Degree college. Besides these they can also avail the opportunities for education of different types at Diamond Harbour where good schools and colleges have been developed. Diamond Harbour is easily accessible to these people by metalled road through which buses ply frequently. It is a remarkable feature that the fishing communities have got a very good inclination towards formal education. Three males one each from Kaibatra, Mahishya and Paundra Kshatriya castes have done Postgraduate degrees from Calcutta University. There are altogether 25 graduates, out of which six are women. The fact that a large number of persons have received education upto Higher Secondary and Madhyamik levels and in these cases the number of females is satisfactory. The dominant fishing caste of the village–the Kaibarta–has progressed considerably in the sphere of education.

Fishing profession everywhere is a well-knit system. It requires the services of diversified human groups which are directly or indirectly related to fishing activities. The fishing economy encircles heterogeneous communities to serve multifarious purposes. There is no doubt about the fact that the lifting of fishes out of water is the essential part of this economy but it will not be completed until and unless the catch is marketed properly and timely. The fishing gears are of specific importance for successful fishing with requisite safety and security of the workers during operations in the unknown waters. In order to procure and maintain these the fishermen are required to make regular contact with the non-fishing personnel. The mechanization process in the fishing operational units, which has become a regular affair amongst the fishermen of the village during the present period, needs some trained up technical personnel for operation and maintenance of the machines worth lacs of rupees. As because fishing activities are conditioned by conspicuous uncertainties and there are every chance of misfortune at each step of the activities, so the fishermen are always shacky from the very advent of their starting for fishing in the deep water. In order to cope with that adverse situation and connected problematic issues beyond human control they, as a matter of course, are to depend on supernaturalism. They regularly arrange to appease various deities and supernatural powers for trouble-free situations in fishing operations as well as for the safety of life. Thus there are personnel who are engaged regularly to conduct ritualistic performance as well as various magical activities.

In Dasherchwak fishing activities are conducted by the Kaibartas, the traditional fishing caste. Table 6 shows that they constitute the highest number (85.26%) of active fishing personnel. Next to the Kaibarta comes the Mahishyas in respect of active fishing. Their traditional occupation is centred round agricultural activities but in this village 9.47% of the population have engaged themselves in active fishing and they have been converted to fishing groups. Four other caste groups like Paundra Kshatriya, Jaladas, Kayastha and Namasudra have taken up the profession of active fishing and which is the result of their continuous mixing with the people of the fishing community. Two Kayastha men were attracted to the fishing in the deep sea by curiosity and ultimately they had been converted to active fishermen. There is no active fisher among the Brahmin and Dhopa castes though three persons from the Brahmins are engaged in fish trade. Agricultural activities are conducted principally by the caste groups like Mahishya, Paudra Kshatriya, Jaladas though a good percentage of them is engaged in some fish-oriented jobs in addition to agricultural work. During slack season when fishing, fish trade and agricultural activities are on the wane people belonging to various caste groups excepting the Brahmin and Kayastha take up the work of daily labour. Eighteen from Kaibarta,

Mahishya, Paundra Kashtriya and Kayastha castes are engaged a non-fish oriented business.

The Kaibartas of Dasherchwak control the total affairs of the village and being economically affluent group they have presented themselves as the Dominant caste in the total village society. Fishing economy in this village does not present itself as a homogenous unit. It has been shown from the Table on occupation patterns that the caste groups other than traditional fishing caste have also made an entry in the fishing occupational system. The history of village tradition indicates categorically that the present Kaibartas have got no specific role in the formation of Dasherchwak. Practically it was a small hamlet inhabited by the stray native fishermen who used to take shelter here after conducting their fishing operations in the rivers and estuaries of the locality. The landmass attracted them for establishing their temporary shelters because of its highly favourable situation for the fishing personnel. From here the rivers and estuaries with promising fish crops were easily approachable through the network of small canals. The topographical situation of Dasherchwak is highly suitable for the fisherfolk. At the very outset this small village was inhabited by some families belonging to Mahishya caste. They had migrated long ago from Midnapur district in the hope of cultivating on the recently reclaimed land. As a cultivating caste they could manage the agricultural work in the new area. They have also got special fascination for fishing though it is of a secondary type of occupation. One Kalicharan Das immigrated into the area and gradually he could develop the region through the proper exploitation of its rich natural resources despite conspicuous adversities. The name Kalinagar Mouza, under the jurisdiction of which Dasherchawk village is situated, had its origin from Kalicharan Das, its developer. Sri Das was the establisher of the Bisalakshi temple at Dasherchawk. In course of time the total area was transferred to Sagar Das who also was one of the fortune seekers from Midnapur. As per villagers, the name Dasherchwak probably owes its origin from the Das family which became the sole owner of this landmass. The total landmass alongwith the habitational unit then came under the Zamindari of Sri Manindra Nath Basu (Kayastha) and under whose administration a good number of fishing families took shelter at Dasherchwak as well as in the adjacent village. One Dinanath Mandal, Dhopa by caste, came to Dasherchwak for the purpose of doing agricultural work. By dint of his skill and labourious attitude he became very close to the zamindar who, understanding his workmanship and sincerity decided to appoint him as his nayab (chief rent collector). After the death of Dinanath Mandal his son, Narayan Chandra Mandal, was offered the same post under the zamindary. As a man Narayan was very simple and obedient. He soon became all in all in the zamindary administration by virtue of his tact and efficiency. At his old age the zaminder was so pleased with him that the wanted to hand over the part of the zamindary at Dasherchwak to him as gift. But Narayan Chandra Mandal did not give his consent as he wanted to pass his life simply and trouble-free. After the death of both the Zamindar and Narayan Chandra Mandal zamindar's sons wanted to quit Dulal Mandal, the son of Narayan Chandra Mandal, from the land at Dasherchwak. As a natural consequence, a conflict of severe nature started between the said parties and ultimately it went to the Court of Law. The decision of the Court came in favour of the zamindar's sons. With the interference of the villagers the zamindar's sons claimed Rs. 40,000.00 (Rupees Forty thousand) from Dulal Mandal in exchange of the land he had been occupying at Dasherchwak. Dulal Mandal, however, collected the requisite money from some of his close inmates in the village and thereby got the sole ownership of the land. In later course, they were given land by Dulal Mandal as repayment of loan. Dulal Mandal then sold two and half bighas of land to the different persons and by means of which he purchased one trawler for fishing, and with this he became a fulfledged fish-oriented businessman having conspicuous fishing units. The goddess

Bisalakshi, though ordinarily considered as the village tutelory deity, yet the shrine practically falls within the landed property of Dulal Mandal and thus he claims it as his family deity. When his fishing trawler became highly profiteering *i.e.* he could earn a lot of money through it, he considered the phenomenon as the grace of goddess. As a token of acknowledgement he constructed a brick-built temple of Bisalakshi with full colouring and decoration replacing the old mud-built and straw-thatched shrine. A permanent Brahmin priest was appointed by him to worship the goddess. The villagers as a whole worship the goddess off and on especially in the event of starting for fishing expedition as well as on their safe return from the turbulent waters. They believe that the goddess Bisalakshi is the guardian deity of the fisherfolk and the fishing personel and she protects them from all sorts of danger. The inhabitants of Dasherchwak come at the temple with reverence keeping aside the question of ownership of this temple, ultimately the Bisalakshitala has been regarded as the common place of worship of the village.

The small hamlet of Dasherchwak gradually started broadening when various fishing groups which took permanent shelter here considering its advantageous situation in many respects. It was just after the partition of India in 1947, a large number of fishermen hurriedly migrated to this part of India from the then East Pakistan through the network of rivers. Many fisherfolk families started settling at Dasherchwak as it was the first settlement they landed after a long dangerous voyage from East Pakistan. The migrated fisherfolk, constituted by both fishing and non-fishing caste groups, started settling by the sides of the traditional communities of the village, the members of which used to practise fishing with the traditional boats and nets having indigenous patterns of fishing techniques. The heavy influx from East Bengal to this landmass abruptly changed the native feature of Dasherchwak. The heterogeneous caste groups centering round fishing profession converted the homogeneous community oriented fishing economy into heterogeneous patterns of fishing profession. The situation brought an end to the tradition-bound fishing by the categorical fishing castes and thereby a new business oriented fishing group developed. In that turmoil a number of non-fishing castes had taken up fishing activities and became identified as fishermen.

Dasherchwak is a typical village of the fisherfolk which is highly characterized by prominent inequalities in the socio-economic status. There are four economic categories of fishermen and these are— (1) Fish merchants and organisors (2) Fishing group leaders (3) Fishermen having technical knowledge and (4) Fish workers. The first category of the people are provided with merchandized trawlers, motor boats and improved types of nets, and have all the qualities in conducting deep sea fishing. Their financial capacities are very strong and they maintain well-organized fishing units with full-fledged office having a number of responsible personnel. These people organise the fish market in the locality and without whose help and cooperation the fishing profession in the region does not receive any momentum. Next comes the middle class fishermen who conduct fishing units and work as group leaders. They have got limited financial abilities but with the help of their knowledge and experience they conduct the fishing units in the deep sea with the expert fishermen. They have got their own trawlers, mechanized boats and nets. Sometimes these are hired from other group leaders or the Fish merchants belonging to the first category. The third category includes the Fishermen who have technical ability to work in the unknown sea and turbulent rivers. They work in the fishing units organized by both the persons belonging to the first and second categories. The Fish workers constitute the fourth category. They work in the fishing units as fish labourers. They are principally engaged in loading and unloading of fishes, in keeping the trawlers, boats and other fishing appliances clean and in order. These four economic categories have naturally possess inequalities in their modes of behaviour inspite of their direct attachment with fishing profession. These four classes of fishing personnel live in Dasherchwak and work in the locality in the midst of conspicuous class consciousness. There are great differences in the general way of life of these specific classes. The Fish merchants occupy the highest priority and with the help of their improved economic position and well-organized infrastructure they control the whole affairs of fishing. They have built palacial buildings in the village with high walled boundary and heavy iron gates. Most of the houses of these people have got extensive courtyards where the workers do their work in connection with fishing. These fish merchants have also got separate office accommodation and private landing spaces by the side of the Kalnagini Khal or other narrow channels. Here various activities like boat and launch repairing, colouring, net mending etc. are done together with the keeping of accounts of their national and international trade organisations. Then Fishing group leaders coming from the middle class families organise their fishing units with a limited fund in their hands. They cannot make expenditures lavishly for the requirement of different needs in long term fishing. They depend primarily on the kin-oriented and neigbhour-oriented fishing personnel in the formation of the fishing units. Their linkage with the unit workers is tradition-oriented rather than money-oriented. When the unit leaders cannot provide cash money they engage the fishing personnel on share basis. The profit drawn out of a particular catch is shared amongst the different personnel according to the prior contract. The Fishing group leaders live in one-storied and in rare cases two storied mud or brick built houses thatched with straw and sometimes baked tiles. They have got no personal landing space for the boats and trawlers like those of the fish merchants. The fishes are unloaded at the common landing ghat away from the village and from where those are marketed through the agents. As because the middle class group leaders have got no personal office accommodation, so they call the persons attached with the unit of fishing to their houses as well as for monetary transactions. The fishermen having technical skill in fishing fail to get proper return of their risk and responsibilities. They live in mud-built thatched houses with limited domestic utensils. They are to work very hard to earn their living. These people are the indispensable persons in the fishing expedition and on their success and failure the whole system of fishing organisation operates accordingly. Fish workers provide their hard labour in fighting with the turbulent waters of the sea and rivers for the purpose of getting a good catch. They engage themselves deeply in the loading and unloading of fishes as well as sorting out these according to specific species. There is conspicuous occupational clash and jealously between the first and the second categories of the classes i.e. Fish merchants and Fishing group leaders. At times, quarrels arise during the time of fishing unit formation. The Fishing group leaders sometimes get efficient fishing personnel in the formation of their units by dint of their traditional kin-based bindings. More often the kin orientations cuts across the financial trend especially in this type of unit formation when all the workers are to spend for a long time out of their homes and away from their family members and relatives. In this situation the fishermen prefer the unit formation based on kin groups for having sentimental consolation for their detachment from sweet homes. But the moneyed Fish merchants sometimes take effective role in breaking down the traditional kin-based units for getting the efficient fishing personnel for the formation of their own units. It is obviously done through the payment of more money to the working fishermen. Being allured by this excessive payment of money a number of fishing personnel find it is no wise to stick to the kin-based groups. In this way the middle class fishing group leaders are facing practical troubles and naturally a conflicting attitude between the two classes has become the result. This economic conflict has found its place in the social life of the village also. The Fishing group leaders call the Fish merchants as the exploiters and dishonest persons who do not follow the norms of fishing but solely look after their profit motive. According to these middle class Fishing group leaders, fishing is such a profession which necessarily needs love for the ecology and biotic environment where the fishes live. It is essential for the fishermen to look into the seasonal variations and the conditions of the different species of fishes to resist wanton destruction of fishes in the name of organized fishing. But the Fish merchants are so much trade-oriented and business minded that they do not bother for these features–they are always after the drawing of profit through the catching of fishes by the adoption of any ways and means they find easy and practicable. Fishing norms are not respected in their fishing activities, with the help of improved type of nets, related fishing appliances and the speedy trawlers together with the technically advanced infrastructure they catch large number of fishes of different varieties. Amongst these a considerable amount of fishes are wasted as these have got no market value as well as demand. These unwanted fishes are thrown away here and there, and most of these die before their re-entry into the water provided they get any chance to do it. It has become the unfortunate issue in Sundarban fishing domain during the present period. Objections are raised occasionally and the traditional fishing communities consider the situation as a suicidal policy of the fishermen concerned but there is no one to pay any heed to it. The Fish merchants are so economically dominant group and they are holding the fish based economy in such a depth-oriented way that the traditional fishermen cannot utter anything against them. But there is always a hidden displeasure in the activities of the Fish merchants. The other two classes of workers viz. the Fishermen having technical knowledge and the Fish workers or labourers hardly go against that mishap as they are always under obligation to work according to the instruction of the Fish merchants and their supervisors of work. The unit leaders belonging to the middle class arrange for the necessary fund through the lending of money directly from the mahajans (moneylenders) who not only charge high rate of interest but also they, most of the time, compel the borrower party to deposit the total catch of the year to them or to their agents under the minimum rate. In this way these unit leaders are being exploited in the hands of the mahajans. On the other hand, the Fishermen having technical knowledge and the Fish workers complain about their ill-fate as regards the meagre payments from the unit leaders as well as from the Fish merchants. From close enquiry it has been understood that inspite of their hard labour and multifarious responsibilities these working personnel get practically nothing. Owing to this, these people who continuously fight with turbulent water and other unfavourable circumstances pass the days in a depressed condition. Within the village society of Dasherchwak reflection of this specific situational context is highly discernible. There is a conspicuous conflicting mentality within the four class fishermen community of Dasherchwak.

The behaviour-patterns of traditional fishing village principally based on caste-oriented fishing activities are not visible in village society of Dasherchwak. Inter-caste relationship patterns have got no effective value here as the caste groups are not in obligatory bindings in the perspective of fishing economy owing to contractual arrangement through the payment of cash. Caste norms are hardly maintained in the manner of fishing. The fishermen here are always in favour of indiscriminate fishing as the mechanization of fish gear has got no chance to make selection in fishing, caste-bound fishing personnel conducting traditional fishing always take specific care to observe a number of taboos and restrictions in the catching of fishes during different times. In the traditional fishing villages the fishermen as per social norms are to refrain from catching specific varieties of fishes during their breeding seasons. But in the business-oriented fishing operations these sentiments have got no value at all and thus a particular ecological norm is being neglected.

Village Beguakhali

Beguakhali is an old and small village at the south-west corner of Sagar Island in the Bay of Bengal. It is situated near (about 4 to 5 km.) the holy confluence of the Ganga with the Bay of Bengal. Further south to this village the sacred pilgrimage of all-India fame–Gangasagar–has been developed. The Sagar Island is famous throughout the world as the largest delta. It has got the greatest geological and geographical importance in respect of its land forms and ecological perspectives. Moreover, Gangasagar is regarded as the famous sacred centre by the people of India especially belonging to the Hindu religious sect. Because of the fact that Gangasagar Island has been formed at the vicinity of the confluence of the Ganga and the Bay of Bengal, so it is full of numerous creeks and channels. As many as thirty seven canlas cross this island which is subdivided into four large and smaller types of islands. There are nearly a dozen roads within the islands which maintain direct connection with the different places. Out of these roads two are of specific importance; one is stretched from Kachuberia at the northern part of the island to the Gangasagar *mela* ground in the south point. Another road starts from Chemaguri jetty ghat at the south-eastern part of the island at the ends of the *mela* ground. The village Beguakhali can be reached after coming through these two roads. A narrow unmetalled road is seen to extend from the main road to Gangasagar which enters Beguakhali.

Beguakhali though not a part of the great sacred complex of Gangasagar yet its inhabitants feel proud to share with the famous mythological events attached with Gangasagar. The legendary background in the establishment of the prominent sacred complex of all-India fame is at times recollected by the people of the village in question and they consider themselves propitious to be in close association with the land of that devotional happenings. It is to be regarded as a territorial religious philosophy that binds not only the people of Beguakhali but also the other inhabitants in the village around Gangasagar. The legendary background has been formed by the thoughts and ideas that go back to the hoary past prior to the period of Ramayana. The famous personality–Sagar–the king of Ayodhya, was the thirteenth ancestor of Rama. Once king Sagar was performing celebrated horse sacrifice ritual popularly known as *asvamedha Yojna* for ninetynine times. Indra, the King of Heaven, had the credit of performing such *Yogna* ritual for one hundred times. He became very much enraged with king Sagar and he took him as his rival and did accordingly. Indra put resistance to the ritualistic programme of king Sagar. He stole the horse and kept it concealed in subterranean spot where Kapilmuni–the famous sage–was totally absorbed in meditation and thus he was not in any active touch with the outside world. Sagar sent his sixty thousand sons to search out that horse. While roaming here and there they could find out horse in the place of its hiding. As it was kept concealed in the room close to the place of meditation of Kapilmuni, so they took it readily that the sage was at the root of that mishap. They assaulted the sage for his misdeeds, as they thought so. At this the pious man suddenly came out of his long-term deep meditation and he readily cursed the sons of Sagar. The enraged sage with his specific mysterious power burnt them to ashes and sent all of them to the hell. After a long time it was so happened that the grand son of King Sagar came out to search his father and uncles. He at last reached the *ashram* of Kapilmuni and through prayer and submission he begged him for the resurrection of the souls of the dead persons. The sage was pleased with the earnest appeal of the grandson of Sagar raj and he instructed that if he (grandson of Sagar raj) could bring the holy water of the Ganga to that spot for sprinkling the sanctified water on the ashes, all would come back to life again. But Ganga at that time stayed in the Heaven under the disposal of the celebrated Creator of the world–Brahma. The grandson of Sagar started continuous prayer before him for his grace in allowing the goddess Ganga to come down on the earth. But before his prayer granted, he died. He had a son–Bhagirath–who continued the effort of his father to make Brahma pleased to send Ganga on earth. He was perfectly successful. Ganga was ultimately released by Brahma, and Bhagirath was thereby instructed to show Ganga the path for coming down to the earth. Bhagirath did so sincerely and after reaching Hatigarh–a place near the sea–Bhagirath declared his inability to show her any further path for reaching the sea. Under that situation Ganga, to make sure of reaching the sea, became divided in hundred mouths, locally known as *satamukhi,* and ultimately reached the ashram of Kapilmuni to wash the ashes caused by the inspired frenzy of the sage. As soon as the holy water of Ganga touched the ashes the said souls of sixty thousand sons of Sagar became resurrected and those were afterward transferred to the Heaven. From that very moment Ganga was recognized as the sacred river whose water was regarded as having spiritual power to wash way all sins in human beings accumulated in them through misdeeds. This concept is still going on unabated and this is why Ganga is known to the people as rescuer of the fallen or *patitpabani.* This sacred spot at the point of Ganga's celebrated union with sea or, in other words, Gangasagar is still attracting huge number of pilgrims from the different parts of India, especially the whole of northern India, on the day of *makarsankranti* when the sun enters capricorn which coincides with the last day of the Bengali month *Pous* and the 1st day of *Magh* (14-15 January). It is compulsory for the pilgrims to take a holy dip on the morning of the *makarsanskranti* at the point of confluence between Ganga and the sea.

As because village Beguakhali is very close to this sacred spot, its inhabitants think themselves to be connected spiritually with that sacred complex. The people here not only visit Gangasagar fair with pious attitude but also they feel it is their specific obligation to pay homage to Kapilmuni as mark of profound gratefulness for making the total landscape glorious and divinity-oriented.

Beguakhali villagers thus consider themselves specifically distinctive and glorified by having been very close to the mythologically tradition-oriented land. Not only so, the villagers irrespective of castes and communities feel sensation as their field of activities are centered round the water of sea which has age-old sanctity. Beguakhali–a tiny village of 443 persons–is divided into two wards or *para*—(1) *Pubpara* of eastern ward, and (2) *Pachipara* or western ward. It falls within the jurisdiction of South Twenty Four Parganas District and Sagar Police Station. It is included within the local administrative domain of Gangasagar Gram Panchayat. Beguakhali has been developed in a fine topographical situation which is very much advantageous in fish-based occupation. In order to understand it the positions of the rivers and sea are to be categorically discussed. The river Hugli or Ganga in its course beside Nurpur–a fishing village already discussed–gradually becomes broadened and after reaching Diamond Harbour it reaches its maximum. In its southward flow the wide mouthed river bifurcates near Kakdwip region at Hairwood point encircling the Sagar Island. The main course, in the name of river Hugli flows by the western side of the Sagar Island, and the branch of the eastern side has taken the name of Muriganga. It is also known by two other names—Channel Creek and Baratala river. Both Hugli and Baratala rivers fall in the Bay of Bengal at the southern point of Sagar Island. Just at the point of bifurcation of Hugli river near Hariwood point there are three small islands out of which one is inhabited by the fisherfolk and the other two are gradually being submerged in the river. The name of the inhabited island is Ghoramara but it is also at the point of danger due to continuous breaking down of its peripheries.

Crossing these islands rivers Hugli flows through the western side of Sagar Island and ultimately it unites with the sea at the southern most point of the said island. Village Beguaikhali is seen to be situated at the south-western end of Sagar Island. The village has vast river mouth and boundless Bay of Bengal which offer a favourable perspective in the fishing pursuits. Beguakhali is well-known for its having a famous light house to help the sea faring ships and other vehicles in getting indication during their voyage. It was constructed here during the early British rule in this part of the country. The village settlement of Beguakhali is dispersed. A narrow road from the eastern side enters the village which is regarded as the way of entrance from outside. After sometime the road has been bifurcated–one has gone to northern side and the other to the southern direction. From these two narrow roads within the village various lanes and byelanes have emerged. The principal road is brick-lined and on which three-wheeled vans can ply–the only vehicular traffic within the village. At the central part of the village there is an old *pipal* tree (Ficus religiosa) under which the people gather at different times for relaxation as well as for conducting village-level meetings. Many a time it is seen that the people simply sit here and gossip for passing their idle moments. There is a small tea stall here which supplies biscuits, bread, *muri* (perched rice) and *ghugni.* Frequently this stall becomes the very important spot of variegated discussions of the villagers. Many of the village problems are categorically discussed here sitting on the wooden platform made by placing a palmyra palm stem on two small brick-made pillers. There is one grocer's shop very close to it which supplies groceries as well as stationeries to the villagers. Because of the presence of the *pipal* tree the place is popularly known as *gachtala* i.e. foot of the tree. Beguakhali is bounded by Narendrapur in the north, Purusottampur in the east, village Gangasagar is situated in the south of it whereas in the northern side there is the vast water of the wide mouth of the river Hugli. From the river small canals have entered the western periphery of the village facilitating the entry of the river and seafaring boats at the village boundary to unload the catch. A large number of boats is to be seen here anchored–some are anchored for unloading the catch, some are waiting for the tide to go outside and some have been stopped here for reparation work. At a distance from the village in the western side there is a big embankment meant for resisting the entry of water of the river during tidal phases. On the embankment there are foot ways which help the people to move from one village to another especially during rainy season. From the village proper the southward embankment pathway leads to the light house. On the opposite side the village Beguakhali spreads from south to north direction. When one proceeds from the south one will meet a grocer's shop and a few mud-built houses, and crossing these Beguakhali Primary School would be seen. The school has got three mud-built and one brick-built houses. It was established in the year 1955. At the school premises there is a tubewell which is the source of drinking water for not only the school children but also for the people of the adjoining households. On way towards the northern part of the village there is a small canal over which there is a narrow bridge. On the other side of the bridge different households belonging principally to the fishing caste groups are to be seen. The village main road at the middle of the village has taken leftward direction i.e. towards western border. Just at the turning point the village Post Office is situated. It is housed in a mud-built structure but having a roof made of asbestos sheets. At the vicinity of the Post Office there are two educational units–One is Pre-Primary School in the name of Udaysagar Sishu Siksha Niketan and the other is Cooperative Junior Basic School. In between these two schools there is a tubewell which caters to the need of many people alongwith the school boys and girls. There are two grocer's shops and one tea stall at this place. At a short distance from this spot on the main village path there is a club named as Beguakhali Pallimangal Club. It is functioning since 1970 having its office in a small straw-thatched mudbuilt house. There are 34 active members in the club who belong to the different age groups. The main functions of the club are centred round different welfare activities of the village especially to protect the interests of fishing communities. The members of the club give special attention in the maintenance of the river embankments, and they inform the relevant authorities if any sort of breakage is seen due to heavy rain and the pressure of current during tidal waves which are very frequent in this ecological setting. It is a registered club under the Societies Registration Act. Another unregistered club is found to be associated with the different activities of the village and the name of which is the Surasangha Young Staff. This club house is situated at the northern corner of the village. It has no shelter of its own. The members of the club sit in the outer portion of the residential house of Sri Akshay Bhuiya, Mahishya by caste. He is the President of the club and he has agreed to provide shelter to this club until it finds a shelter of its own. Just by the side of this club house a grocery-cum-stationery shop is found which supplies requisite materials to the people of the northern part of the village. There is always a keen competition amongst the different shops of the same nature. There is one shop in the village just at the central part, where the people assemble for passing their lazy moments, which is meant for selling the different accessories in relation to the fishing implements including materials for petty boat reparation. Thus it serves the fishworkers in conducting their instant reparation work. It is, no doubt, advantageous to a great extent. But some complain about the price rates of the different materials which differ greatly from the outside market. The shop owner, a Paundra Kshatriya by caste, has developed a monopoly business taking the advantage of the immediate need of the fisherfolk specially at the advent of their starting for fishing in the rivers and sea.

Beguakhali is famous for the Shrine of the goddess Ganga at the northernmost corner of the village. The river Ganga is worshipped by the people as the Divine Mother because of the fact that, according to them, the life and property of these fisherfolk are being saved at the grace of the Gangamother. Thus her image is installed in a specially built temple at the northern entrance of the village. The temple, constructed by local bricks, faces the river Ganga and it is regarded as the sacred duty of the fisherfolk to go out for fishing after seeking blessings from the goddess for a successful catch as well as safe return after struggling with water. The fisherfolk in Sundarban, as a whole are dependent on the Mother Ganga as most of their fishing activities are centred round the river Ganga and its tributories. They pay respectful homage to this goddess regularly in addition to the annual worship on the day of *dasahara.* But from the study in Beguakhali it has been noted that because of their living at the horrible point of the Ganga's union and at the face of various uncertainties in working in the vast open watery atmosphere the people of the village have developed a special attitude of veneration towards the Goddess Ganga. During fishing operation in distant river and sea these fisherfolk praise in the name of Ganga in the hope of resisting any sort of untoward event. During staying at home after successful return from fishing activities they invariably go to the temple in the evening for singing devotional song jointly. The womenfolk from most of the households offer burning mustard oil lamps to the deity especially when the male members of their families are out for fishing. They jointly pray for the safe and successful return of their family members. Thus the temple of Ganga has become the effective centre for socio-economic as well as psycho-ritualistic life patterns of the people of Beguakhali. During the annual worship all the people contribute according to their abilities to the central fund for *puja* festival which is enjoyed by the people to their hearts' content.

Besides the temple of Ganga here there is a temple of Hari. It is also a small mud-built shrine within which there is a small altar where the clay image of Radhe-Krishna is installed. In Sundarban region the impact of Vaishnavism is greatly seen. Visalakshi mandir is another important religious centre in the village which is situated at the central region. It is a mud-built shrine having a small door. Inside the shrine there is small mud-built altar on which the clay image of the goddess is placed. It is practically a folk deity and the fisherfolk are her main patrons. There is a strong belief amongst these people that Devi Visalakshi protects them in water and jungle. Thus she is regularly worshipped by the people who move about on water and travel through the jungle-infested regions. Then there is an earthen shrine under the shade of tamarind tree (*Tamarindus indicus*) which is meant for the goddess Manasa–the snake deity. The goddess Manasa is represented here, in an open shrine, by a vermilion-oriented piece of stone. It is said that the goddess Manasa does not like any covered temple, she prefers to live in the open. Therefore, the villagers have not made any attempt to build any temple for her. The village people, irrespective of their occupational nature are to move about in the darkness as well as they are to enter into bushes and jungles to collect fuel and other materials of life. In these circumstances there is every possibility that they may face snakes which are present in abundance in the rural environs of Sundarban region. Thus it is quite natural that in order to get rid of the snakes these people would pray for blessings of Manasa–the presiding deity of snakes. The villagers jointly worship the goddess Kali annually but there is no permanent shrine for her. On the eve of the annual worship during the month of *Kartik* (October-November) the villagers constitute an Organising Committee in a general meeting which is held under *gachtala.* The Committee then makes preparation for the worship. A temporary shed is erected at the central part of the village in a fixed spot in which the clay image of the goddess Kali is installed. This puja performance is observed with due respect and splender. All the villagers, irrespective of caste groups, actively participate in the various performances. The puja ceremony is held for two days and during which the villagers behave as members of the same family. A Sutradhar family of the village prepares the clay image of the goddess but it does not receive any payment for the service. Of course, the materials like colour and objects of ornamentation are supplied by the Puja Committee. Most of the time the villagers arrange for *jatra* performance in which the local players take active part. It becomes enjoyable to all sections of the villages. On the second day of worship a communual feast is held in which all males, females and children of the village take part to give it a shape of thoroughly public festival.

From the above observations on the deities, their shrines and sacred performances it is clear that despite the smallness of the village and very simple type of socio-economic organisation Beguakhali is enriched with the philosophy of sacred complex. Every phases of life and activities of the villagers are specifically governed and moulded by the different gods and goddesses. This trend is substantially reflected in the social philosophy of the people. Living in the midst of mysterious rivers and sea as well as in the background of the boundless horizon these people have comparatively become more sensitive to the divine world and as a result of which their dependence to the gods and goddesses is on the increase.

Beguakhali is inhabited by 443 people belonging to 9 Hindu caste groups and 1 Muslim community. There are altogether 30 families. The total population of the village is comprised of 254 males and 189 females. Table 1 and 2 depict the detailed picture of the number of families and total population pattern according to caste and community groups.

Table 9
Distribution of Families According to Caste/Community Groups in Beguakhali

Sl. No.	*Caste / Community*	*Total Families*	*Percentage*
1.	Mahishya	27	30.00
2.	Paundra Kshatriya	19	21.11
3.	Jele Kaibarta	10	11.11
4.	Bagdi	7	7.78
5.	Kantra	4	4.44
6.	Sunri	3	3.33
7.	Tanti	3	3.33
8.	Sutradhar	4	4.44
9.	Kayastha	1	1.11
10	Muslim	12	13.33
	Total	90	100.00

It is seen from the Table 9 that the Mahishya caste group possesses the highest number of families in the village and after which comes the Paundra Kshatirya caste. The Muslim community comes to the third position. The Kayastha caste stands lowest in the number of families, there is only one Kayastha family in the village.

Table 10 gives the details of the total population of the village according to caste/community groups. From the population trend it is seen that the Mahishya and Paundra Kshatriya castes are numerically predominant. Then comes Jele Kaibarta. From Table 11 the distribution of the different family sizes according caste and community groups would be found out. In this village most of the families are medium-sized; out of 90 families 61 families are of medium-sized in nature. Next comes small-sized families; the large-sized families run almost parallel to the small-sized. But the very large-sized families are rare.

Table 10

Caste/Community wise Distribution of Population in Beguakhali

Caste Groups	*Total Population*	*%*	*Male*	*%*	*Female*	*%*
Mahishya	120	27.09	64	25.20	56	29.63
Paundra Kshatriya	100	22.57	63	24.80	37	19.58
Jele Kaibarta	52	11.74	23	9.06	29	15.34
Bagdi	42	9.48	26	10.24	16	8.47
Kantra	30	6.77	19	7.48	11	5.82
Sunri	20	4.51	11	4.33	9	4.76
Tanti	19	4.29	11	4.33	8	4.23
Sutradhar	13	2.93	8	3.15	5	2.65
Kayastha	5	1.13	2	0.79	3	1.59
Muslim	42	9.48	27	10.63	15	7.94
Total	443	100.00	254	100.00	189	100.00

The Mahishyas of Beguakhali is a dominent caste having the highest population in the village. The history of the development of the village indicates that these people are the ancient inhabitants in this village. The Mahishyas, the traditional agricultural caste group having inclination with fishing in Midnapur district, migrated to Sagar Island long ago. During the British regime when the reclamation of agricultural lands was started in the jungle infested Sagar Island, many caste groups in Midnapur district became highly inspired by that venture. Many of them took the risk of coming over here in the hope of getting benefit in the newly reclaimed areas. Between Sagar Island and Midnapur district there is a very broad river–the Hugli, with its characteristic high tides and cross-currents. At that time the said river was very rough and dangerous. Neglecting all those adversities a number of people belonging to Mahishya caste group crossed the river with the help of country boats. It was a very riskful activity but they dared to face that situation with strong determination. One Mahishya gentleman from Kanthi (Midnapur district), named Biseswar Bhuinya crossed the high waves of the river Hugli to reach Sagar Island to find some lands for cultivation in the newly reclaimed areas. He was accompanied by two of his assistants in his agricultural domain at Midnapur–his original homeland. He, like a few other fortune seekers, reached the more of less lonely island during the early twenties of the last century and became bewildered to live here, even temporarily, in the midst of so many calamities. It was very difficult to pass the day to day life there especially due to the want of drinking water. The fear of ferocious animals including snakes made the life all-along shacky and frightful. But Biseswar Bhuinya could manage to overcome those troubles with his daring attitude of mind and capacity for making adjustment with the hostilities. Gradually he settled down at Beguakhali region facing the wide open Hugli river. He made arrangements with the then administrative authorities to get the ownership of land for habitation as well as cultivation. For the work of cultivation he had to bring the trained agricultural workers from Midnapur–his homeland. At that time the family men did not like to come to the Sagar Island because of the total uncertainties in living. But Bisewar Maity could inspire a good number of working persons in his native village area on the condition that they would be released just after the work of cultivation so that they would be able to come back home. As per condition they had to visit the island during the time of harvesting of crops. Gradually the area started developing into a prospective region for agriculture which attracted other people also. With the conduction of agricultural activities on the land taken through an agreement on lease from the administrative authority Biseswar Bhuinya gave specific attention to the field of fishing which had a conspicuous prospect. It was for that reason he with the help of his assistants, already reached, Sagar Island with him, started inshore fishing in shallow water with nets and boats. Those twin activities related to the economic sphere made that Mahishya gentlemen affluent within a short period and he made up his mind to make permanent settlement in that part of the island. In addition to the prospective field of agriculture and fishing that part of the island had a special attraction to him–it was close to the mythologically famed *ashram* of Kapilmuni at the point of confluence of the Ganga and the sea. With the effective endeavours made by the British administration a greater part of the island became cultivable which was done through the continuous efforts of deforestation and putting of high embankments to resist the salt-infested water of the river and the sea in inundating the lands cleared and brought to agricultural activities. Those double-sided approaches ultimately could recover the land from the grip of dense and dangerous forests and made it habitable to some extent for conducting the economic activities based on cultivation and fishing.

In course of time the renovated areas started being populated, of course very slowly but effectively, due to the specific possibility of growing of crops especially paddy and catching of varieties of fishes. In the meantime Beguakhali took the form of a tiny human settlement with the workers and relatives of Biseswar Maity. Small hutments were raised with the locally available materials. A Gangamandir was erected by Sri Maity to get the blessing of the goddess Ganga in his various efforts to make the place habitable. It is the oldest shrine of Beguakhali raised by the founder's family of the village though the original structure had been destroyed long before. But the impact of the deity is still pulsating in the minds of not only the descendants of the original Mahishya family but also the whole village very keenly feel the legendary background of the deity established during the formative stage of the village and very actively offer their reverential homage.

Table 11
Distribution of Family Size on the Basis of Caste/ Community Groups in Beguakhali

Different Caste & Community Groups	*Small-sized family (upto 3 members)*		*Medium-sized family (from 4 to 6 members)*		*Large-sized family (from 7 to 8 members)*		*Very large-sized family (10 members and above)*		*Total*	
	No.	%	No.	%	No.	%	No.	%	No.	%
Mahishya	7	46.67	17	27.87	2	16.67	1	50.00	27	30.00
Paundra Kshatriya	–		17	27.87	2	16.67	–		19	21.11
Jele Kaibarta	1	6.67	7	11.48	2	16.67	–		10	11.11
Bagdi	–		4	6.56	3	25.00	–		7	7.78
Kantra	–		2	3.28	1	8.33	1	50.00	4	4.44
Sunri	–		2	3.28	1	8.33	–		3	3.33
Tanti	–		2	3.28	1	8.33	–		3	3.33
Sutradhar	2	13.33	2	3.28	–		–		4	4.44
Kayastha	–		1	1.64	–		–		1	1.11
Muslim	5	33.33	7	11.48	–		–		12	13.33
Total	15	100.00	61	100.00	12	100.00	2	100.00	90	100.00

The next caste group that came to Beguakhali was the Paundra Kshatriya. As a dominant caste of North 24-Parganas District it has been taking special endeavour to become associated with the reclaimed areas of the southern part of the district. In the meantime the people belonging to the Paundra Kshatriya caste made themselves expert in the work of cultivation. Naturally their attention was always directed to the newly renovated area for getting much scope for flourishing in agricultural activities. It was so happened that one Paundra Kshatriya gentleman in a village of North 24-Parganas District accidentally came in touch with a member of the founder's family of Beguakhali. In consequence of a friendly conversation with his friend of

Beguakhali the Paundra Kshatriya person named Brajesh Sardar became very much convinced with the possibilities of the newly developed village and he then and there took the decision of coming over there. He did so with two of his family members and all of them became convinced with the beautiful situation of the village for conducting both the agricultural and fishing activities simultaneously. The visit was resulted in the migration of a number of families of Paundra Kshatriya caste to Beguakhali for taking permanent settlement there. In later years they purchased lands in the vicinity of the village and started constructing their habitations in accordance with the ecology and environment of the region. Gradually they could attract a number of families belonging to their own caste group from the northern part of the district to come and settle in the southern end of the district. The people belonging to Paundra Kshatriya caste in course of time became acquainted with the nature and extent of the land and thereby to utilise it properly for getting good crops. Together with the Mahishya people they could grasp the technicalities underlying the mystery of fishing in Sundarban rivers, estuaries and sea. In this way the two agriculture based caste groups in a different setting became specially conversant with the raising of crops in the saline soil as well as fishing in the turbulent water infested with various aquatic animals of ferocious nature. It was a sort of active effort for adjustment with the surrounding unfavourable ecological settings and the people concerned could develop that capacity to make it perfectly successful.

In order to make the fishing pursuit more successful and highly effectual the agriculturist caste groups like the Mahishya and the Paundra Kshatriya felt the necessity of taking positive help from the traditional fishing caste having age-old experience in the domain of fishing in Sundarban rivers and estuaries. Successful fishing needs total conception over the behaviour and movement of fishes and the ecological perspective of the Sundarban regions. The rivers and estuaries which have created complicated network are not like the ordinary rivers and canal found in other parts of the country. Considering all these matters with profound seriousness the dominant caste groups of Beguakhali inspired a number of families belonging to Jele Kaibarta and Bagdi castes to settle in Beguakhali and engage themselves in fishing activities. Those people were promised by the original settlers of the village to get facilities of various types for constructing their houses as well as for building or purchasing the different kinds of fish gear. It was effected during the thirties of the last century. These two fishing communities migrated from the different regions at different times after being attracted by advantages given to them by the original settlers of the village, on the one hand, and by the fishing prospect at the point of union of the Ganga with the Bay of Bengal, on the other. After reaching the village these people gradually settled down and formed homogeneous fishing groups. Their traditional fish based understandings and indigenous knowledge were extensively used by the original settlers belonging to the Mahishya Caste together with the Paundra Kshatriyas. In course of time these two fishing communities became the inevitable factors for the fishing organisation of the village. These fisherfolk did their level best in bringing an effective atmosphere in the domain of fishing activities of the village. The Jelepara or ward of the fisherfolk gradually took the distinctive look. The people became very much busy with courageous activities conditioned by unabated struggle with the turbulent waters. It was the result of their joint venture to establish a shrine for the deity Bisalakshi in the Jelepara during the earliest phase of their migration. They believe that Bisalakshi is a roaring deity having all-rounded influence on the work and movement of the fisherfolk. The principal fish gears–nets and boats–were purchased from the market outside the island or those were locally made. For nets it was all right. They collected threads from the local market. Those were made of hemp. The fisherfolk had got the ability to prepare nets themselves in their indigenous way. The women in the fisherfolk households proved themselves as expert net menders. But for the boats expert workers outside the fishing community became inevitable. The boats were needed to be repaired off and on as well as new boats were to be built for making the fishing pursuit effectual to a considerable extent. Considering the total situation the people belonging to the fishing community considered it was essential to get the service of the carpenter caste having the indigenous technological skill to make and repair boats and other accessories on the spot. Thus they took the leading part in inviting a Sutradhar family to settle permanently in Beguakhali for taking responsibility of all the works related to boat making and reparation. The invitation thus made to the Sutradhar caste by the fisherfolk was actively supported by the dominant caste groups in the interest of the fishing economy.

The immigration of the Muslims to Beguakhali was effected long ago when the fishing economy in the village took a developed form. They belonged to the northern part of the 24-Parganas District and reached here with the intension to get themselves involved in fish-oriented business. Though initially they were attached to the fish trade yet they made a slow entry into the agricultural domain of the village. When they could earn a lot through fish trade some of the families started purchasing agricultural lands and turned themselves in agriculturists which was prestigeous than fishing profession. The Muslims though live in a particular ward exclusively meant for them but there has always been a trend of free mixing between the Muslim and the Hindu communities. A give and take relationship always prevails amongst these two communities and not only so one stands by the side of the other during any kind of misfortune. Rest four caste groups like Kantra, Sunri, Tanti and Kayastha immigrated to Beguakhali during the forties of the last century being attracted by the two-sided economic patterns of the village which were characterized by effective possibilities.

Beguakhali is a fringe village in the Sagar Island and being more or less detached from the main land and staying away from the populous locality the different caste and community groups here could form an integrated whole despite diversified life-ways and thought-ways. This integration has been specifically reflected in their village-level economic understandings mainly centred round fishing. The village was never enlightened by formal education as there was considerable lack of opportunity. But during recent times some positive measures have been adopted in establishing educational institutions within the village. It is due to this the present generation of people here are getting the advantage of receiving formal education. A trend has recently been identified in this village which is associated with the encouragement for educating the children in most of the families. Though the effort for getting higher education is not seen amongst the people but a good number of persons have received education upto class-X standard. After passing the Madhyamik examination they fail to continue their studies because of the lack of opportunity in getting themselves admitted to the Higher Secondary course. Table 4 shows that out of 291 persons after completion of their Madhyamik standard only 5 passed Higher Secondary examination. Out of them 4 persons belong to the two dominant castes in the village i.e. Mahishya and Paundra Kshatriya, and the rest one belong to the non-fishing caste like Sunri. There is no tendency amongst the villagers to send their children to the educational institutions outside the village. It is true that due to economic stringency the people depending on the uncertain income in fishing activities cannot provide for the expenses that are incurred in sending the boys and girls to the institutions of higher studies. But the economically affluent castes like Mahishya and Paundra Kshatriya also do not send their children outside the village for receiving higher education. The trend of female education in the village is rather encouraging. Out of 291 persons passed Madhyamik Examination there are 102 females.

So far as the caste and community groups and the occupations are concerned, in this village, it is seen that 9 castes and 1 Muslim community have associated themselves with the fishing activities directly and/or indirectly. There are 27 land holder families in the village which are engaged in agricultural activities. Alongwith them the landless families also take part in these as workers. There is always a good reciprocal understanding between the landholder and the working groups. All the caste groups and Muslim community are directly or indirectly related to agriculture. But what is important is that the village with its 10 caste and community groups, having their specific traditional occupations, work as a homogeneous unit of fishing pursuit. The life and philosophy of these people with heterogeneous caste and community affiliation have been mingled with the patterns and perspectives of fishing economy. Table 5 shows that out of 10 castes and community groups persons from 7 castes are engaged in the work of active fishing–these people have converted themselves to the fishing personnel. All the caste and community groups are found to be related to various fish-oriented jobs as well as in trading of fish. It is to be noted that though there are definite fishing castes in the village and the fishermen have been taking various measures to fish in the turbulent water through the rivers and sea, but the fish based economy is being controlled by the two non-fishing castes like Mahishya and Paundra Kshatriya. Not only so, they have dared to accept all the hazards and anxieties of fishing in the distant rivers and sea. Many of them work as active fisherfolk which is their occupational linkage but as per social norm they are non-fishing groups of people. Thus Beguakhali have prevailed an effective field for the transformation of the occupational background which has been pin-pointed by the social norm and legislation following the traditional pattern.

Unlike other developed fishing villages with heterogeneous occupations centering round fishing Beguakhali is solitary as well as calm and quiet. Because of its situation at the furthest point of the island near the sea it is less visited by the outsiders. It is also not visited by the urban traders having no linkage with the occupation of fishing. Thus there is no broad-based interactions here between fishing and non-fishing groups of people. The fish traders do visit Beguakhali but all of them belong to the local merchant class each of whom has sentimental linkage with the profession of fishing. Thus the life philosophy of these traders does not differ from that of the fisherfolk engaged in active fishing pursuit. Life in the village is simple and there is person to person understanding despite their economic and social differences. The fishermen here still conduct their fishing activities following their indigenous knowledge and perception in respect of fish behaviour and nature of water on which they work. There is no touch of mechanization of the fishing process here. Two years ago there was a proposal from the Fishery Department to arrange for a mechanized trawler to fish in the deep sea under government subsidy but it could not be made possible due to very bad financial position of the villagers.

At the vicinity of Beguakhali there is a prospective dry fish centre with which some fishermen of this village is closely connected. Along the sea shore near the confluence of the Ganga and the Bay of Bengal three or four dry fishing units are set up at every season of the year. It is the winter time fishing. These units are locally known as *shabar*. All the fishing units are organised locally and the working patterns are conducted through the establishment of fishing camps known as *Khunti*. There are a few natural creeks at the sea shore in this region which are the inevitable factors for harbouring the boats after fishing in the sea. Here the *Khunti* starts right from the western point of the Kapilmuni's *ashram* at Gangasagar and is extended towards the whole of western part along the sea coast. It ends at the extreme western end where village Beguakhali is situated. The Bahardar or owners of the *shabars* are generally migrants from the other adjacent districts. They are no doubt economically well-placed or they have got the capacity to arrange for requisite money from the financiers. In the fishing units that have been developed in the said sea shore most of the workers are of local origin. A conspicuous number of fishermen from Beguakhali join these fishing units every year. They get various opportunities in drawing substantial income by working in different categories of working personnel. There are six expert boatmen from Beguakhali who are appointed every year by the Bahardars to fish in the sea. The fishing operations in these *shabar*-based fishing are highly technical in character. The movements of the boats in varied currents during spring tides as well as in ebb tides are to be properly controlled on which the fate of the expedition depends. Being born and brought up very close to the wide open sea having dreadful state of affairs as well as working continuously against the different phenomenal adversities these fishermen could develop a specific strength of mind to fight out the unfavourable circumstances. Moreover, through a continuous training received from the elders having considerable indigenous knowledge in fishing activities and ready-wit to control the fish gear in adverse situations these fishermen could have been able to make themselves fitted to sea fishing in varied circumstances. Therefore, they are in great demand in those dry fishing units. During off seasons, these fishermen conduct group fishing in rivers as well as in sea. The fisherwomen including other women having experiences in fish based work from Beguakhali join these dry fishing units as fish sorters. Fish sorting is a specific art which needs the power of recognition of fishes, swiftness and perserverance. These women fish sorters have earned reputation in the work assigned to them. The fisherfolk of Beguakhali have got the ability for conducting fishing activities for getting fresh fish as well as dry fish.

The fishing administration at Beguakhali is conducted by an intra-village body constituted by seven eminent fishing personnel belonging to four castes like Mahishya, Paundra Kshatriya, Jele Kaibarta and Bagdi and the Muslim community. It is a traditional administrative unit the member of which come through selection. There is a village-level convention that both the dominant castes e.g. Mahishya and Paundra Kshatriya would send two members each and one would come from each of the three groups like Jele Kaibarta, Bagdi and Muslim. The main functions of this traditional administrative unit, named as "Beguakhali Matsya Kendrik Sampradaya Samiti", are the following:

(1) to look into all the norms and social legislations that have been imposed on the operation of fishing,

(2) to assists in the formation of fishing groups,

(3) to solve the problematic situations arising out of any conflicting affairs in the domain of fishing,

(4) to examine minutely the condition of the river embankments and sea dykes especially during the spring tides when there is every possibility of breakage.

This traditional administrative unit holds a high esteem amongst the people irrespective of caste and community groups. It also performs the function of general village administration that are not directly related to fishing devices. After the formation of Statutory Panchayat under Panchayat Raj Programme the activities of the traditional administrative unit has not been diminished or disturbed. In Beguakhali, both the traditional and statutory administrative units are running parallel to each other. It has been possible because of the fact that the occupation of fishing has made the homogeneity of the village so rigid that the people's philosophy here is efficaciously influenced by inter-dependency and friendly understanding. The indigenous patterns of life-situation have been so well-integrated through time and space that there seldom occurs any situation of fighting amongst themselves–their continuous struggle has been set against various uncertainties of life.

Brick-lined Path in a Fishing Village

Boys Being Trained up in Van Pulling

Two-storied House of a Middle Class Fisherman

Well-decorated Building of a Trader-fisherman

A Poor Fisherman's Family with the Boat

Floating Light Indicator–essential for Night Fishing

Conference of the Fishermen and Fisherwomen

Scene of a Group Interview– the Author is seen at the Extreme Left

A Group Discussion on a Fishing Problem

4

FISH-BASED ECONOMY AND ADHERENT ETHNO-ECOLOGICAL PATTERNS

Sundarban region is not only enriched by having a large number and complicated system of rivers, rivulets, estuaries, creeks and the vast open sea water in the name of the Bay of Bengal but also these are resourceful to the highest order of excellence. This southern part of the West Bengal is characteristically low land area. The network of rivers and channels in this world famous deltaic landmass provides ample opportunities to fish during the different periods of the year. The up-stream water of the rivers is sweet, but in the lower Sundarban it is brackish. The main course of Hugli river is little saline in comparison to the other like rivers in the neighbouring regions. In this brackish water special varieties of fish flourish in large quantities. These have got special taste and naturally their demand is very great in the market centres. The mighty rivers like the Ganga and the Brahmaputra fall on the placid bosom of the Bay of Bengal through the media of numerous big and small channels. This situation of Sundarban rivers has given the fishermen ample opportunities in smooth fishing. Another factor is that these channels, estuaries and creeks of this region are fed with diversified food materials constituted by both plant and animal organisms including various microscopic species. These are heavily flourished during monsoon months through tidal action. Also, in consequence of this tidal action in the sea, the channels, creeks, rivers and estuaries are filled up with salt-water. It results in the higher yield of most valuable fishes and crustaceous animals. The physiographic structure of the region processed in combination with south-west monsoon and other climatic conditions causes a powerful determining influence on the character and abundance of fishes in Lower Bengal and on the migratory movement of fishes as a whole.

Fishing in Sundarban region is regarded as the second important economic activity next to paddy cultivation. It is true that a large section of the people here is dependent on one crop paddy culture on the fertile deltaic alluvium. But production of paddy many a time becomes minimized in the fragile environment due to salinity of soil, cyclonic storms, tidal waves leading to breaking down of embankments by the side of the river or sea resulting in the inundation of the paddy fields by salt water. Similarly fishing in Sundarban region is also characterized by such uncertainties. Sundarban rivers and Bay of Bengal are unpredictable. Sudden cyclonic disorder spoil all the efforts made by the fishermen with huge expenditures and hard labour. Fishing in the sphere of deep forested region are full of constant risk–at any time the greedy jaws of the tiger or crocodile may result in a very unfortunate situation. Sundarban rivers are full of cross-currents and the formation of alluvial land here and there cause great disturbance and sometimes these bring disaster to human life and property. Despite all these acute adversities the fishermen never hesitate to respond sincerely to the call of danger proned rivers and estuaries as well as the greeny reflection of the dense mangrove forests. But it is to be noted that the situation needs the united appeal of the fishermen as well as integrated working pattern of the different fishing units. There is no denying of the fact that out of two principal modes of economy viz. agriculture and fishing, the later one is very troublesome, tremendously riskful and at the same time it is adventurous and prospective.

Fishing in such a varied and riskful circumstances, no doubt, requires the united activities of a large number of persons as well as considerable arrangements for capital. Fishing is based on three principal categories— (1) actual fishing performances on water through the formation of fishing units, (2) financial provisions to meet varied experiences in the arrangement for and conduction of fishing far away from homes, and (3) marketing of the catches in the regional and central fish markets in the country and occasionally in abroad. Thus fishing economy is said to be a very complicated process in which not only fishermen but also a large number of non-fishing personnel are involved. Until and unless these two ends meet, the fishing performances can never be made successful. Thus in the totalistic fishing pursuits there are conspicuous arrangements based on mutual understanding as well as services–remuneration factors. These factors are originally centred round traditional norms and culture patterns though there are always provisions for instant arrangements beyond the scope of the traditional perspectives considering the urgency of the situations that may develop during the course of work.

The first and foremost procedure in fishing activities is the formation of fishing units. Success in fishing depends solely on the nature and composition of the units. Fishermen are of opinion that the fishing units must be made after fulfilling all the required formalities. They consider that the following features must be associated with the making of the unit concerned— (a) Recruitment of the fishermen as well as the boat operators should be made considering the experience and total understanding of the situation, (b) the members of the fishing units may be kin-oriented or non-kin-oriented, but care should be taken to see that there must be a disciplinary attitude in the day to day activities, (c) the fishing personnel as well as other members of the unit must possess required courage and strength of mind to face the challenges of adversities, (d) there must be a good understanding between the owner of the boat and the employees working under him, (e) the fishing unit while working in the distant rivers or sea must not be faced with any shortage of provisions, (f) it is essential for the members of the fishing units to maintain strictly all the taboos and restrictions that are earmarked in the social system of the fishing communities.

Sea fishing as well as deep river fishing require a number of technicalities and in these concerted group activities there are basic points on which the total success depends. Thus at the very first instance, the *mahajan* (jaidar) or the boat owner recruits the fishing personnel and the conductors of boats. Generally an experienced and dependable fisherman is selected and according to his advantages as well as in favour of serving the actual interest in fishing the boatmen are recruited. He serves as leader of the unit, known as *majhi*. Majhi must be an expert boatman as well as fisherman. He should have got the through knowledge on fish behaviour, water currents and weather conditions and also he must possess the requisite personality to guide all the fishermen under his disposal. The fishermen in a particular boat are very often kin-related–failing which they are purposefully recruited from the same village unit so that there will be a friendly understanding among them. Also intimacy amongst these people minimizes the mental hazards and anxieties during their work and stay far away from homes and in an atmosphere of uncertainties. The smaller fishing units meant for fishing in the neighbouring rivers and creeks are constituted by less experienced persons. Many a time novices may also be recruited here which serves the double purposes. It is regarded as beneficial on both the sides–the owner and the boatmen. In this case the owner of the boat has got the privilage in paying less than what is given to the experienced persons. The novice persons get ample opportunities to learn the different techniques of fishing in the practical field. In this near-the-shore fishing units persons from both fishing and non-fishing castes are also taken as workers. But this affairs is only restricted to the river fishing only.

Fishing operation requires a long-term planning for the accumulation of technical equipments and to fulfil the essential requirements relating to the diversified activities in water for a considerable period. It is evident from the integrated activities, and through implementation of the programme for fishing by the different fisherfolk of the world. Firth's observations on the activities of the Malay fishermen depict a well-knit picture in this regard. The fisherfolk of Sundarban have little thought over it as they have to work with various financial constraints. It is difficult rather impossible for them to provide for nets and boats to serve their purpose. They also do not have any elaborate preparation to meet the different challenges throughout the season. Those who have either net or boat or both are on the look out for collecting men for forming a fishing unit. The owner of a boat or net, in the first place, seeks the other persons on hire basis during the season and then form a unit for the pursuance of fishing operation. Fish trade bring immediate money on the spot as it bears no credit business and it is its advantage over the agricultural activities. It is for this reason many persons are attracted towards the fish-based activities. But in spite of the getting of instant money the fishermen cannot reach prosperity because of complicated expenditure they are to meet on various affairs. The first thing is that the income from fishing is quite uncertain. The fisherman is to think of the payment of debt in the market, for he will not get things afterwards, if he does not clear it up. He cannot think of setting aside an amount after keeping the money for daily consumption. A fisherman also faces the problem in regard to storing the excess amount of fish which requires some special arrangements as to hire a space for keeping it in safe custody and purchase of ice. Above all the obligation to the *jaidars* to whom he is perpetually indebted creates the basic pattern of this problem. Thus the fishermen cannot keep any excess amount with them. The most distressing problem that the fisherfolk encounter is the procurement of capital goods, boat and net, which are regarded as the principal factors for fishing operations. Once the boat and net are lost by continuous depreciation, they find it very much difficult to regain these. They have either to hire these or ask the fishermen, who have net and/or boat, to join in their group. Otherwise, they have to wait until they are able to make a net or purchase a boat by taking loan from a *jaidar* who acts as a capital-rentier.

They establish an economic relationship with the capitalist-rentiers who invest money to the fishermen in order to have his permanent client who will regularly supply them fish. The capitalist-rentires oblige the fisherfolk so that they may be ensured with a regular income. Relationship also grows in that they get financial assistance from the capital rentiers as they occasionally help them or give them money on loan for running their families. In this case, they do not have to pay any interest. It is indirectly realised through the sale of fish. Besides their obligations to the *jaidars* the fishermen are to depend on different neighbouring castes for their maintenance during the period when fishing cannot be profitably conducted. During the lean months a fisherman engages himself as a daily labourer in the agricultural fields, in the excavation of tanks and in the construction of roads etc.

The fishermen living on traditional fishing pursuits require to form small units for fishing expedition to eke out their sustenance. This fishing unit has obviously got a relationship with the *jaidar* in organising the fishing activities. The commodities in question are taken over by the wholesalers and sometimes the retailers also, through auction, which is arranged by the *kantader,* who receives the whole catch with the help of their middlemen through an on-the-spot auction. Ultimately these are brought to the market by the wholesalers and/or retailers for public consumption. The fishing unit is directly connected with the *jaidars* to whom the fishes are sold, who then send to the retailers for onward transmission to different markets. In respect of making contact with the *jaidars,* there are often some men who work in his trade either as weighman or clerk who keeps account of fish. These people sometimes act as the agents of the *jaidar* for organising fishing units for him.

The fisherfolk, however, after being able, try to escape themselves from the *jaidar* and make direct contact with the retailers who also lend money temporarily on the condition of getting the whole catch until the amount taken by the fishermen concerned is fully repaid.

All the fishing units are temporary in nature. The agreement that is made continues for one fishing season. A fisherman in any fishing unit is at liberty to discontinue at any time provided he is not under the obligation of any debt to the owner of the unit. But it is the general principle of the fishing unit organisation that nobody should go off the work during the season of fishing. There are many occasions to see that a particular fisherman in spite of his freedom to vacate has been working in a specific unit for years together. When controversy arises between the fisherman and the owner of the unit, the local fishing committee takes the responsibility to settle the matter. This is done in the interest of the total fish-based economic perspective. When it is seen that a fisherman leaves a particular unit without caring for the debt to the owner/mahajan, the Committee imposes exemplanary punishment on the offender. In general cases the fisherman concerned is fined, the amount of which varies according to the nature of offense.

The fishermen in general are very much poverty striken. This is the main constraint in taking the risks and responsibilities for exploring new dismensions in the fishing sphere. Everything goes on in a monotonous and traditional way. It is the poverty of these people which causes to fell them in the grip of the unscrupulous moneylenders and the unit leaders. There are some fishermen in the traditional fishing villages who cannot afford even to engage themselves in fishing in neighbouring rivers owing to extreme poverty. They are, therefore, in search of securing the capital equipments by bringing even land to market either for sale or mortgage by which they can procure money; even they run the risk of borrowing money from different *mahajans* to whom they are directly linked up. Members of such groups with these capital equipments try not to part with, except in cases of disputes, as there is then little chance to find another group to join.

The boats and nets which are regarded as fixed capital equipments by the investment of which production of fish is made, do not remain as such with a particular owner all through the time. They find a transit from person to person on various occasions, the main cause being that the fishermen are to stay in a tremendous economic stringency. These fisherman when in an urgent need of money for marrying away their daughters or to meet the expenses of the funeral ceremony find no other alternative but to sell the boat or net or to keep these in mortgage. Moreover, at the death of a fisherman if there is no male member in the family the boat or net may be handed over to another fisherman in share term. On the other hand, like the landed property, the net is also divided amongst the descendents of the dead, of course not in the process of making it into pieces, but the shares are divided through a mutual understanding amongst the partners.

On formation of the fishing groups the leader of it sets his members in repairing work of the nets. The work of reparation is generally done by the professional women net menders, and if the said work is limited to small parts of the nets, these are done by the members of the fishing groups themselves. Boats are repaired by the carpenters. The nets are dipped in the juice of *gab i.e.* mangosteen (Diospyros peregrina) and bark of *garan* (Rhizophora sp.) to make the threads very much stronger. The method is time consuming and labourious to some extent. The fruits and barks, as mentioned above, are boiled in water for the extraction of juice, in which the net is boiled part by part for sometimes and then dried up; after this the parts are stitched together. When the fishermen return home after conducting their fishing operation, it is the essential duty of them to examine the nets and boats. The torn parts are detected and these are placed for mending properly. If any breakage is seen in the boat, it is readily repaired by the persons engaged for that purpose. The expenditures incurred in the large scale repairing work are borne by the *jaidar* or leader of the unit and afterwards *i.e.* following the sale of the catch these are adjusted.

Sailing out in rivers for the purpose of group fishing requires a good deal of preparation to cope with the various situations in distant rivers for which each member of the group has to carry out some specific duties and responsibilities. All the essential commodities like rice, vegetables, mustard oil, spices, tobacco, *bidi*, kerosene oil etc. are collected as per requisite quantities considering the appropriate number of days to be spent on the rivers and sea. Drinking water is also taken in large-sized earthen pitchers. Provisions are also made for taking crockeries, oil lamps and torch light alongwith the necessary materials. On the eve of starting a list is prepared by the head of the group in consultation with the other members for purchasing and collecting the materials essentially required for that trip. Cooking is done on the boat while it is sailing on water. The fuel wood is collected from neighbouring forests. Before starting for fishing it becomes the essential duty of the fishermen to make arrangement for the daily family expenditures that are to be incurred during their absence from home. Most often the fishermen find no other alternative but to take loan from the different sources or they may approach the owner of the unit for this purpose. Sometimes local shop owners are requested to supply the requisite commodities to the families concerned the prices of which are paid after their return from fishing. But most of the time the village shops fail to comply with that arrangement because of their weak financial position–it becomes impossible for such shop owners to supply materials on credit for a long time. There is another important factor working behind this situation. Fishing activities are akin to a kind of gambling. Thus it may be the fact that after a fishing expedition the fishermen are being returned empty handed. In this specific case it would be almost impossible for the fishermen to make payment to the shop holders. On this issue it is the owner of the unit who becomes the saviour of the unfortunate fishermen but this situation makes the fishermen concerned to be fallen in continuous obligation in serving the owner of the unit for the years to come.

Prior to sailing out in rivers and estuaries, the primary thing to be taken into specific consideration is the season of fishing in sequence to the weather. Those who actually run the risk of catching fish almost throughout the year, cannot do away with the adversity of the weather in the fishing region. The most favourable weather when fishes of varied types can be caught in good quantity, commences from the middle of September and continues upto March. In the tenure of fishing the fishermen try to remain ensured of not to encounter the inclement weather for which they take every possible precautionary measures during the rainy season. On the other hand, they always expect a good catch during the period, rarely it is out of expectation. In this time, that is during the middle of the season, they are put to much troubles due to cold as they are in acute shortage of clothing. They try to keep their bodies wrapped with only a part of the cloth worn or in some cases with the help of a cotton wrapper, when the cold conditions is accompanied by rains and gusty wind, their misery knows no bounds. At this time, they find no other alternative but to remain at shore by anchoring the boat. During the cold period varieties of fishes are available which fetch a considerable amount. The fisherman are to work in the face of diversified adversities. In the troublesome and monotonous life on the boats and launches there is no specific provisions for their recreation. But they find out their own ways to pass the idle and dull moments which have been categorically mentioned below. An on-the-spot survey amongst 199 active fishermen belonging to the three different villages studied supplies the following information as presented in the Table 1.

Lean season starts from the month of April at the approach of spring when south wind begins to blow hard. Moreover, at the middle of April, when nor'wester exerts its influence, there is a fear of drowning of the boats. The other factor is that during this time the fishing ground in the rivers moves away. This period continues upto the month of July

Table 1
Adoption of Different Ways and Means for Recreation

Name of Villages	*Number of Fishermen Interviewed*	*Playing of Cards*		*Playing of Baghbandi*		*Singing of Folk songs*		*Singing of Kirtans*		*Solving of riddles*		*Listening to Religious Texts*		*Simple Gossiping*	
		No.	*%*	*No.*	*%*	*No.*	*%*	*No.*	*%*	*No.*	*%*	*No.*	*%*	*No.*	*%*
Nurpur	89	23	25.84	19	21.34	14	15.73	9	10.11	11	12.36	5	5.62	8	8.99
Dasherchwak	81	19	23.46	13	16.05	21	25.93	6	7.41	12	14.81	6	7.41	4	4.94
Beguakhali	29	11	37.93	5	17.24	6	20.69	3	10.34	2	6.90	1	3.45	1	3.45
	199	53	26.63	37	18.59	41	20.60	18	9.05	25	12.56	12	6.03	13	6.53

and August, after which they set out again and at this time there is a great possibility of getting fish, especially Hilsa (*Clupea ilisa*). During this time, the fishermen encounter the weather opposed to the operation. As Hilsa enters the estuaries in swarms at this time, the fishermen, even taking risk of difficult sailing, go out for catching the species. In the early part of the season the price of Hilsa remains high which induces the fishermen to sail out even when there is frequent rains. Besides Hilsa other fishes like bhola (*Sciaena coitor*), bhangar (*Mugil tade*) etc. are caught during the rainy season. When in distant river the fishermen do not hesitate to catch fish at night. They do not like to lose time except of lunch and diner time. If required, they keep themselves awake throughout the night when there is a possibility of good catch. Sometimes, however, they set back to fishing when they fall either in a rush of current or an eddy. This situation happens when the rivers are in spate during the rainy season. They also sail here and there for exploring a new fishing ground for the purpose of which they even enter into the jungle-infested region of Sundarban. The fishermen, however, are prevented from doing their job if any member of the group falls seriously ill. They do not usually take the risk of keeping such a serious patient as there is no arrangement for treating him in the boat. But in case of sudden illness of any of the members in the unit, the diseased person is not kept without treatment. The disease is, most of the time, combated with the help of different recipes provided by the fellow members of the unit. But mostly it is done through the traditional folk and rural medicinal systems. Sometimes a few common types of allopathic medicines are kept by the leader of the unit which are applied for immediate relief. The following table gives the ultimate picture of the efforts made by the fishermen concerned to treat the different types of diseases of their co-workers who fell ill during last year's different fishing trips.

In every net group the owner of the boat usually becomes the haulman, who is generally regarded as the headman having good command over the nature and movement of the different species of fish. He possesses the capacity for recognising the particular types of fishes from the typical sound emitted by them. The headman also understands the depth of water in which the different varieties of fishes swim. Hilsa and Bhetki (*Latis calcarifor*) generally swim at a considerable depth, while tangra (*Arias nenga*), Paayrachanda (*Pompus Chinensis*), falui (*Notopterus notoptrus*) do not go at depth. Shrimps, pabda (*Callichrous pabda*), fansa (*Engraulis hamiltoni*), Khoira (*Clupia fimbriata*) and topsia (*Polynemus paradiseus*) fishes swim at the shore. The parses (*Liza parsia*) make prattling sound or a ripping noise in the turbid water, while the sound becomes less in clear water. There is rather a buzzing sound created in water by the swarm of fish, which is felt as the beating sound on the under surface of the boat. The crew then sails his boat to his neighbourhood by directing the drift of the net towards it. A very good quantity of fish can be caught by this way. Tangra fish makes a chattering sound in the water while they go down the surface as if there is a beating sound of the boat or the hawking sound of man. After a while the swarm come up to their level of water with their same original chattering sound. As the bhetkis live in deep water, a large sized fish, makes a sound similar to that of firing of a gun. This kind of sound is heard in either turbid or clear water. The Hilsa fish makes slopping sound by beating water with its lashing tail. When a swarm moves, a sound of continuous slapping is made. While doing this they move round underneath creating a whirlpool. The pangas fish (*Pangasius pangsius*) gives a sudden jerk of its body after coming on the surface of water. The swarm of shrimps make a dashing sound against the water while swimming. The dashing sound of the oar too, at the approach of the boat, helps the bhangar to mimic in the similar way to run away from the haunt of the fishermen.

After understanding the exact position of the fishes and also by recognising their specific types through his indigenous power the expert begins his operation alongwith his colleagues. The owner of the boat and net, who has

Table 2
Various Modes of Treatment of Diseases

Name of Villages	*Number of Fishermen Interviewed*	*Traditional Magical Medicines*		*Herbal Medicines*		*Taking of Vow to Curedeities*		*Taking of Western Medicines*		*Going without any Medicines*	
	No.	*No.*	*%*	*No.*	*%*	*No.*	*%*	*No.*	*%*	*No.*	*%*
Nurpur	89	32	35.96	28	31.46	9	10.11	11	12.36	9	10.11
Dasherchwak	81	16	19.75	28	34.57	6	7.41	28	34.57	3	3.70
Beguakhali	29	10	34.48	5	17.24	8	27.59	2	6.90	4	13.79
	199	58	29.15	61	30.65	23	11.56	41	20.60	16	8.04

acquired varied experience in course of his extensive tour through the rivers, estuaries and sea acts as the expert. Sometimes other persons of the group with similar experience may take this responsibility. But the owner of the boat has got full command over the situation by virtue of his position. The other members of the group, as a prevailing custom, abide by the directions of the headman. They may give their opinion and differ from that of the headman/expert, for the formers too are acquainted with the movement of the fishes in different situations. The headman, all the time, does listen to others, if logical. Contradiction in the opinion is cast off by reaching a concensus agreement after a discussion as they move on a cooperative basis with a background of sharing the sale amount. The headman/expert has, however, no authoritative mentality, rather he believes in coordination with the members of the group as fishing is always considered as a group activity.

The fishermen with the help of one another fit the *bintijal* by dipping one margin into the water through the application of weight to it. The two ends are allowed to remain floating and the other margin is fixed in the boat. They then go on sailing the boat for a considerable distance. When it is felt that a considerable number of fishes have been entangled, the fishermen lift the net on the boat. In this connection, mention may be made of *berajal* which may be of considerable length (about 200 ft.); it is used by a large number of fishermen in the turbulent water. The net is fitted across the river, with its one margin loosely fixed underneath the water by means of bamboo and wooden poles at intervals, while other end is stretched along and tied to a number of boats. At least three fishermen remain on the boat awaiting for the swarms of fish. The boats and the poles act as the floats as they are tilted to and fro when the fishes fall into the net. The men immediately pick up the poles and the dipped margin is rolled up to enclose the fishes. Large-sized fishes like bhetki, rahu (Labio rohita), katla (*Katla buchanani*) are caught in this manner. During rainy season when hilsa fishes swim down the rivers and estuaries, the same process is adopted but a different method is applied to net these. When the swarms, being hindered by the impediment formed by stretched net, swim away to the opposite direction, the fishermen impel them to the direction of the net by constant beating of the water. The fishes, then, being frightened, impeded again into the net, when the fishermen readily lift the net. If there is a chance of having considerable amount of fishes, the fishermen increase the duration of their stay whereby they produce their necessities by the sale of fishes on the spot. There are carrier-boats which ply regularly to shore to carry fishes to the market. At times motor launches also are found to be engaged in transferring fishes from the catch area to the market on transport basis. There are also some agents on the launch who directly buy fishes on the spot. But for the precondition as made previously between the fishermen and the owner of the unit, the former strive hard to catch fish apart from previous catch, to bring a quantity of fish by which their loan repayment is made. It is an imperative task on their part to make themselves relieved of the loan taken at different times.

Sea fishing is different from river fishing, as it requires specific knowledge and techniques. It starts when the river fishing activities are over. The personnel engaged in river fishing do not necessarily go out for sea fishing. The fishermen who conduct river fishing belong to the traditional fishing villages having indigenous fishing abilities. Sea fishing demands conspicuous skill on the movements of the water currents, sufficient courage to face the devastations, physical strength to fight with natural calamities as well as sharp presence of mind to take decision during the time of need. Considering these situations the owner/*mahajans* of the sea fishing units are compelled to recruit fishermen having the above qualities and for this they are to go beyond the territorial limit. Sea fishing units are always constituted by the heterogeneous people. In addition to the expert fishermen there are experienced technicians in the sphere of driving of the water vehicles over the sea in different weather conditions. These technicians should have got requisite knowledge for instant reparation of vehicles for the smooth fishing on sea water. Care should be taken to see that due to mechanical and/or technological failure the fishing programme must not hamper, because day-to-day expenditure in sea fishing is a heavy burden. Thus even one workless day on the sea means a tremendous loss to the fishing unit. Therefore, in sea fishing unit everything must be kept ready at hand and naturally a heavy expenditure is incurred in organising the sea fishing group.

Sea fishers must have got practical experience over their immediate environment which is inextricably interwoven with the sea and the marine fish besides the allied natural phenomena. For successful hauling of fish and at the same time for keeping their lives out of danger they are to cultivate a broad-based knowledge on the topography of the sea bed, nature and extent of sea water including tidal waves, various types of fish in marine ecology and their behaviour patterns are to be looked into with due importance in instanteous perspective. The sea bed is characteristically uneven. The soil condition of the sea bed and the direction of movement of the shoal of fishes are considered as the most important criteria to set the net prior to fishing. The depth of the sea bed differs from place to place. The depth of the sea gradually increases starting from the shore. The sea bed in some region is seen to be risen above the sea level which is called by the term *char*. It remains above water level even during the high tide. In some places the water is very shallow. This particular area of the sea is known as *dubachar*. The *dubachar* in course of time becomes prominent with the gradual accumulation of silt over it. Due to these sorts of undulations of the sea bed the current of water become different at different times. Waves in the sea occur as a result of diverse under currents. The fishermen by dint of their long association with the sea, supported by the knowledge they have inherited from their ancestors, could distinguish these waves separately. These waves have got direct relationship with the shoal of fish. From their indigenous knowledge the fishermen can specify what kind of wave is favourable for the movement of what type of fish and on understanding this they set their nets to lift these fishes out of water.

The fisherfolk hold that the colour of the sea water does not show uniform pattern in all the places. The colour of water has a linkage with the presence of fish. The usual colour of water is bluish but it may sometimes become blackish. Fish become abundant when the colour of the water becomes murky due to continuous body washing of the shoals of fish. Thus the colour examination of sea water becomes one of the most important and effectual procedure in detecting out the presence of fish in an area. It helps the sea fishers to save unnecessary movement over the sea and thus it protects them from doing excessive labour and spending money and energy needlessly. It is demanded that the water gives fishy smell when the fishes are abundant in it. The colour of the water in that case would be like fresh fish-washed water. Sometimes it is noted that if the shoal of fish move in the water, it generally emits a fishy smell. On the basis of this criterion the fishermen can detect the route of the movement of the shoal of fish. The presence of sharks and crocodiles in the water of a particular spot in the sea can be detected by smelling the water. The sharks give oily smell while crocodiles present fleshy smell. The movement of the hilsa fish is invariably understood through the detection of pinkish oily substance in their route on the surface of water. Most of the experienced fishermen can easily understand the presence of hilsa fish in large number from the condition of the water in the sea. As they move in great number the water becomes very much disturbed emitting a specific sound which is the specialty of hilsa.

II

The study on the behaviour of fish is an important achievement of the fisherfolk. It is inevitable for the fishermen working especially in deep sea to make fruitful attempts in fishing. The fishes in the mid-sea move according to currents–some varieties of fish like to go against the current and others prefer to move in favour of the current. Their movement is also related to the directions of the wind. There is a month-wise variation in fish movement. When water flows down through the different tributories to the sea in the rainy months the sea water becomes light at the point of mixing. But when the southern wind starts blowing, the heavy water in the mid-sea commences its flow towards the shore. This natural process of movement of sea water influences the movement of sea fish. The variation of this movement is largely affected by seasonal characteristics which are more or less perfectly determined by the fishermen. Thus good hauling of fish is only possible if these factors of fish movement are categorically observed. As this observation pattern is intimately associated with the economic existence of the fisherfolk, so they not only take this trend of observation with due seriousness but also it is passed on to the next generation and thus it is influenced by the flow of transmission through generation giving it an age-old traditional shape.

The fisherfolk, irrespective of their places of fishing, are closely associated with the regular natural phenomena like tide (*joar*) and ebb (*bhata*) which is directly connected with the lunar position. The fisherfolk in general, are to remain well-informed about the lunar position throughout the month as on the information of this the total success in fishing depends. It is said that the hauling of fish increases during the ebb in comparison to the tide. As in tidal phenomenon the back pressure and the volume of water increase, so it results in the scattering of the shoal of fish in various directions. During ebb the back pressure of water decreases and the volume of water becomes less, and as a necessary consequence of which the shoal of fish move towards the *khari* (maximum depth of water where nets are set) where nets have already been set. The fisherfolk have an indigenous perception, which has been developed through time and space, regarding the celestial position of the moon and its direct impact on the water of the sea and rivers.

Each month is broadly divided into two different halves–brighter half or *sukla paksha* and darker half of *krishna paksha.* The current of water becomes stronger on the new moon day *i.e. amabashya* than on the full moon day *i.e. purnima.* The nature and pattern of both the tides are calculated on the basis of their indigenous knowledge over the celestial bodies and their interactions.

Another important indigenous system lies on an inevitable sphere of movement in the broad-based sea. It is the ascertainment of time and direction exclusively during the period of busy fishing and also exploring varied dimensions. It is a fact that during their long-term staying over the vast open sea and especially during the night there is every possibility of losing the direction of the shore. Mention may be made that they uptil now do not carry watch with them for finding out time as well as they are devoid of any mariner's compass to locate the direction of the different sides. But they manage the whole situation through the adoption of indigenous scientific principles on the rising and setting as well as the position in the sky of some of the eminent night stars. Thus their knowledge as regards stellar system is an inevitable factor for coping with the problems relating to the determination of time as well as the direction of sides. The stars on which the fisherfolk exclusively depend for serving their purpose, just mentioned, are *Dhrubatara* or Polester, *Nishitara* or Nightstar, *Sat Jalitara* or Great Bear, *Suktara* or Morning Star etc. Through continuous observations and discussions amongst themselves these stars have become very much well-known to them. The most interesting thing is that surrounding each of the stars in the stellar system there are compact folklore depicting the way of life and functional patterns of them. Through the close-set discussions about these amongst themselves they have developed close intimacy with these celestial bodies as if these are their well-wishers and saviours. When these stars go out of vision during the cloudy and rainy nights they certainly fall in troubles, but it is overcome by observing the flow of water during tide and ebb. Thus it is seen that for the great part of their life and activities the fisherfolk are exclusively dependent on their immediate environment. The nature-man interactions in the fishing pursuits conducted in the unknown sea are highly conspicuous and these give rise to the multi-dimensional views on the work and intellect of the fish-centred human communities.

Fishing in water is not an easy task and if the water is characterized by extreme depth, heavy cross-currents and prominent tide and ebb condition, it becomes very much troublesome to cope with the situation especially when it turns rough. To catch fishes from water thus requires some specific technicalities which have been devised by the fisherfolk themselves through a continuous process of trial and error. It has needed a long-term observations on the ecology and environment of the whole region together with the assessment of the fish behaviour in its totality. All these have jointly given rise to a specific issue what is known as folk technology. Since time immemorial man had been trying to develop ways and means to devise different procedures which could help him fight out the adversities of life with the help of his superior brain power and the specific capacity to observe the surroundings. Man could learn many things from his immediate nature so extensively exposed before him. In course of time he could apply his tireless effort to shape the things according to his necessity. In course of his continuous confrontation with the surroundings he could gradually win over the success in finding out some effective techniques to meet with the unfavourable circumstances. As a natural consequence that technology was based on the primitive inquisitiveness and oriented with the primitive mental situation as well as the effort of these people to explore the mystery of the world. The technology thus adopted by the preliterate people goes by the name of folk technology as mentioned above. The specific feature of this type of folk technology is centred round not only on the categorical native scientific principles, but also it is seen to be effectively influenced by supernatural understanding. In all these technological principles and procedures native science and the supernaturalism walk jointly hand in hand.

The economic pursuits of the rural society was characteristically processed with variegated ritualistic performances, taboos, traditions, beliefs and superstitions besides the realistic technological devices. All these have jointly made an integrated whole surrounding the folk life and philosophy. The fisherfolk had to face, from the very beginning, forces of tremendous adversities while fishing in turbulent rivers and sea. The living as well as non-living circumstances of nature many a time become hazardous and those went to the extent of exerting death blow to them. But they could not remain idle, rather they collected requisite power and courage to resist the unfavourable situation as their economic existence was rooted to the pursuit of fishing. The ultimate results of these devices found their expression in the designing and making of fish gears the principal types of which are the net and the boat. In the discussion of the fishing gear we do not like to go to the time consuming affair like descriptive study of the technological details but to restrict ourselves in the pointing out of the definite patterns and the human interactions with these. The nets are no doubt processed by superb technology which is exclusively marked by indigenous scientific principles. The Sundarban fisherfolk principally use five definite types of nets like, (a) Stationary net, (b) Floating net, (c) Trawl net, (d) Cast net and (e) Drag net. The former two types of nets require large number of persons for setting in the water. As these are very large and expensive, so these are always put under joint ownership. Thus there develops an organisational environment centering round a net of such type. These large types of nets are not available in the market but these are to be knit by the fishermen themselves. The requisite threads are purchased from the market, but formerly these were spun by the fishermen in the fishing villages. Recently these cotton threads have been replaced by synthetic fibres. Though the nets made of synthetic threads are costlier than the nets prepared from cotton threads but these are better in quality and last long. The knitting work are mostly done by the old fishermen who do not accompany the fishing trips. They conduct the work of knitting sitting at home or while gossiping in the village shop or at common public place. They are paid by the active fishermen on daily wages basis or it may be according to the contractual system. The large-sized nets require strong and massive ropes which are fitted to the top and bottom portions of the net. The ropes are always made of plastic yarn and purchased from the market. These stationary nets are set in the deep water of the sea with the help of sinkers and floats as well as bamboo poles. A number of bamboo poles are tied together which work as float-cum signal locally known as *bhasan*. The stationary nets as *selejal* or *khuntijal.* Then comes *Chhandijal* or a kind of floating net. It is a kind of gill net and is operated from the boat which may even be used in shell fishing. A large number of pieces of nets sewn separately and then fitted together horizontally giving it a very longer type. Floats and singers are essential in the operation of the *Chhandijal.* Generally polythene balls and circular burnt earthen pieces are used as floats and weights respectively. These nets are set horizontally in water. These are not fixed at one place, but float from the surface of water and proceed in the direction of the current.

Trawl net is like a large bag having a wide open mouth and a long tail like structure. These are extensively used in trawlers. Recently mechanized trawlers with high capacity have been introduced by the comparatively well-to-do sections of the fisherfolk. These nets are exclusively prepared by hard nylon threads and these are of different sizes. All these nets are made to order and for this purpose experienced net workers are employed. These persons are also engaged in reparation work of their nets when needed. These are meant for sea fishing and especially used in deep water. Owing to heavy pressure of currents and cross-currents of sea water these nets are very often torn out despite their strongest mesh-work with highest quality materials. It is for this reason the organisers of the mechanized big trawlers always keep some experienced net menders ready in the launch or mechanized boats for instant mending of the trawl nets. Trawl nets are not composed of separate parts–these are made of entirely as single pieces. Thus its owner would be very naturally a single person. Many a time it becomes an excessive monetary pressure. Large-sized trawl nets are presently found only in the possession of the well-to-do section of the fisherfolk most of whom belong to the non-caste-based and non-traditional fishermen.

Cast net or *Kheplajal* is an individual-oriented net which is used in catching fishes in shallow and motionless water in rivers and tanks as well as ditches. It is cone-shaped and generally made of cotton yarns. But now-a-days there is a tendency to use nylon threads for the preparation of these nets. These nets are also used together with the large-sized siene or *berajal* very often put in entangling fishes in shallow water of the sea, rivers and big tanks. Besides this a few types of hand operated nets are very much popular amongst the Sundarban fisherfolk, the most important of which is the Dragnet or *hatjali*. It is rectangular in shape. Two bamboo poles are fitted vertically to the two sides of the net made of cotton threads. It is generally used by the womenfolk of the fishing communities who supplement their family income through this type of fishing. Two persons on at each side are needed for operation of this net. Then there are Dipnet or *vesal* which is triangular in shape. The three sides of the net are bound to the bamboo poles. The two sides constitute an acute angle and these are placed on the gunwale of the boat or these may be attached to the fixed bamboo pole planted in the river. These principal types of nets are again divided or sub-divided into varied sub-types according to the different requirements and ecological set up. The fisherfolk working actively in the Sundarban rivers, estuaries and sea are always found to be alert in setting their course of work as per circumstances. Thus they are seen to be continuously engaged in remodelling and improving the existing nets to fit the total situational context.

Boats constitute the inevitable media to move on water during fishing. These are specially constructed to fit the situation of diversified currents of water and the total planning of boat construction is of indigenous in nature. The fisherfolk, though do not personally make boats, have got specific knowledge in the technology of boat making as per their patterns of interactions with the currents of water. It is a perfect example of folk technological affairs which has developed through time and space. The boats are prepared by some professional carpenters with whom the fisherfolk have got socio-economic linkage. Sometimes it is seen that migratory boat makers from different districts reach this fishing zone for the purpose of getting work on boat making. Occasionally the fishermen make a call to the boat makers from Hooghly, Howrah and Midnapur districts. They stay in the fishing villages for months together to conduct the work of boat making on contract basis. Boat making is necessarily a technical job and only the experts in this line are engaged. As because successful fishing is greatly related to the boat, so every possible steps are taken to fashion the boats to fit the different environmental situations. In addition to it a special step is taken up to observe a few ritualistic performances in connection with boat making. The boat building work must be started on an auspicious day and it is followed by a short ceremony that is held at the house of the boat owner. On the prow of the boat a slit is made in which a dust of gold and silver is put after which it is sealed up with a piece of wood. During the period of boat making it is customary that the owner of the boat should observe purity in life and he must be abstained from practising any sexual activities–it is a rigid taboo. The carpenter making boat is to follow certain restrictions. He must take his bath before he engages himself in boat making activities. All through the time of boat making there exists a profound amicable relation between the owner of the boat and the carpenter. On completion of boat making the carpenter receives his due remuneration in cash. Also he is very often rewarded with brass-made pitcher and a new *dhuti* as well as a napkin.

The boat is built by precious wood. Very often *sal* (*shorea robusta*) and *segun* (*Tectona grandis*) are used. The requisite wood is purchased from the market. The structural pattern of the boat is highly processed by different technicalities. The concerned carpenter becomes heavily concentrated in the work of measurement which is done according to indigenously defined way. At the very first stage the keel of the boat is prepared. In order to make the necessary bend which cuts through the water, the wood is tempered with fire. It is a very hard job and a lot of pressure is to be applied to make the bend. When the keel is ready, wooden planks are then fitted on both the side ways one after another. In this way total hull is surrounded by the planks. The fitting of the wooden planks are done by the application of special types of flat iron nails. Formerly these were prepared by the blacksmiths who used to supply these regularly to the fishermen families concerned on payment in cash as well as in kinds. But now-a-days all types of nails are available in the market. The small gaps that are found in between the planks are packed up with jute fibre and then the whole structure is painted with coal tar which protects the boat from the direct influence of water. The application of tar makes the boat leak proof. The maintenance of the boats is a regular affair in the system of fishing. The boats are heavily affected by the rough currents and the saline water of the sea and estuaries. Thus these are to be constantly looked into and minor repair works are to be conducted every now and then. The smaller repairs are done by the experienced fishermen themselves whereas in case of broad-based reparation the expert carpenters are to be called in. On the eve of each trip the condition of the boat is thoroughly checked up and when it is seen all right, the boat is brought down to the water. These boats are not regarded as the simple water vehicles–these not only help the fisherfolk to cover a long distance over water, but as the living embodiment which is needed such a behaviour that is befitting to human beings. Owing to the significant part played by the boat in the very existence of the fishermen, these are propitiated with full esteem. The indigenous pattern of belief in highly effective in the sphere of fishing gear that all the items included in it are treated with great care and respect. When the boats are anchored at the landing ghat and are lying idle, these are never looked as inanimate object lying haphazardly. They are regularly venerated by the womenfolk, belonging to the boat owner's families concerned, with burning lamps in every evening. Besides these the boat is compulsorily worshipped by the Brahmin priest on the eve of the fishing trip. Generally two principal types of country boats are common among the fisherfolk in this region. The *nauka* or *nao* is the most common type. This boat is constructed by placing the planks on the both sides of the keel which has been noted earlier. The height of the hull of the boat is dependent on the condition of the water current where the boat is engaged as well as the concerned fishermen's advantage in the easy handling of the net floating on the surface of water. But always a specific minimum height is maintained to avoid drowning of the boat when it is tilted during the winding up of the spread out nets at the time of collecting the catch. The size of these boats vary according to the nature of service to be conducted by it. Boats are provided with sail, locally known as *badam*. Oars are also in action and these are tied along both the edges of the boat. Then there is steer which is operated by the crewman who remains perfectly attuned with the exact planning of the total fishing expedition. During some specific occasions dug out canoes are in use. The special feature of these canoes is that these are made from a single block of wood. These are given the shape of boat by the carpenters through the fixing of semi-lunate shaped wooden bars within the cavity at regular intervals for giving it proper strength in fighting with the water currents. The two sides of the dug out canoes are raised further by placing wooden planks longitudinally. In these work no iron nail is used–everything are fixed on the body itself and, if necessary, these are tied up with the help of strong string. Owing to the non-availability of requisite wood the making of dug out canoes has been going down and ultimately the effort is being stopped.

Of late, mechanization of boats has changed a great deal the indigenous pattern of the fishing gear. Though it has not yet been the broad-based phenomenon in the fishing pursuits of the region, but a specific trend of change has been started to set in. The well-to-do fishermen have already invested huge amount of money to purchase mechanized launches and trawlers which have helped a lot in fishing in the distant sea on a large scale. There are occasions when it is seen that some influential and moneyed men belonging to non-fishing castes have made arrangements for mechanized fishing vehicles and after forming fishing groups they are conducting fishing activities. The recruitment of the workers including the personnel engaged in direct fishing is done in such a way which does not bother for the caste-oriented economic pattern. These persons may come from different caste groups and thus the fishing groups in the mechanized fishing gear are mostly heterogeneous. In these groups the fishing as well as non-fishing castes work side by side. Thus the atmosphere of mechanization has caused a great deal in attracting non-fishing castes to the domain of fishing. The indigenous country boat centred fishing unit has always been caste oriented as well as kin-oriented. The fishing unit is headed by a particular group leader who looks after all the affairs of the fishing pursuits. Then in the indigenous system of fishing utilising country boats there always prevails an atmosphere in the maintenance of local traditions and customs as well as native taboos and restrictions in fishing activities. Most of the time the owner of the boat works as the group leader who recruits all the personnel keeping in mind their ability in the work of fishing together with their loyalty towards the leader. This type of fishing unit, therefore, is processed by homely atmosphere and is influenced by close cooperation and mutual understanding. But it is to be noted that despite all these favourable circumstances the fishing in country boats is conditioned by limitations and it has been very much acute during the present period. Owing to the silting of Sundarban river system the inward movement of the fishes from the sea has become decreased to a great extent and thus there has developed a present need to be engaged in deep water fishing which becomes difficult with simple country boats and having comparatively smaller nets. Considering this specific situation mechanization is, no doubt, a welcome venture. In this system of fishing a large scale attempt neglecting most of the barriers of ecological and climatic hazards can easily be made and very naturally the output becomes satisfactory. The impact of mechanization in Sundarban fishing pursuits is not so effective as is felt in other parts of the coastal fishing activities especially in Southern India. But its slow introduction into the total system certainly has resulted a lot of change over though in a very limited perspective. In a specific survey work amongst the fisherfolk an attitude study was conducted as regards the phenomenon of mechanization of fishing gear and the allied matters. The respondents, belonged to the three villages, studied for the purpose, put forward their opinions both in favour and against the process in the perspective of their own understandings. These have been summarized systematically in the following table. The economically solvent fishermen, principally migrated from the then East Pakistan, are the main organisers of the mechanized boats, launches and trawlers. This basically business-oriented people could develop effective infrastructure which has been profitably utilised in fishing in Sundarban rivers, estuaries and the Bay of Bengal. In this mechanized fishing system a large and strong group is necessary. The members of the group are broadly divided into three categories— (1) the mechanical experts who drive the mechanized water vessels as well as the repairers whose services are needed during the time of mechanical failure; (2) the expert fishermen completely devoted to the fishing activities depending on their indigenous skill and intellect; (3) the ordinary fish workers who exert their manual labours in spreading the nets over water and in drawing the catches. Thus amongst the working personnel in the mechanized system of fishing there is conspicuous classification of workers. These workers are recruited from any social status *i.e.* caste categories are not the primary consideration here. It is to be noted that the active fishermen are mostly, if not wholly, belong to the fishing castes. The personnel in this sort of heterogeneous group are always found in a clash between tradition and modernity. As because the mechanized fishing units are principally based on the conditions of immediate economic profit so these do not bother for any socio-cultural restriction on the fishing pursuits. According to the organisers of these fishing units, they are to invest lots of money for the fishing units and for the maintenance of the machineries which incur a heavy expenditure, so they are always in the tendency of catching any sort of fish at any time. The indiscriminate fishing has become a compulsion for them to fit the total situation. If there is any species-based and time-oriented selection in the expedition of fishing, they would suffer a great loss and, in the long-run, they would not be able to run the establishment. Thus there is a conspicuous interaction between the indigenous and the mechanized fishing activities. In addition to the private enterprises in the introduction of mechanization in fishing there are also some concrete measures for giving the benefit of mechanization to the indigenous poor fishermen who have been facing lots of troubles since long time past. Considering their plight the Government of West Bengal made an arrangement to provide mechanical trawlers to the fishermen in Sundarban. At first a net group was to be formed from amongst the active fishermen in a particular village or from neighbouring villages. Generally the net group was constituted by 8 to 10 members. The beneficiaries were selected by the Gram Panchayat which was confirmed by the Panchayat Samiti. But the final approval of the net group was given by the Dept. of Fisheries, Govt. of West

Bengal. The total cost of the trawlers was forwarded to the authorised net groups concerned. Fifty per cent of the total amount is the government subsidy and the other fifty per cent was to be repaid to the Bank with interest in 20 equal quarterly instalments by the members of the net group. The subsidised trawlers have no doubt opened a new vista in the domain of fishing in Sundarban. Alongwith the trawlers they were given nets and other related fishing appliances together with the advanced cost of food as well as fuel. The mechanization of fishing gear has definitely brought abrupt changes in the sphere of traditional indigenous fishing activities. The fishermen concerned have been able to visit the far off sea without any risk; their tension has been minimized and the uncertainty in fishing has to some extent been vanished. But a specific factor has become the result of such mechanization and which is the clash between traditional indigenous and modern mechanized fishing. The indigenous caste-based fishermen are characteristically governed by traditional norms in fishing which they generally do not like to violate because of their special regards to the social legislation. But in mechanized trawler fishing there is hardly any scope for observance of any such norms and restrictions. Thus with the mechanization of the fishing gear they have to face a kind of cultural clash because of the interactions between the indigenous and modernized systems. It is true that these fishing units having mechanized trawlers are in a better position in the domain of fishing in Sundarban rivers and sea because of the fact that they can cover a very wide area on the water even at a greater depth. But in spite of getting the requisite facilities of purchasing trawlers through the subsidy provided by the government these people have failed to maintain the fishing units thus formed in active organisational perspectives. In these units due to the clash of leadership the activities within these could not be maintained in the proper order and ultimately most of the net groups had been disorganised. It was thus made them unable to repay the bank loan released to the net groups. Due to the lack of proper maintenance

Table 3
Attitudes of Fishermen towards Mechanization

Name of Villages	*Number of Fishermen Interviewed*	*Accelerates Catch*		*Uncertainties Vanish*		*Resists Superstitious beliefs*		*Destructs ecosystem*		*Neglects traditional Customary laws*		*Causes indiscrimi-nate fishing*		*Fishermen loss freedom of thinking*	
	No.	*No.*	*%*	*No.*	*%*	*No.*	*%*	*No.*	*%*	*No.*	*%*	*No.*	*%*	*No.*	*%*
Nurpur	89	32	35.96	17	19.10	13	14.61	10	11.24	6	6.74	7	7.87	4	4.49
Dasherchwak	81	36	44.44	14	17.28	11	13.58	9	11.11	4	4.94	5	6.17	2	2.47
Beguakhali	22	11	37.93	3	10.34	2	6.90	8	27.59	1	3.45	2	6.90	2	6.90
	199	79	39.90	34	17.09	26	13.07	27	13.57	11	5.53	14	7.04	8	4.02

and in most of the time the want of efficient personnel to look into the technicalities the mechanized trawlers failed to exert proper service. In most of the cases these net units could not compete with the private trawler organisations. There are occasions when the fishermen in the government subsidised trawlers take shelter in the private trawler system due to stringent economic situation. The basic problems relating to these and their overall impact on the Sundarban fisherfolk have been discussed elsewhere in this book specially meant for prospects and problems.

Some fishermen are engaged in catching fishes in the sea which are meant for drying up through a particular process. There are specific fishing devices which are followed by the fishermen who are expert in sea fishing. Fishing units, known as *shabar,* are formed and most of these are family-oriented or kin-oriented. This sort of fishing is to be done on the shallow water of the sea, but the main point is that the prospective spot on the sea is to be searched out, otherwise all the efforts would be ended in dispair. The experienced fishermen can do the job very efficiently–it is based on traditional knowledge that runs down through generations. Two wooden posts (Khunti) are planted vertically on the sea bed and two boats are tied longitudinally with these. A funnel-shaped big net is tied up in the space between the two boats. The fishes coming through the current of water are passed into the net and accumulate in the lower and narrower end of the net. In this sort of fishing the fishermen are to stay in a very troublesome situation because the boats continuously swing by the heavy waves created in the sea. Thus they face acute problems in keeping the balance in the boats. But with the help of their inborn skill and profound courage they can manage the total situation whatever may be its severity. The operating fishermen wait in the boats with the hope of getting a good catch. During this time they make necessary arrangements for tightening or loosening the nets according to the situation with the help of the string fastening to the nets. After the spring tide or ebb tide when the water of the sea becomes almost static, the mouths of the nets come above the water level with their floats. The operators then pull out the lower ends of the nets over the boat to collect the catch and this is done by opening the ends. In this type of fishing the fishermen are needed to be alert in utilising the proper time of collection of the catch. The catch must be removed within a short transitional period. The period between the end of the spring tide and the beginning of the ebb tide or the end of the ebb tide and the beginning of the spring tide are the specific times of collection of the catch. The nets are set close to each other so that the collection work may be done hurriedly during that short transitional period. Other members of the unit wait on the shore where the camp has been established. This type of fishing camp is locally known as *Khunti.* It is seen that all the inmates in the *Khunti* are passing their time anxiously for the arrival of the catch. On the safe return of the boats all the members of the *Khunti* feel enjoyment and they get themselves ready to conduct their specified duties. The boats are anchored a little off the shore and the members of the respective *Khunti* go to the boats with the carrying baskets and hangers to collect the fishes. Two persons are needed to carry the baskets on their shoulders. On reaching the *Khunti* the fishes of the baskets are spread over the mat which is spread on the ground for sorting the fishes.

The sorting work of the different varieties of fishes are done by the professional sorters most of whom are the aged women. These sorters constitute two different types–one type is local and the other is migratory. Generally the migratory sectors comprise the greater part of the sorting people. These migratory sorters come from the neighbouring districts during the season and settle temporarily at the vicinity of the fishing camps. The local sorters visit the *Khunti* daily and after the completion of their day's work they return to their homes. The sorting of the fishes are done according to typological similarity–in this case size of the fishes does not get any importance. The sorters sit side by side keeping heaps of fishes at the centre. The sorters generally receive some amount of mixed varieties of fishes as remuneration.

Sometimes they are paid in cash. The nature of remuneration varies according to the locality as well as the organisational pattern of the *Khunti*. After sorting the fishes are dried up separately according to their typological nature. These are spread out under the sun. In some cases the fishes are hung up on the string stretched on two poles implanted vertically on the ground. Occasionally the fishes are stuck mouth to mouth through their gills and then hung over a horizontal bar. Some varieties of fishes become too much flattened if spread over under the sun which diminishes market price. So they are hung upon the bar to keep their shape intact. The dried up fishes are sent to the *aratdars* or the agents of the *aratdars* for onward transmission to the markets. Sometimes the men of the *aratdars* arrange to collect the dried up fishes directly from the *Khunti*. The dry fishes have got a broad-based international market. Despite the conspicuous economic prospect through integrated trade pattern the procedure of catching fishes and system or drying these up are still going on in the age-old indigenous way and no scientific method has yet been applied in this domain.

III

The fish trade is centred round a unique organisation which is comprised of a number of personnel, principally non-fishing, and trading units. Right from fishing in the turbulent waters of the rivers, estuaries and sea upto the distribution of the catches to reach the different households for consumption through the different markets, there is a chain of close-set activities governed by financial relations as well as norms and traditions.

Fish market, it is to be noted, is the centre of focus of all the fishing activities because of the fact that until and unless the catches are sent to the market the riskful and labourious efforts of the fishermen would be meaningless. Thus all the attention of the fish workers is always directed to the fish markets developed at the different urban and semi-urban centres.

On the eve of the fishing season when different preparations are made for continuous work in water the owner of the boat as well as the leaders and *bahardars* of the fishing units are in the necessity of taking advance payments, known as *dadan*, from the *aratdars* or owners of the godowns. It is not only mere necessity but a compulsion. The Sundarban fisherman are highly poverty striken and in no circumstances they can manage to conduct fishing activities without getting financial assistance from outside. This situation puts them to work under the *dadan* system. Under this particular system the *mahajan* or moneylender provides them with money as per their requirements through their agents. It is a kind of interest free loan. But there is a specific condition behind this system. The *bahardars* are in the obligation to supply all the catch during that season to the agents of the respective *mahajans.* The amount of *dadan* may be from Rs. 6000.00 to Rs. 20,000.00 which vary according to the region of fishing as well as the prospect of the fishing unit concerned. The catch is collected from the different landing ghats by the fishermen themselves or with the help of their hired labourers, and these are stored in the *arat* of the *mahajan* in the fish market. Here the fishermen concerned wait for hours together for selling the fishes through auction. At this place the total catch supplied by the fishermen are kept by putting ice over these and which is provided by the *aratdar*. If there is insufficient catch in a particular year due to circumstantial reason or for any other mishap, the *aratdar* considers the situation and help the fishermen under his disposal by advancing loan to manage the ill-fated situation. But this help is not sufficient for their existence. Still, the fishermen are always under the compulsion to remain in the grip of the *mahajan* as there is no alternative way to save themselves in the face of calamity.

Auction of fish is conducted before the fishermen concerned and the amount is paid by the *aratdars* after deducting some amount according to the trade system. In all the fish markets in Sundarban locality the fishermen who come for selling their catch are to add 50 grammes of fish to every kilogram of fish sold. The buyers get the entire extra amount. The *aratdars* deduct, in each sale proceeds, the subscription of 13 to 15 paise, for accounting 20 paise and for gift 50 paise. In addition to these commission of 8 paise per rupee is levied from the total sale. These deductions are more or less same in the different fish markets of the region. Both from the buyers and the sellers the *aratdars* draw their profits. It has been seen that the *aratdars* charge 5 paise per kilogram of fish from all the buyers. The *aratdars* become encouraged with these profits and in consequence of which they do not hesitate to invest their capital amongst the fishermen. The fish thus purchased by the buyers are speedily transported to Kolkata for getting a network of markets inside and outside this city. The *aratdars* are the essential factors in the fish-based economy. But they also are to work under various problematic situations. During the period of survey as many as 98 *aratdars* from the three leading fish markets were interviewed individually to find out the nature of problems faced by them. The result of that investigation is seen to be reflected in the following table.

There are a few dominant and organised fish markets in the Sundarban region which play the essential role in the functioning of the fish-based economy of the total area. These markets are like the following– (1) Canning market (Canning), (2) Nagendra market (Diamond Harbour), (3) Birendra market (Kakdwip), (4) Namkhana market (Namkhana). These are permanent fish markets in addition to some smaller seasonal markets which develop instanteously during the period of need. But the above-noted four markets function throughout the year though during the slack season these become less active. The fish market at Canning is not only a famous but also it is an age-old market. Being developed at the bank of Matla river Canning fish market could depict itself as the prosperous centre for fish trade from the earliest period. It regularly draws a large number of fish merchants from the different places. The fish workers visit the market regularly to make direct connection

Table 4
Types of Problems Faced by the Aratdars

Name of the Fish markets	*Number of Aratdars Interviewed*	*Various*				*Problems*									
		Transit of fishes to urban centres		*Regular giving of dadan*		*Fishermen fail to maintain conditions*		*Getting no regular financier*		*Irregularity in fish supply*		*Unscrupuls agents for fish collection*		*Unhealthy competition among aratdars*	
	No.	*No.*	*%*	*No.*	*%*	*No.*	*%*	*No.*	*%*	*No.*	*%*	*No.*	*%*	*No.*	*%*
Diamond Harbour	31	11	35.48	9	29.03	8	25.81	7	22.58	3	9.68	1	3.23	2	6.45
Kakdwip	24	5	20.83	3	12.05	4	16.67	6	25.00	5	20.83	1	4.17	–	–
Canning	43	3	6.98	11	25.58	12	27.91	8	18.60	5	11.63	2	4.65	2	4.65
	98	19	19.39	23	23.47	24	24.49	21	21.43	13	13.27	4	4.08	4	4.08

with the trade situation and thus plan their activities accordingly.

The fish market here comprises of the *aratdars,* locally known as *jaidars* or *jiuni* belonging to the different caste groups like Brahmin, Kayastha, Kaibarta, Mahishya and also they may belong to the Muslim community. The *jaidar* is associated with one *muhuri* who performs two-fold functions– (i) he is to keep the full accounts of the trade, and (ii) he is to keep watch over the stock of fishes. Then there is one *Kantadar* who also has got two-fold duties– firstly, he calls bid at auction, and secondly, he weighs the fish. The persons performing the activities of these two workers may come from any caste. Sometimes they may belong to the fishing castes. The *Kantadar* actually works as a middle man. These people attend the market before the coming of the fishermen. The wholesalers, too, from the different places, assemble there. The fishes are put to auction, the maximum price is settled between the *jaidar* and *kantadar*. The Kantadar calls out the price among the wholesalers present there. The price of different varieties of fish rises according to the type and quality. It is to be mentioned that the price of fish does not remain static throughout the year–it varies according to the season, and also it is dependent on the supply and demand factor.

The *muhuri* works with the *jaidar* not as a paid man but as an associate who helps him in keeping the accounts. He gets remuneration for his service and it is deducted from the sale proceeds. The other amount is deducted as *aratdari*– a commission in literal sense of the term. The *Kantadar* is, however, a paid man on the average remuneration of Rs. 350.00 per month. The *jaidar* who lends money to the fishermen levies no interest on the amount *i.e.* on the borrowed money, but it is deducted from the fishermen as commission. The term may suggest that the *jaidar* acts as a commission agent but actually the *muhuri* may be said to be a really commission agent and also a middle man who acts as a liaison between himself and the wholesalers. The *jaidar* realises his invested amount thus in the form of commission which varies usually from 15 paise to 20 paise per rupee, which is determined according to the quality of fish brought to him. Sometimes the amount of commission may be lowered; the fixation of the commission is, however, a personal discretion. All these amounts of expenditure taken together are deducted from the sale of every catch. The rest amount is then handed over to the headman of the group. This amount is then divided amongst the five persons, the boat and the net being taken as one of the co-sharers. Therefore, the amount is actually divided into seven equal shares. The share of the boat and that of the net goes to the respective owners. If a fisherman owns both boat and net, he actually gets three shares at a time, one for the boat, one for the net and the other one for himself.

There is a complicated economic relationship amongst the *jaidars*, the *muhuri*, the *kantadar* and the wholesalers and even with fishermen related with fish apportioned from the whole quantity disposed of. At the time of weighing fish, the *kantadar* lifts up some quantity of varied types of fish brought to the *arat* for sell. The *kantadar* and the *muhuri*, each gets one-fourth of the lifted fish, and the *jaidar* gets half of it. Keeping aside a required quantity for domestic use, the rest is sold out at the market price. The fishermen are to loose 50 gms. of fish per kilogram as the wholesaler gets this exemption, that is, he pays the price of 950 gms. instead of one kilogram. In that sense, if a catch weighs 40 kilograms, the fishermen get the price of about 38 kilograms, 2 kilograms having been accrued to the profit of the *jaidar*. From the sale of 38 kilograms of fish, the fishermen get their respective shares. The *jaidar* takes half of the 2 kilograms of fish, and the other half is shared equally between the *muhuri* and the *kantadar*.

On the other hand, in the process of laying out money, apart from giving loan to the fishermen for fishing operations, the wholesalers ask for money from the *jaidars* to meet the expenses to the incurred for the running of their families or for buying fish on payment. This is in consonance with the verbal discussion between the *jaidar* and his clientale as the letters sometimes come with small amount of money. When the transaction is persistant for a considerable period of time, the *jaidar* does not hesitate to pay a liquid cash to the fishermen and fish traders in addition to the amount already paid at the time of going for fishing, or giving out the fishes to the wholesalers on a loan in part of the whole amount of sale.

There are two types of investments made by the *jaidar* and the *muhuri* viz., on lending money towards the fisheries and fish trade., When the investment is made on the first type, a *chati* of 1½% per day is deducted of which 1% goes to the *jaidar* and ½% goes to the *muhuri*. When it is made on the second type, 4% interest is deducted of which 2% is meant for the *jaidar*, 1% for *muhuri*, and 1% for the establishment of the market. For the clerical job, the *muhuri* gets 1/3rd of the 2% realised in share for the *jaidar*. The realied money is kept with the *muhuri* as he maintains the accounts of all the money invested. The *jaidar*, however, enjoys 1% of interest as privilage, even he does not keep the account.

Nagendra bazar at Diamond Harbour is a famous fish market which comes next to Canning market as regard its trade pattern. It was established in 1977. Formerly, there was no fixed and organised market place here. Fishes were auctioned at different meeting places according to the convenience. But with the increase of the amount of catch especially sea fishes, there had been a specific necessity to start a regular fish market here. This market at Diamond Harbour sits at 7 in the evening and continues upto the midnight regularly and it caters to the needs of the fishermen covering an excessively large area. The location of this market is very good. It is situated very near to the landing ghats of the Ganga. Moreover, the broad metalled road from Kolkata to Kakdwip passes touching the gateway of the market. This market is meant only for wet fish. The stalls are arranged more or less in a circular way. At the middle of the circle there is an open space. All the requisite arrangements have been made within the market and the stall holders i.e. *aratdars* can easily perform their business. Most of the *aratdars* have come from outside. They have got direct and constant linkage with Kolkata market centres. There are facilities for ice supply to prepare fish packets for onward transmission. This market is to bear a great pressure and especially during auction people of different categories pour in the market. The fishermen find a good atmosphere of bringing their merchandise for sale. Most of the *aratdars* here have definite number of fishermen who are under the obligation to deposit their total catch to the concerned *aratdar*. As Diamond Harbour is connected with Kolkata–the principal trade centre–through road, railways and water ways, so Nagendra market in spite of some limitations has been developing day by day as an important market place. This market has specific prospect but no modern technical equipment has ever been introduced to make it fitted to the present situation. Care has also not been given to make the market place clean–there are heaps of garbage here and there which needs clearance for the benefit of the fish trade as a whole.

Birendra market at Kakdwip is another effective centre for fish trade through it is not so extensive in structural pattern. Having been situated at the bank of the Kalnagini Khal, which has got direct link with the Muri Ganga river as well as the Bay of Bengal, this market is always fed by the different varieties of sea as well as estuarine fishes. There are more than 30 stalls within the market space which are owned by the local as well as migrated *aratdars.* Five of the *aratdars* belong to some places outside West Bengal. In addition to these stalls constructed permanently within the market enclosure, a number of temporary stalls have been grown up at the outskirts of the market place. The number of these increases during the favourable season when fishes are caught in abundance. The workings of this market start in the very early morning and continues upto noon. All the workers here are casual in nature. Just at the gate of the market there are number of stalls vending groceries, bedding materials, cheap cosmetics, furnitures etc. These are totally dependent on the fish market *i.e.* fishermen as well as their agents who come regularly to this spot from the different villages are the principal purchasers. Amongst the *aratdars* as well as the fishermen and their agents there is a good number of persons migrated from Bangladesh. Formerly, Birendra market was biweekly in nature. Now it has become a full-fledged daily market. People attached to it are considering to make an extension of the time of its work because of its heavy pressure. The market was started in 1977. As because Kakdwip is gradually developing as an important fish trade centre owing to large scale migration of fisherfolk, so the market in question has been facing conspicuous changes from its traditional nature.

Namkhana fish market though sits daily yet it is not at all a full-fledged market having all the characteristic features of a fish market. It is practically a road-side market having seven authorized *arats*. But however small it is the market is functionable due to its situation near the landing ghats of the famous river Hatania Doania through which a large number of fish-loaded boats, launches and trawlers reach Namkhana. It is seen that most of the fishes unloaded from the various water vehicles are sent directly to the outside markets through road transports. Namkhana is well connected by motorable roads with various urban and semi-urban market centres of the region. All sorts of transports, big or small, can load the fishes right from the very landing ghats. Very small quantities out of the total catch which are unloaded here come to the riverside market at Namkhana. The individual oriented catches are principally sold here. There is no fixed market time but generally it remains open from early morning and closes before noon.

Besides these regular markets dealing with fish there are a few instant fish markets at the sea shores like Bakkhali, Frasergunge and Gangasagar where principally dried fishes are purchased from the agents of the fishermen. After purchase these fishes are transported to the urban centres for their final sale to the consumers–both in the country and in abroad. In the sphere of dry fish trade the concerned people do not depend on the local market–they simply sell these to the individual or group merchants directly who send these to the different distant markets through their own enterprise. Some *bahardars* or owners of the dry fish units have got their own cargo boats or they may hire these to send their finished products directly to the dry fish markets. Amongst the different species of dry fish the dry shrimps have a great demand, the large portions of which come from Sagar Island. The principal purchasers of dry fishes belong to all the varieties is located at Kolkata having the head quarters at Teriti Bazar from where these are distributed to their all India centres. After processing these are exported to different foreign countries.

The trade on fish, both fresh and dried, is thus based on a specific chain organisation. At the source i.e. at the point of catching there are the primary producers constituted by the fishermen who are principally traditional caste-based fishing personnel. Right from the production centres to the final markets for consumption there has developed varied middlemen who are originally non-fishing personnel. Like all other occupational system fishing occupation is heavily characterized by the influence of the persons in the middle stage. But in fishing economy the specific feature is that the middle men have engulfed most of the spheres of it. The distance between the production centres to the actual consumers is so great in fishing economy that it characteristically needs the active interference of the middle men. Not only so, as because the merchandise is perishable and which requires swift movement from one centre to another, so there must be well-organised and mutually compatible machinery of personnel having various duties and responsibilities. Until and unless the chain of persons is well-integrated the fish-based economy would paralyse. In this chain, it is to be noted that, the primary producers *i.e.* the active fishermen are the worst sufferers. In spite of their riskful activities and hardest possible labour they get very little return out of the total catch even if it is a successful venture. In the other side of the chain there are non-fishing personnel who mediate between the production centres and the consumers' market. The active fishermen, working day and night in the estuaries, rivers and sea neglecting all sorts of barriers in the land and water of Sundarban, have been facing ill-fated condition all through the time. In the every step of their life they are to face financial stringencies and because of this reason these people fall in unbearable debt. The indebtedness of the fishermen in Sundarban is their destiny. All of them, excepting a negligible few, have come from very poor families and thus it is not only difficult but impossible for them to cope with the heavy expenditures that are incurred in making the arrangements for fishing activities. The owners of the fishing boats are always in need of money for boat reparation, purchasing of nets and other accessories on the eve of their starting for fishing activities. They are to lend money from the *aratdars* on hypothecation of their total catch in that season. The *aratdars* provide *dadan* to the fishermen to meet the multifarious expenditures for the preparatory stage for fishing expedition. But this amount of money does not cover the day-to-day expenses during the work of fishing away from homes. Moreover, they are to arrange for providing ready money to their respective families to meet the day-to-day expenditures during their absence from homes for weeks together. In order to fulfil these essential requirements the fishermen lend money from the *mahajans* or money lenders on high rate of interest. Sometimes the fishermen borrow money from the boat owners under whom they work. Also, they at times lend money from friends as well as kinsmen.

Fishing is such a profession which is highly influenced by uncertainties. It is largely dependent on the conditions of nature. In the event of poor catch/the owners of the boats fail to repay the loan amount to the *aratdars*. On the other hand, the active fishermen under the owner would not be able to repay their loans taken from the concerned owner. Loans can also be drawn from the professional moneylenders but in these cases certain securities are needed. Thus at times of emergency the fishermen find no other alternatives but to take loan from the moneylenders against securities which may be gold ornaments, brass or bell-metal made

Table 5
Various Purposes Behind Indebtedness

Name of Villages	*Number of Fishermen Indebted*	*For meeting day-to-day family expenditure*		*For the Performance of daughter's marriage*		*For medical treatment*		*Owing to boat accident*		*For purchasing fishing appliances*	
		No.	*%*	*No.*	*%*	*No.*	*%*	*No.*	*%*	*No.*	*%*
Nurpur	232	82	35.34	14	6.03	22	9.48	12	5.17	102	43.97
Dasherchwak	221	47	21.27	8	3.62	10	4.52	28	12.67	128	57.92
Beguakhali	81	19	23.46	6	7.41	8	9.88	11	13.58	37	45.68
	534	148	27.72	28	5.24	40	7.49	51	9.55	267	50.00

Table 6
Various Sources of Indebtedness

Name of Villages	*Number of Fishermen Indebted*	*From Relatives and Friends*		*From Private Mahajans*		*From Aratdars*		*From Local Inhabitants*		*From Cooperative Society*		*From Bank*		*From Other Sources*	
	No.	*No.*	*%*	*No.*	*%*	*No.*	*%*	*No.*	*%*	*No.*	*%*	*No.*	*%*	*No.*	*%*
Nurpur	232	46	19.83	112	48.28	57	24.57	12	5.17	3	1.29	–	–	2	0.86
Dasherchwak	221	39	17.65	86	38.91	61	27.60	–	–	11	4.98	18	8.14	6	2.71
Beguakhali	81	12	14.81	43	53.09	25	30.86	1	1.23	–	–	–	–	–	–
	534	97	18.16	241	45.13	143	26.78	13	2.43	14	2.62	18	3.37	8	1.50

Table 7
Different Extents of Indebtedness

Name of Villages	*Number of Fishermen Indebted*	*Loan upto Rs. 500.00*		*From Rs. 501.00 to Rs. 1000.00*		*From Rs. 1001.00 to Rs. 2000.00*		*From Rs. 2001.00 to Rs. 4000.00*		*From Rs. 4001.00 to Rs. 6000.00*		*From Rs. 6001.00 to Rs. 10,000.00*		*From Rs. 10001.00 to Rs. 20000.00*		*Rs. 20,001.00 and above.*	
	No.	*No.*	*%*	*No.*	*%*	*No.*	*%*	*No.*	*%*	*No.*	*%*	*No.*	*%*	*No.*	*%*	*No.*	*%*
Nurpur	232	136	58.62	73	31.47	14	6.03	3	1.29	5	2.16	1	0.43	–	–	–	–
Dasherchwak	221	96	43.44	62	28.05	10	4.52	17	7.69	16	7.24	14	6.33	6	2.71	–	–
Beguakhali	81	43	53.09	24	29.63	9	11.11	2	2.47	2	2.47	1	2.23	–	–	–	–
	534	275	51.50	159	29.28	33	6.18	22	4.12	23	4.31	16	3.00	6	1.12	–	–

utensils and sometimes their fishing nets also. Those fishermen who have got no valuables to work as security are out and out denied of any loan by the professional moneylenders. Almost all the fishermen of Sundarban are indebted to a large or small scale and this indebtedness passes through generations. The three tables given here, show a clear picture of the nature and extent of indebtedness which are the results of a survey conducted amongst 534 fishermen in the three villages studied in details for this work.

The causes for indebtedness of the fisherfolk are, no doubt, many. In the villages studied these causes can be broadly grouped into five categories, and the fishermen all the year round approach the various sources for getting money as loan to solve their immediate financial problems. The Table 5 is meant for forwarding such an idea.

In addition to the professional moneylenders the needy fishermen approach a number of other sources for lending of money. There are instances when they do not hesitate to go to their relatives and friends for borrowing of money. The Table 6 depicts the multiple sources for getting loans during the time of need.

The Fishermen here belong to the different status and thus according to their capacity and pattern of work they borrow money from others which ranges from small to large amount. The Table 7 would illustrates this situation.

It is a matter of great concern that there is no scope for any form of alternative economy here by which the fishermen can draw some sort of income when the fishing pursuit fails to support them wholly or partly. There are occasions that the poor fishermen have lost their material possessions including boats, nets and other fishing appliances due to acute indebtedness. This unfortunate situation has made them out of the traditional profession as they cannot procure the essential fund any more through borrowing or getting of *dadan*. A large section of them has been turned into daily labourers. Fishing is always uncertain and in recent years Sundarban rivers have become less productive due to large-scale pollution, ecological damages as well as indiscriminate fishing by the non-traditional fishermen. The fishermen as a whole are completely landless people and they have got no practical knowledge about cultivation. Thus they are not directly involved in the Sundarban's another principal economic pursuit like agriculture. During off-seasons the traditional fishermen of Sundarban are compelled to work as daily labourers in road construction work, in the fields and barns of the agriculturists, and a few, finding no other alternative, dare to accompany the team of the honey collectors. In this way the traditional fishermen having close-set link with the domain of fishing are gradually transforming into daily unskilled labourers from the skilful profession of fishing which they have been following through generations.

Fishermen in Net Making Activity

Training in Net Making for Future Workers

Boat Making Work is In-full Swing

Boat Repairing is a must in the Onset of Fishing

Fishing Launches need Regular Servicing

A Fishing Launch–ready to Soil

At the Landing Ghat–ready to Unload Catches

Fishes are Being Transferred to the Market

On the Way to Fish Market

Entrance to the Fish Market

Fishes are Being Auctioned

Carrying of Fishes to the Drying Ground

A Busy Moment of Fish Sorting Work

Fishes are Displayed for Drying up

Men, Women and Children Engaged in Sorting Work

Fish Sorting Work in a Rapid Pace

5

RITES AND RITUALS INTERFACING ECOLOGICAL MILIEU

Each and every society has its ritualistic perspective which is characterised by age-old customs and traditions. The innate philosophy of life has found its place in the development of the various stages of ritual performances. The ritual life of a particular community is the outcome of time-long experience about the world and its different features that have been gained by the people as members of the society. It is due to this fact, the reflections of thoughts and ideas of the society concerned are to be felt in the nature of observances of various rituals. The beliefs and ideas of different societies are very often formulated in their rituals more strikingly than in any other cultural trait. On this ground, the study of the various performances in connection with the ritualistic aspects is essential to understand the actual view of life of a particular community. The fisherfolk under study observe a conspicuous number of rites and rituals that are centred round the different fishing activities with which their holistic life and philosophy are intimately associated.

Supernaturalism is characteristically associated with the fishing activities. Everywhere in the world, it is seen that, the fishing communities are to face various uncertainties; they are to meet with hazardous climatic and associated natural irregularities which may jointly result in the complete failure of the catches. Sometimes these exert dead blow to human life and property. The uncertainties caused by natural disasters are out of human control and even these are beyond avoidance when the fisherfolk enter the water of the turbulent rivers and sea. Fishing in these waters is always full of insecurities. These unfavourable and unknowable circumstances give rise to a sort of supernaturalism and the concerned people explain the hazardous situations in course of their work as the creation of some mysterious powers which by nature put obstacles in the smooth conduction of their work. As these are unforeseen elements and cannot be explained through rational background, so they are compelled to proceed in a mysterious way to solve the adversities.

Amongst the fishermen working in Sundarban ecological settings a large number of ritualistic performances is seen to be conducted, both individually and collectively, at the various stages of their fishing activities. The fisherfolk in this region are to meet with the acute uncertainties in catches like their counterparts elsewhere but unlike others they are in a constant dread of death caused by natural calamities as well as sudden attack of ferocious animals which abound in the whole of Sundarban mangrove ecosystem. Fierceful Royal Bengal Tigers, sharp-jawed crocodiles and highly poisonous snakes alongwith other ferocious animals create a horrible atmosphere in the field of the fisherfolk's work all through the time. While working with this ecological setting human life may be extinguished at any moment by the attack of any one of these animals. There is no way of evading this terrible event–they are to go to the mouth of danger to eke out their existence. Therefore, in this place of work there is a continuous fight between existence and death–it is the basic essence of philosophy of the fisherfolk in Sundarban. They are always in the daring attitude to face the perilous situation. This bravery is the result of their immediate support by supernaturalism to which they have been in an age-long contact and dependence. In this way the world view of Sundarban fishermen is highly conditioned by fatalism.

The fisherfolk of Sundarban region are in the habit of performing a large number of rituals right from their preparation for fishing expedition. At the one hand, they worship various forces and factors responsible for good catches and propitiate the fishes directly, on the other. They believe that the fishes can never be caught by the net until and unless the fishes allow the fishermen to catch them. So they are in favour of the "kindness" of the fishes and to get this the fishermen worship the fishes at different occasions. Boat worship is an inevitable factor which allows the fishermen to go to the water where fishes stay. It is the boat which not only helps them to fish in the turbulent water but also it does a great deal in their safe return to the shore. To them, boat is thus the living embodiment–it is not the mere structure of wooden pieces but it pulsates with life-force. This life-force must be awaken right from its time of construction and the process should be continued all through the time by the observance of sacred performances and through the observance of different taboos.

The boats are constructed by the carpenters who must lead sacred life during the time of construction. He starts work after propitiating the presiding deity of his community–Viswakarma. At this moment the concerned fishermen arrange for worshipping Kastha Devi–the presiding deity of the boat. It is a kind of family level worship. The womenfolk in the family concerned take active part in the worship. The worship is conducted by the traditional priest of the fishermen. Most of the time he is a degraded Brahmin. The boat is constructed by the carpenter stage by stage. The laying down of the keel of the boat is an important event which is observed by a particular ceremony. In this ritualistic performance a promise is made before the goddess of wood to keep herself sacred by presenting the boat with sanctity. In return, the fishermen are prayed for trouble-free journey over the waters and good performance of fishing. An efficient crewman must alert himself in keeping the body and mind fit for the voyage of uncertainty. If in any case he deviates from the line of the sacred way of life, the whole trip would be futile. Thus the life of the boatman is full of responsibilities; it is his all-sided approach which bring prosperity to the whole fishing group. It is essential that the fishing boat should be given a ritual bath with the sanctified water, prepared by the priest, before it departs from the landing ghat. After requisite worship of the boat the owner of the boat, in association with the priest, breaks a cocoanut and pours its water at the head of the boat following which the boat becomes animated. Through the adoption of this process the boat is given the ceremonial responsibility to save the life and property of the fishermen concerned during their movement over water.

Like boat, net is also an essential part of fishing. Success in fishing is dependent on proper placement of the net, and not only so, the nets must be effective. Nets are also regarded as the living embodiments which need care and respect. A number of taboos and restrictions are to be followed for the sake of successful fishing operation. When a new net is prepared, it is ceremonially welcomed by five married women, from the fisherfolk community, with the *baran dala* having a burning oil lamp. *Baran dala* contains turmeric power, vermilion, mustard oil, a few betel leaves and betel nuts and, if possible, small pieces of silver and gold. *Baran dala* is also provided with a water pot filled with water and having a mango twig with seven or nine leaves on its month. One iron nail is also kept with the materials in *baran dala*. It is believed that the iron nail has a magical influence. There is a strong belief amongst the fisherfolk that the water of rivers and sea is haunted by a number of evil spirits which sometimes take the form of gigantic animals that enter into the net and may torn it to pieces. Naturally, it spoils the whole effort. The bundle that is tied with the net alongwith an iron nail saves the net from the evil effect of the malevolent spirits. On returning from an unsuccessful catch (which may be due to multiple reasons) it is customary for the fishermen concerned to purify the ill-fated net through a purificatory ceremony. There is a belief that if the net becomes sterile due to the loss of life-force in it, the fish will slip out of it. In this situation the net concerned should be animated through a continuous ceremonial function. The loss of life-force of a net may be caused due to violation of taboo related to the net by the net owners or it may occur due to the attack of an evil spirit which engulfs the life. The *ojhas* or medicine men in the locality who are related to the fishing people very often called in to search out the cause or causes of malady. After finding out the exact cause of mishap he tries to drive away the evil influence of the malevolent spirit through supernatural way. The *ojha* performs the magical activities in the house of the net owner. He brings out a few short length threads from the net and then he utters magical spells over these. After a long-term procedure of magical performance he draws out the evil spirit from the net and then he proceeds towards the river (not on the landing ghat) to ceremonially throw it in the water and warns it not to repeat the evil act. The *ojha* then washes his hands and feet in the river water and returns to the house of the net owner for further work. He pulls out the tied up old nail from the net because it has lost its quality to resist the evil spirits. He changes it for a new one which he has brought with him. This concludes his work of driving out the evil spirit and he is paid in little cash and in kinds. The kinds include one kilogram of rice, 250 gms. of pulses, a few vegetables, 50 gms. of mustard oil and vermilion.

There is a strong belief amongst the fishermen as regards evil eye and evil touch. Boats, nets and associated implements must be kept out of evil eye possessed by some persons. In case the fishing appliances are influenced by evil eye these are bound to cut a sorry figure in fishing expedition. Similarly, the fishing appliances should not be allowed to touch by the different persons outside the group as because the touch of some persons is ill-fated which may cause a calamity in the fishing effort, and in serious cases, the whole unit may fall in danger. Thus the fishermen are always alert to avert these consequences and for this reason there are some sorts of supernatural methods which are followed and controlled by the *ojhas*. Generally jalpara or charm-influenced water collected from the akata tank, *i.e.* the tank which is not connected with other water sources by canal and also which is devoid of any outlet for water, and is sprinkled with incantations over the fishing appliances. The unit leader supervises the whole procedure and takes a serious note of everything. The *ojhas* claim that they have ample knowledge regarding the various unknown creatures in the sea which cause a lot of disturbances by their supernatural actions. These creatures cannot be brought under control through any other means but the following of supernatural way. The *ojhas* prescribe very often a kind of amulet which is to be tied on the right arm of the person going out for fishing. Thus supernaturalism exerts marked influence on the working patterns of the fishermen and the cause of which is principally the lack of proper scientific knowledge on the different affairs of the unknown sea and rivers. Their long association with the mysterious waters as well as traditional age-old struggle in the unfavourable circumstances with the help of their indigenous fishing gear have made their supernaturalism orientation so specific and all rounded.

Through a continuous struggle with the adverse ecological settings in course of their work in the mangrove ecosystem the fisherfolk have been able to develop various ways and means to adjust with the surroundings. Sometimes the state of affairs becomes so tense and complicated which cannot be averted through the adoption of realistic methods. As because these situations are out of human control as well as beyond perception, so there has developed a number of deities encircling these mysterious happenings which, it is thought, work as the effective measures to cope with the unforeseen circumstances.

Ganga–the water deity–is regarded as the most important deity for the fisherfolk. The fishermen, as per their nature of work, are to fight continuously with water. In the watery environment that has been developed extensively in the midst of network of rivers, estuaries and sea the river Ganga's contribution and influence are very broad-based.

Therefore, a cult of goddess Ganga has come into the conspicuous picture amongst the fisherfolk of this region. She is regarded as the guardian deity of the workers on the waters of the rivers and sea. Therefore, everybody working in this watery situation as well as the inmates of their families want the grace of the Ganga for smooth work and trouble-free life. The goddess Ganga is worshipped on community level of the different villages in Sundarban on the *Dasahara* day.

An idol is made out of clay. The deity is seen to be in the standing position on a shark provided with a proboscis and this is why she is known as *makarbahini* or carried by shark. There are a number of fishermen's villages where *Gangapuja* is held with pomp and elcat. In this annual worship not only the fisherfolk participate but also the people of the region irrespective of casts and communities join deliberately. The important village centres in this region of study where *Gangapuja* is observed on village level are Beguakhali, Namkhana, Kakdwip, Frasergunj, Chemaguri, Nurpur and Sultanpur. In these villages there are either permanent temples for the deity or special shrines are erected at the time of worship. The actual worship is done by the Brahmin priest who is assigned to serve the fisherfolk. In the worship pattern there is seen a distinctive blending of both shastric and non-shastric concepts. Indigenous modes of thinking have been intermingled with the Brahminic ideas. It is pin-pointed by the fact that all the people of the villages keeping aside caste, class and community affiliation think *Gangapuja* as the part and parcel of their life. This deity of the fisherfolk has been universalised in the river dominated region of Sundarban. Here everybody need the protection of the Ganga to save them from devastating flood which very often inundate the villages in consequence of cyclonic storms, earthquakes and even heavy rains. In each and every shrine where *Gangapuja* is arranged by the fisherfolk many non-fishing families send their sacred offerings in the form of sun dried rice, fruits, vegetables, sweets and a few coins. Some persons offer new cloths and napkins to the deity. The festival is held for two days. In every evening there is an arrangement, in most of the shrines, for various recreational activities that are held in the evening and sometimes it continues throughout the night. These may be *kirtan* songs, local *jatra* performance, *kabigan* and different folksongs of the region. All the people belonging to the different age group enjoy these recreational programmes to their hearts' content.

Gangapuja is performed by the fishing groups invariably on the eve of their departure. Before going to the distant rivers and sea for weeks together it is essential for the fish workers to propitiate *gangamata* on group level. On this occasion the idol of clay is not prepared but *gangaghot* is placed ceremonially representing the deity. An earthen pot is filled up with water in the name of the goddess. A small mango twig is inserted at the mouth of the pot and then a cocoanut is placed over it. The body of the earthen pot is wrapped with a red coloured napkin. The worship is generally held at the house of the leader of the group or *manjhi* or it may be conducted in a public place. Whatever may be the case the womenfolk of the families of the fishermen concerned take active part in the organisation of worship. It is not generally attended by outsider. The leader of the fishing group supervises every steps of the *puja* performance and he observes fasting till the worship is completed. After the completion of worship he sprinkles the sacred water to the attending persons which is meant for peace and success in life. The *manjhi* or leader arranges for a feast on that day to entertain all his crewmen. The *gangapuja* is continued till the departure of the boats from the landing ghat of the village. When the boats are being ready with all the fishing gears, food staffs, drinking water and all other necessary materials, it is the perfect time for the priest to perform a short but effective ceremony on the boat to worship the mother Ganga. He oints vermilion with mustard oil on the two ends of the boat. Some turmeric paste is also applied on the boat and then the two ends of it are garlanded. The attending women coming from the fishermen's families make a ceremonial reception showing the *baran dala* with a burning mustard oil *lamp*. They make the sound of "oolu" and blow the conch shell (*Sankhadhwani*). On completion of all these the attending persons, males and females, bow down before the boat in honour of the Mother Ganga who has been ceremonially placed within the boat so that she will continuously bless the fishermen and protect them from the untoward happenings in the water of the rivers and sea. During the long absence of the malefolk owing to fishing outside the womenfolk regularly promise *telsindur* (oil and vermilion) to the Mother Ganga to get her kindness so that the male members of their respective families, engaged in fishing, may not face any disaster and also they pray for their safe return. In every fishing village it is seen that during the days of spring tide the womenfolk go to the river to show regard to the *gangama* by offering betel leaf, betel nut oriented with vermilion. Some quantity of mustard oil is thrown over the tidal waves drop by drop as a symbolic attempt to pacify high waves.

Sundarban region is characteristically the abode of the different varieties of snakes, some of which are highly poisonous. During rainy season these perilous reptiles become the objects of terror to the people. The people of the different villages who are principally cultivators and fishermen are to come out of their homes to work in the fields and water in the rivers, estuaries and sea. During the rains the snakes come out of their hiding places and move about here and there. Most of the time these shelterless creatures enter the households and take temporary shelter there. Thus the people of this region are to remain in a continuous terror–striken condition because of these deadly creatures. Snake-bite instantiously cause hazardous situation; many a time it brings an end to life. Thus it is a complicated problem before the working people of the region. From the study and analysis of cultural perspectives it is seen that man did not sit idle in that problematic situation. They were to come out, move about here and there for the sake of their economic activities–there was no way out of these. But they could find out a specific way to adjust with the surrounding dangerous situation. It was a kind of cultural adaptation. Continuous fear about these deadly creatures forced these people to think of a saviour who could be appeased regularly to get rid of the danger in their daily life. Ultimately, through the age-long tradition of the folk, they could identify a presiding deity of the snakes. The deity concerned was named Manasa and in course of time she was given a special place in their culture. The myth relating to it penetrated into the modes of behaviour which ultimately found place in the value-attitude system of the rural folk. The folk culture of this region is heavily characterized by the propitiation of the goddess Manasa celebrated at a large scale during the rainy season. The snake deity is adored with great veneration and a large number of ballads composed by the local composers are sung in a chorus with the accompaniment of the characteristic musical instruments. People observe a number of rites and rituals in the praise of the deity of snakes. A number of folk ballads and folktales have been composed by the people at different times which enhance the magnanimity of the goddess. A number of narratives depict her range of influence over the diverse human groups irrespective of castes and communities. All of these are so vividly and carefully arranged that the people cannot pass even a single day without asking her grace to tide over the crises. The Manasa Cult is a direct response to the people in the midst of terror-striken situation arising out of the activities of snakes. This particular cult has been so conspicuously intermingled with the life of the rural folk that it has formed a definite cultural background and the main intention of the cult is nothing but an attempt to cope with the unfavourable environmental circumstances. Variegated rites and rituals in connection with the deity and their analysis would readily explain the fact that various patterns of thinking of the people about Manasa cult are centred round one point which is the utmost prayer and heart felt request of the people to protect them from the deadly reptiles like snakes. In this way the rural folk develop various means to make adjustment with the environment.

The Sundarban region is characterized by broad-based spread of Manasa deity. In this region there are so many villages which have been linked up with the name of Manasa. There are villages like Manasatala, Manasabari, Manasadanga, Manasabere, Manasadanri etc. In the Sagar Island there is a broad region known as Manasadwip.

Fishing caste groups are specifically the admirers of the goddess Manasa. She is practically the household deity of these people. They propitiate the deity daily specially in the evening by the showing of burning lamps. Wherever any untoward situation arises, they sing in the name of Manasa. It is believed by the fishing communities that Manasa not only protects them from the sudden attack of snakes, but also she saves them from many other crises of life in land and water. Idol worship of Manasa takes place in large number amongst the fishing communities and other related people on the last day of the month of *Sravana* (August-September) or on the last day of *Bhadra* (September-October). In all these fishing villages there are *manasa than* or shrines of Manasa where the annual worship is performed. She is worshipped by the Brahmin priest serving the fishing caste groups. The worship is attended not only by the fisherfolk but all other people assemble at the shrine because the grace of the goddess is specifically needed for all the people to save themselves from the attack of snakes.

The fishermen working in the jungle-infested parts of Sundarban are always afraid of the Royal Bengal Tiger whose line of action is very difficult to understand. These majestic, highly powerful and skilful hunters are the part and parcel of the Sundarban ecosystem. They have exclusively adapted to the saline ecological settings and have developed into a specific type which differs from all other species of tigers found elsewhere. The tigers are not habitually gregarious, they move alone and rarely they are seen more than two together. They have well-developed senses and are extremely suspicious in nature. They drink very well the salt water from rivers and estuaries like all other animals in the region. The people of Sundarban especially those who work in the forested regions like fishing, collection of honey, fuel collection, crab hunting etc. regularly encounter with tigers. This situation has developed a terror-oriented mentality in the life and behaviour of the people dependent on forest resources. The fishing groups as well as the honey collectors are exclusively related to the direct forest connected professions. The fishermen engage themselves in fishing in the network of rivers and estuaries of the region, and very often they are to enter into the dense forest knowing fully well that they would at any moment be attacked by tigers. If a tiger aims at his human prey in the fishermen's boat, he would do it readily and nobody would be able to resist the tiger. Thus the fishermen perform the activities of fishing in these localities taking a tremendous risk of life. But despite that very risk they do not lag behind because of the fact that it is their traditional occupation. Moreover, there is no way out from it as there is no other choice of occupation for them. This is perfectly true in respect of the other professional workers also in the sphere of forest. Thus these people are always in a struggling condition–the struggle to get rid of the mighty jaws of the tigers. Mention may be made that this struggle does not relate merely to the strength of arm or devising of any technological procedure to challenge the tiger as they believe firmly that the tiger is not only a living creature of the forest but also a symbol of supernatural power. Thus it must be tackled in a supernatural way. Tiger is regarded as the symbol of unlimited power which can be brought under control through the adoption of certain miraculous procedures. Therefore, these people depend very much on the magical activities of the specialised persons having supernatural potentiality to empower the activities of the tigers. These people are known as *fakirs*, *bauley* or *gunins*. The fishing groups as well as the honey collectors take with them one such expert to work in the supernatural domain to save them from the claws of death. It is believed that by the magical activities of these experts the movement of the tigers will be stopped–they will be inactive for that period.

In course of time there developed a full-fledged tiger cult in the whole of Sundarban region, and a presiding deity has been associated with that cult tradition. Dakshin Roy became the famous figure in the sphere of tiger cult. He is the controller of tigers. Thus, if he is appeased properly, the tigers would not be in the attacking mood and, therefore, the life will be saved. The spread of Dakshin Roy cult is to be seen throughout the Sundarban locality but it is more compact and effectual in the jungle-infested part of the region. Dakshin Roy is the household deity of the fishermen and the honey collectors. Almost all the villages especially the fishing villages posses a particular spot of worship of Dakshin Roy known as Dakshin Roy *than*. It is a mound of earth raised under the foot of a tree. In some villages there may be special altar within a mud built temple. Dakshin Roy is worshipped in two forms– (1) the idol of a worrier , having sword, gun, bow and arrow in his arms. He is seen to be seated on a tiger worrier or sometimes on a horse. The idol is made of clay; and (2) a trunkless human head having a decorated head dress. In this form the deity is termed as *barathakur*. This tiger-god is worshipped on the *makar sankranti* day i.e. on the last day of the Bengali month *Pous* (December-January). During the annual worship the fishermen compulsorily take active-part. They remain fasting till the worship is completed. Amongst these people there is a tradition bound belief that if they get the blessings of Dakshin Roy during this time they would be able to keep themselves away from the attack of tigers while working in the tiger-prone areas. During the days of worship the fishermen do not go out for fishing. They pass these days alongwith the women and children of their respective families in joy and merrymaking. The worship is done by the Brahmin priest and he observes both the Sanskritic and indigenous methods of worship. The specific feature of the cult of Dakshin Roy is that in the performance of worship all the people belonging to the different categories of caste groups give active participation. The people belonging to the Muslim community also come to join directly in the worship.

Thus Dakshin Roy by virtue of his specific power of subsiding the terror of tiger in the midst of the working people could cut across the caste and community differentiation. Besides annual worship Dakshin Roy is worshipped during the different times of the year when such need arises. At this time the *bara* idol is placed ceremonially on an earthen mound and is worshipped by the people themselves in their indigenous ways. Dakshin Roy is regularly worshipped in a symbolic form by the womenfolk of the fishermen's families during the latter's absence from homes for the conduction of fishing activities in rivers and sea. The worship is sincerely done by these women to keep their male members in safe position by dint of benison of the celebrated tiger-deity. Thus the cult of Dakshin Roy is inextricably interwoven with the life and work of the fisherfolk of Sundarban.

Banbibi–the Sylvan deity–is worshipped throughout the length and breadth of Sundarban region. As a guardian deity of the Sundarban her grace is essential for the people who enter the forest for drawing their sustenance. Banbibi is represented by a figure wearing a skirt, a trouser, a crown on head, a garland of wild flowers, necklace, shoes on legs and having a child on her lap. Banbibi is seen to be carried by a tiger. Sometimes a hen is seen in place of the tiger. As per legend, Banbibi once saved a widow's son, Dukhe Sah, from the jaws of the tiger and, therefore, from that moment she came to be known as the saviour of the poor and ill-fated people. Thus Banbibi is still regarded as the protector of the poor section of the society the members of which are exclusively dependent on the forest resources. Within the Sundarban forested region there are a number of *thans* for the worship of Banbibi. When a group of workers enters the forest, there is a regular practice of offering *puja* to Banbibi on these *thans*. She is propitiated jointly by the Hindu and the Muslim devotees. People of both the communities pray before the deity from the same platform for their protection while at work in the forest. Besides this the annual worship of Banbibi is held at different times starting from *makar sankranti*, and it continues throughout the Bengali month

Magh (January-February). The annual ceremony connected with Banbibi is popularly known as *jantal*. No Brahmin priest is required for the worship of Banbibi. All are allowed to approach the deity according to their own way. The principal purpose of this worship is to beg for her kindness as the guardian deity of the forest for getting success in their respective endeavours as well as safe return from the forest.

Bisalakshi is regarded as the mother of the forest. The people who draw their sustenance from forest resources or forest clad fields are the principal admirers of this deity. Bisalakshi acts as the inevitable factor in the folk religion of Sundarban. As a folk-oriented deity Bisalakshi does not need the service of the Brahmin priest. The experts from the down-trodden communities may be at liberty to worship her. The annual worship is held throughout the months of *Vaisakh* (April-May) and *Jaistha* (May-June) besides the daily worship in the individual families. In addition to numerous *thans* or small shrines throughout the Sundarban region there is a conspicuous number of brick-built temples of Bisalakshi in some of the villages. The terror of the landed part of Sundarban is tiger, similarly in the water dominated region crocodiles create tense situation. The large and extremely sharp jaws of the crocodiles are very difficult to avoid when the fishermen are busy in work. When they set the large and heavy net in water, move here and there on water keeping their full concentration on the total planning of fishing, the crocodiles may stealthily move on and attack the fishermen at work. Thus there is always a panicky atmosphere at the time of fishing. Similar is the case with the honey collectors also. In order to get rid of the attack of crocodiles there has developed the specific pattern of propitiation of the presiding deity of crocodiles–the Kalu Roy. The idol of Kalu Roy follows the trend of Dakshin Roy to some extent. He wears a dress like the worrier-deity of the *Purana*. Two of his hands are provided with battle axe and shield. A number of weapons hang from his belt. On the back there are bow and arrows. Kalu Roy is worshipped by the forest goers and the fishermen in the indigenous way. They offer him jungle flowers with deep regard and pray for total protection from the greedy jaws of the crocodiles. Annual worship of Kalu Roy is held in some villages on the special *than* on the night of *makar sankranti*. There is a regular practice of offering rice beer to this deity.

Makal Thakur is the presiding deity of the fish and, therefore, the fishermen are the chief admirers of him. Makal is the god of the marshy lands. All the traditional fishermen are seen to worship Makal Thakur with special regard. There is no idol of the god and no fixed date of worship is observed. He is represented by one or two clay lumps prepared at the bank of a tank or river immediately before worship. Any man from fishing community may work as the priest. He offers to the deity some amount of sun dried rice, banana, wafers, etc. together with a few forest flowers. The fishermen believe that the tanks or rivers depict infernal region. The god Makal may give protected shelter to the fishes in the midst of water and submerged soil if he so desires. If such thing happens, fishermen would never be able to get any trace of the fishes in spite of their painstaking fishing activities. Thus to satisfy the Makal Thakur the fishermen do their level best, and it is done through the performance of his deep-based worship.

The fishermen irrespective of castes and communities visit occasionally the *majars* of the Muslim *pirs*, when they are staying at their homes after the fishing expedition, and prays for the grace of the *pirs* to tide over different crises in life. In Sundarban region there are conspicuous number of *pirsthan* or the shrines of the Muslim saints who became famous by dint of their love and sympathy for the suffering human communities. These saints are believed to possess extraordinary spiritual power through which they could control the activities of the ferocious animals in the forest. After their holy departure from this mortal world they have become conspicuous in their respective places of meditation known as *pirsthan*. In these *pirsthan* the mortal bodies of the saints are generally buried, and these take the name of *majars* of the *pirs* concerned. One such famous *majar* in connection with a Muslim saint with variegated supernatural power is to be seen in the eastern Sundarban region. It is the place of meditation of the great Muslim saint Pir Mobarak Gazi. After travelling through the different places in this country Gazipir reached, by a divine instruction, Bansra village developed in the basin of Piyali and Bidyadhari rivers. He came to this part of Sundarban when it was densely forested and inhabited by a large number of ferocious animals both in the land and in the water. Lower Bengal at that time was being heavily plundered by the Portuguese and the Mug pirates and due to which the life and property of the local inhabitants were at stake. Local people started vacating the extensive areas of Lower Bengal out of fear. During that period the whole of Sundarban region was devoid of any source of drinking water. Gazipir was very much shocked to see the acute distress of the people. The wood-cutters and fishermen who used to depend exclusively on forest failed to continue their line of work due to the atrocities of the Portuguese plunderers. Gazipir with the help of his supernatural power helped the local working people to continue their activities in the forested region without any sort of trouble. It was for that reason the wood cutters and fishermen in that vast region became highly obliged to Gazipir. In course of time Gazipir's spiritual capacities spread throughout the country and the people started to approach him for the instant relief of their distress. There is a popular belief that Gazipir dedicated his life at the feet of the Almighty to make arrangement for drinking water to the suffering humanity. The pious site where Gazipur used to conduct his deep meditational activities is known as Ghuntiari Sharif. On the 17th of the Bengali month Sravana (July-August) every year a large fair is held here to observe the *urs* ceremony of Gazipir The people of the region belonging to both the Muslim and the Hindu communities are under obligation to visit the *majar* to show reverence and gratitude to Gazipir for his kindness to the suffering people. The fishermen of the region cannot think to go out for fishing without uttering his sacred name. When in danger on the river or sea or within the dense forest the fishermen and the wood cutters as well as the collector of other forest resources gratefully utter his name in the belief that they would ultimately be saved from all sorts of danger through the spiritual assistance of Gazipir.

From the discussions of the aforesaid deities and spiritual powers it is seen that the fisherfolk of Sundarban including other workers in land and water are exclusively dependent on these divine forms for trouble-free drawing of their sustenance from the natural surroundings as well as for keeping themselves away from dangers created by environmental hazards and ferocious animals. The origin and development of a conspicuous number of deities in consequence of their direct interactions with the unfavourable circumstances are needed to be analysed to understand the nature and extent of struggle, in the cultural perspective, of these people declared against the uncertainties and dreadfulness. The numerous rites and rituals encircling these guardian deities have been intermingled with the cultural patterns of the people giving a picturesque background of human-deity interactions. Fishing is principally based on uncertainties because in this system of economy there are a number of factors of different nature which work in distinctive state of affairs. If all these factors do not meet according to close-set understanding, there is every possibility that the total operation would be abortive. It is for this reason the fishing pursuit is generally equated with gambling. The fluctuations of the catches have made the fishing people destiny-oriented and thus there has developed an integrated pattern of supernaturalism. Their dependence on supernatural forces and in observances of various rites and rituals to appease these powers beyond perception and control are always in the process of unabated continuity. In addition to the usefulness of rites and rituals for bringing the uncertainties as well as troubles and tribulations under effective control these play an essential role in the fostering of friendship and in establishing a close-set understanding amongst the members of the fishing group coming from different households and more often from different villages. These rites have got a tremendous psychological effect on the fisherwomen. These women are to live and work in the respective families during the absence of the male members for the cause of fishing. It is a very critical phase of life of these women. At this time they are to shoulder all the basic responsibilities in running the family and in addition to these they find themselves in a severe mental disturbance when they think the fate of their male members fighting continuously with the turbulent water. In all the fishing villages in this region it is seen that the womenfolk individually and jointly observe a number of rites and rituals centering round the propitiation of different deities in the locality as well as they sincerely obey different restrictions and taboos. These jointly help a lot in gaining mental strength and in resisting the overall anxieties for their male counterparts. The organisation and observance of the different phases and elements of the rites and rituals unitedly on ward level or village level do a great deal in developing group behaviour which minimize the worries and anxieties to a considerable extent.

A Trouble Free Catch Needs Ritual Performances

A Ritual Site in a Fishing Village

Mother Ganga–the Presiding Deity of the Fisherfolk

Serpent Deity Manasa–a Saviour from Snake-bite

Kali Temple at Dasher Chalk–a Fishing Village

A Sacred Corner in a Fisherman's Family

Symbolic Worship to Avert the Evil Spirits

6

FISH AND FISHING IN MANGROVE ECOSYSTEM—PROBLEMS AND PROSPECTS

The Community of fisherfolk has been working from time immemorial in the perspective of Sundarban mangrove ecosystem but the people belonging to this community have been facing conspicuous problematic situations through the ages. The problems are, not doubt, multi-dimensional which vary according to time and space. From the very earliest time the fishermen have been conducting their fishing activities with the simple technological equipments which are devised indigenously. It has been shown in the different discussions in this treatise that the fishermen are the victims of abject poverty. Sometimes it is so tense that in spite of their inhuman labour and risky attempts they are compelled to sell out their personal fishing gears especially during the time of scarcity. Fishes are not available throughout the season and also the occupation of fishing is specifically characterized by uncertainties. This particular situation has created a basic problem in the life of the fishermen concerned. Fishing profession needs regular flow of money to meet the different expenses prior to fishing expedition as well as during the operation. Moreover, the fishermen are to arrange for the family expenditures to be incurred during their total absence from home. The fishermen working under a group leader, who is also a fishermen, take advance payment as *dadan*. But the group leader cannot be able to meet all the necessary expenses of the fishermen concerned.

What he does is to satisfy the part of the requirements. Thus, the fishermen are compelled to borrow money from other sources that are invariably the local *mahajans* or professional money-lenders. It is true that they sometimes try to borrow money from their kinsmen and friends but the attempts become most of the time futile because they fail to provide any substantial help in this regard. Thus the ordinary fishermen owing to stringent economic position are bound up by the two specific obligations. By the bondage of *dadan* they are to work throughout the season as per contract with the owner of the boat. They cannot move out as per their convenience. After their return from the trip they are to repay the loan or pay the interest, the rate of which is exorbitant. Many a time it goes to such an extent that they out and out fail to keep the contract. The ultimate result is that they are forced to borrow money from another *mahajan* to cope with the calamity and gradually they fall in the deep ditch of debt. The leader of the fishing unit, in turn, is also bound up by the condition of *dadan* received from the respective *aratdar* who lends a large sum of money to manage the total expenditures that are generally incurred in organising a seasonal fishing unit by forming a fishing team. But the *aratdar* puts a strong bondage of obligations. The owner of the fishing unit is to hypothecate all of his future catches. Thus through the taking of *dadan* the owner of the group loses all his freedom to dispose of the fruits of his hard labour and riskful activities. If a fishing expedition fails to be successful, he finds no other alternative but to make a fresh contract for the ensuring season with the *aratdar* on the similar conditions as laid down in the earlier one. In this way a group leader may be turned into something like a bonded labour. His traditional knowledge in fish and fishing, efficiency in organising the fishing team and a strength of mind to resist all the worries and anxieties while working on the turbulent waters are of no avail when he falls in the clutches of repeated indebtedness. These people do not get any facility for taking loan from the bank as they fail to fulfil the rigid conditions in their miserable assets and living circumstances. There is no cooperative society for making arrangements for loan to these ill-fated but genuine workers in the water of rivers and sea. From the study it was gathered that in one year as many as 18 group leaders in the region had been compelled to dispose of their fishing gears together with the landed properties to repay the series of loans taken from the professional moneylenders. In most of the cases repeated failures in hauling good catches were the cause of that misfortune.

The fishes caught after a long turmoil and through the making of complicated expenditures must be marketed in time and there should be a regular procedure in dealing with the *aratdars* within the fields of their work. Though there are a number of fish markets here, yet the fishermen attached to the pursuit of direct fishing hardly get any opportunity to send the catches immediately to the market. There is an arrangement for collection of the catches from the landing ghats by the persons working under the *aratdars*. But most of the time they are not regular and, as the fishermen complain, their unscrupulous nature puts them in great monetary disaster. As because everything depend on their whims, so it appears to be very difficult in organising the whole thing *i.e.* the sending of the catches systematically. There is always a specific demand to maintain a close link between the landing ghats and the fish markets, and this link must be regular and instanteous. Sometimes the owners of the fishing troop are in compulsion to dispose of the catches on the boats to the mobile agents of the urban *aratdars* who take the opportunity of helpless condition of the owners of the boats and exploit them by purchasing the total catches through the payment of a very law rate. When these owners of the boats are in the distant rivers and sea for a long time and due to paucity of ration and drinking water cannot continue their stay over there, these agents approach them with provisions and water for drinking and instigate them to spend much of their time in fishing. But in return they compel the owners of the party to sell the fishes to them and naturally, in this situation, they invariably exploit the poor fish workers.

Fishing is mainly the caste-based occupation of the Sundarban fishermen and it is the only reason for them to stick to that profession. There is no other alternative prestigeous profession for them here to make a change over. Fishing occupation in course of its age-long journey in this region has penetrated into the value-attitude system of the fishermen surpassing its economic character. During the present situation of the national economy fish-based business has got a very broad dimension which most of the time is extended to the foreign markets also, and thus it is economically highly prospective. But it is a matter of great regret that the workers in waters who devote themselves exclusively for the lifting of fish from water are in a unspeakable distress. The calamity is for-reaching which cannot be solved, even to a smaller extent, if they are not saved from the greedy clutches of the professional money-lenders. The study reveals that as much as 87 per cent of the fishermen have fallen prey to such a mishap. Most of them have lost their personal boats, nets and in consequence of which they have become the hired fish labourers working under the non-fishing owners of the fishing units. Having profound love for and sentimental attachment with the fishing pursuits as well as possessing the indigenous expertise in fishing in the mangrove ecosystem it has become the irony of fate that the traditional fish workers are gradually being converted to mere labourers in the Sundarban rivers, estuaries and the sea. Thus, there is always a conspicuous question of survival of the traditional fisherfolk.

And in answering this basic question of survival the fishermen leave no stone unturned to traverse through the network of Sundarban rivers and creeks neglecting the devastating tidal waves and the ferocious animals especially the tigers and crocodiles. Very often the fishermen enter into the core areas of the Sundarban mangrove ecosystem to overcome the failure in catch. In this field of work they are greatly exposed to the man-eaters which very often becomes fatal to the fishermen. Despite this sort of riskful activity the fishermen are compelled to engage themselves in compact struggle simply to earn something for the maintenance of their families. It is the minimum expectation of these indigenous people but they cannot achieve this aim due to obvious reasons.

The indiscriminate fishing by mechanized trawlers with finely prepared large nets alongwith other devices resulted from technological advancement of the fish merchants has opened up a new problematic issue. It is true that these fish merchants with the help of trained fish workers have developed a commercial fishing procedure in Sundarban both in estuaries and in rivers as well as in deep sea which could not be reached by the indigenous fishermen with their insufficient technological devices. The commercial fishing methodology of the fish merchants differs basically from that of indigenous fishing on the points that the formers catch hurriedly all the aquatic species alongwith their wanted as well as unwanted categories of fishes with the help of their efficient netting technique. The mechanized system of fishing neglects the caste-based tradition of controlled fishing. According to this tradition, there should not be any haphazard fishing. In order to maintain the ecological balance of the biological species fishes and other related aquatic animals should be put under selective catching programme. The breeding seasons of the different varieties of fishes must be noted properly and these should not be caught during that time. The social legislations prevailing amongst the fishing communities working here through the ages are needed to be properly and effectually followed for the betterment of the faunal atmosphere as well as fishermen's way of life. On the other hand, the personnel belonging to non-fishing caste groups working principally in the mechanized fishing launches and trawlers do not bother to pay any heed to these traditional restrictions. They catch all the aquatic animals within their capacities and after taking the commercially useful fishes they reject all other organisms then and there. The traditional caste-based fishermen feel this untoward situation with great concern but they cannot actively resist this because of the fact that the owners of the mechanized fishing units are economically much better and they are successful businessmen practically controlling the total fishing pursuits here.

Because of the existence of low fish population in the buffer zones of the network of Sundarban rivers the fishermen both in the mechanized and non-mechanized units feel the necessity of entering into the deep sea for getting a better catch. Taking of the risk of this kind, many a time, provides a good return and thus the attempts for conducting deep sea fishing are on the increase. It has already been noted that while working on sea there is every possibility of crossing over the international border line between India and Bangladesh. If it happens even unintentionally, the fishermen with their fishing gears and the total catches would fall in a very critical situation to be dealt with the international law. The frequent incidences of dacoity on the different rivers and sea have become an acute problem to the fishing communities as a whole. Those dacoits are very much organised and their sudden attack on the fishermen's boats, launches and trawlers make these people penniless instanteously. All on a sudden they loose all the catches–the products of their tremendous labour–valuable nets, ready cash and even the water vehicles. From the long time past these robbers have been continuing their evil activities. The fishermen from Kakdwip and Canning complain that these evil deeds have been going on unabated despite some resistances made by the Police force under the Govt. of West Bengal. Sundarban rivers and attached sea have now become the fertile fields for the anarchy caused by the pirates. There are numerous instances of snatching and hijacking of trawlers and other mechanized and non-mechanized water vehicles. These pirates and hijackers move throughout the Sundarban mangrove ecosystem without any sort of resistance. The network of rivers and small creeks and estuaries help them in hiding themselves. There are instances when the trawlers alongwith the fishermen are hijacked by the pirates and then they went into the deep forested regions. After a few days these mischievous persons send their agents to make secret contact with the owner of the trawler or with the allied office to pay a lumpsum amount for the liberation of the captives. These plunderers are not only of local origin but a large section of them belongs to Bangladesh and other countries. Many a time the demand for money for the purpose of liberation of the hijacked men and materials is excessively high which becomes impossible for the concerned owners/agencies to comply with. But finding no other alternative in saving the life and property they are bound to follow the instructions of the hijackers. If these hijackers are challenged, the fishermen concerned will never be able to conduct their activities of fishing any more. There are concrete instances of such kind of threatening. The fishermen complain that despite regular and continuous attack on the life and property of the fishermen the administration is inactive. All the mishaps had been reported in details to the local police stations and the attention of the higher authorities was properly drawn but to no effect. The atrocities are going on as before, rather, these are increasing day-to-day. The two important employees' union and Fishermen's Association like Sundarban Matsyajibi O Matsya Karmachari Union, and West Bengal United Fishermen's Association approached the allied administrative authorities for taking of immediate measures for resisting the evil activities of the pirates which are not only spoiling the fishermen's only means of subsistence but also these are causing irreparable loss to the national economy. All the Fishermen's Associations in Canning, Gosaba, Kakdwip, Sagar Island, Diamond Harbour have expressed the fact with great concern that during the recent period the price of petrol and diesel, nets, machinery parts of the water vehicles as well as the provisions has been escalating day by day and which is causing a great economic involvement of the fishermen concerned. If, in this situation, everything is looted by the plunderers, how the fishermen will survive to add their contributions to the national economy? Fishes have got an international market and especially a few varieties of fish and aquatic species viz. prawns, crabs etc. have got a great demand in the different foreign countries. Until and unless positive steps are taken to create healthy atmosphere in the domain of fishing and all the worries and anxieties are averted, the prospective development in the sphere of international market would surely be stopped.

The life of the fishermen faces dangerous situation if they are not informed of the weather condition at the proper time. Sundarban rivers become furious because of devastating water movements during cyclonic condition. If the cyclone signal is not timely and properly transmitted, there would be a great havoc. Sundarban fishermen still depend on their indigenous system of understanding of the emergence of cyclonic storms and for their devastations they exclusively rely on their destiny. There is no arrangement for weather forecast to cater to the specific need of the fishermen. They are to depend on the AIR weather bulletin which transmits general weather report. The fishermen working in the Sundarban river system and the Bay of Bengal feel the necessity of regular transmission of the area wise weather conditions in details so that they would be able to move to the safe locality while working in the total area of the mangrove ecosystem. There is an essential requirement to know the nature and extent of the weather condition beforehand to plan their work programme smoothly. Still today there are many events of missing of the boats and launches with the fishermen on board caused by cyclonic disaster. Sometimes the lost fishermen are rescued but many a time they are untraced which causes heart rending situation in the families of those fishermen concerned.

Sundarban fish population is characterized by conspicuous diversities. This largest deltaic landmass criss-crossed by numerous rivers with dominant tidal waves is regarded as the gold mine for fishery. Sundarban fishes are noteworthy for their abundance, variegated nature and economic importance. In the Sundarban estuary system marine fishes dominate. It is to be noted that these fishes have got tremendous physiological adaptability in marine, estuarine and fresh water environment. Some marine fishes regularly visit upstream estuaries and fresh water rivers during breeding season. Hilsa fish is the best example. Similarly there are some species of fish which migrate from fresh water to saline estuaries for the purpose of breeding. Different kinds of eels are in the practice of this type of migration. Thus various rivers and creeks having tidal saline water with the flushing of sweet water form the unique ecological niche for speedy reproduction and excessive multiplication of fishes. From time immemorial different local and migrant fishermen engaged themselves in the sphere of fishing to procure these multitude of fishes through the devising of various indigenous means. It is surprising to note that the indigenous methodology of fishing is highly characterized by close set observations on the behaviour-patterns of fishes and not only that there are also different trends of understanding the background of ecological setting of land and water which create the birth and living places of fishes in an ideal way. The study of the fish behaviour by the local fisherfolk is so acute and intelligible that they have given significant local names to all the fishes in Sundarban rivers, estuaries and sea.

The gold mine of Sundarban fisheries is new facing troublesome situation due to multiple reasons and in consequence of which both the fishes as well as the fisherfolk are now in a situation of great disturbance. Sundarban rivers and creeks are in a rapid process of pollution. The Hugli river has been carrying the refuse of numerous factories developed on both the sides of it for a long distance along its course. It is going on unabated for a considerable period of time. Moreover the burnt oil and mobil exhausted from the mechanized vessels and ships which ply throughout the river mouth are causing defilement of water. This polluted water have naturally become unfit for the healthy growth of fishes.

Unable to cope with the unfavoúrable habitat fishes are moving to the deep sea region. Thus the propitious surroundings for the ideal habitat created by the natural phenomenon like the flushing of fresh water in saline water has been heavily affected due to obvious reasons. Moreover, owing to water scarcity in the Hugli river the flow of water has been minimized causing silting of the mouth of the river. This situation prohibits easy movement of the fishes from deep sea to the river, from saline to fresh water. It is because of this particular phenomenon fishing in the Hugli river and its mouth by indigenous appliances has become conspicuously unprofitable. It ultimately has been developed into such an acute state that the native fishermen who work through indigenous methodology have been failing to meet their day-to-day expenditures through the occupation of fishing.

During recent period Prawn industry has taken a conspicuous place in the international market. Sundarban is in abundance with both *bagda* i.e. prawn (*Penaeus monodon*) and *galda* i.e. lobstar (*Macrobracium rosenbergi*) which are being heavily exported to different foreign countries. In this connection, a very unfortunate happening is occurring now-a-days in the domain of fishing in Sundarban. Prawns breed in plenty in Sundarban rivers and creeks. The *bagda* spawn are seen in considerable number in the water of the rivers and creeks near the shores. These spawns, commonly called *Bagdamin* by the local people, are now in excessive demand amongst the *bagda* rearers throughout the region; even the traders from Bangladesh extend their greedy hands secretly. These rearers collect *bagda* spawns from the local people in exchange of hard cash. These are then reared up as per necessity in their personal reserved tanks after which these are sold to the agents in the country or are sent directly to the international markets. Being allured by the direct cash payments a large number of people in the locality, irrespective of men, women, adults and children, have engaged themselves full time in catching *bagdamin*. These *mins* are largely and easily available in the Sundarban rivers when there is the influence of southern winds. This particular wind is seen to be blown from February-March to May-June every year. It is the favourable season for *bagdamin* collection though these are collected more or less throughout the year. The collection is made by a specific technique, but it is very simple, and in it technological requirement is minimum. *Min* collection work starts from the sunrise and it continues upto the sunset. Thus throughout the whole day a large number of people is seen to be very busy along the both sides of the rivers and creeks. They use a kind of long net, one end of which is wide mouthed and the other end tapers to a point. The net is made up of mosquito net type of meshing. It is planted in the shallower water of the shore with the help of a few wooden logs facing the mouth of the net against the current of water. *Bagdamins* as well as a large number of fish spawns and other smaller aquatic animals are flown down the nets and are entangled. Even the minute animal forms cannot go out of the net because of its very fine texture. The nets are kept in water for one or two hours as per circumstances, and then the manipulators come down to the knee-deep water and lift the nets. The entangled *bagdamins* are then collected alongwith a huge number of different species of fishes and other smaller aquatic organisms. It has been observed during field investigation that the collectors get from a single catch only 3–20 *bagdamins* and during this time not hundreds but thousands of aquatic species are being spoiled as these are thrown away in the land where the nets are cleared. In this way an ecological imbalance is being created in the Sundarban rivers, creeks and sea which, if continues unabated, would surely abolish, to a large extent, the fish population in Sundarban region in near future. The natural food chain and symbiotic relations amongst the aquatic animals in Sundarban are thus breaking down causing a death blow to the whole of the Sundarban ecosystem.

Of late, a conspicuous number of multinational organisations from India and abroad have been allowed to fish in the Sundarban river system and the sea principally for export business. These organisations are provided with sophisticated modern technological equipments and with the help of which these have been devised noval ways for large-scale fishing. In this region, in the deep watery environment especially at the bottom of the sea and rivers where the water remains calm and quiet, a special type of water weeds grow within which the female *bagda* (*Penaeus monodon*) lays eggs. This is the most desirable environment for the laying of eggs of this species of aquatic creature. The personnel belonging to these multinational organisations first try to search out these specific spots and then they, with the help of modernized trawlers strain out all the *bagda* spawns and other similar types of aquatic species as per their necessity. Alongwith these spawns huge number of other fries and smaller aquatic species are caught by the very finely meshed nets of the trawlers. Out of these heavy quantities of aquatic species they select only the precious ones and tons of other species are thrown carelessly over the water which start floating. These huge quantities of floating fish fries and other aquatic species ultimately get putrefied causing environment pollution. Owing to this sort of activities of the multinational companies the ideal fish breeding and growing centres are being destroyed on the one hand, and the polluted sea and river waters are greatly affecting the very existence as well as the breeding activities of the fishes, on the other.

There are more than a dozen of active Fishermen's Associations/ Workers' Union in the whole of Sundarban region which have started thinking seriously the fate of this fishing operation in the total Sundarban mangrove ecosystem. In a few recent united conventions these Associations have decided to raise their voices against immoral activities of the outsiders to serve their business interest, the large scale pollution of the rivers and sea make these unfertile for fish growth, as well as these are gradually destructing the fish based economy, so long reared by the traditional fishing communities. In a joint deputation these Associations have drawn the attention of the administration on the different categorical issues as have been detailed below. With the presentation of these specific issues to the relevant authorities the Associations, in a body, have demanded proper solutions of these. The Memorandum of Associations contained the following points:

1. In no circumstances the rights of the traditional fishermen in fishing throughout the region in the Sundarban mangrove ecosystem should be taken away.
2. The bonafide fishermen should be issued legal permit by the administration for fishing.
3. All sorts of pirates doing their evil activities in Sundarban region must be severely dealt with by the administration.
4. The fishing activities by the multinational organisations in Sundarban region by trawlers provided with finely meshed nets must be stopped.
5. The fishermen incurring a loss due to cyclonic disaster should be given proper compensation. When the fishermen become victims of environmental hazards and are lost in the vast sea or in the network of rivers, they must be searched out with due seriousness.
6. The victimized fishermen should be given immediate relief and requisite monetary help.
7. Physical and mental atrocities done by the personnel of the Tiger Project to the fishermen working in the neighbouring region of the core areas should be immediately stopped. All the captured boats, nets etc. must be returned without delay.
8. The concerned families of the fishermen died either by the attack of tiger, crocodile, shark or by the natural disaster must be given proper and instant monetary help. The rate of compensation must be raised upto the minimum level of Rs. 1,00,000.00 per person.
9. For the framing of any policy in relation to the fishing in Sundarban the administration concerned

must sit with the Fishermen's Associations for requisite discussions.

10. The fishermen should be supplied with petrol and diesel at subsidised rate by the administration concerned considering the poverty-striken condition of the fishermen.
11. The sales tax should be excused when the purchasers are the fishermen themselves.
12. Positive steps must be taken by the government to save the poor fishermen from the clutches of the pattern of lending of money by the private money-lenders which is conditioned by tremendous rate of interest and inhuman treatment.
13. Provisions should be made to help them financially through the taking of loans from Banks with the minimum rate of interest as well as nominal formalities.
14. Arrangements should be made to introduce the system of Life Insurance Policy in which the life of all of the fishermen working in rivers and sea should be insured. Their life is always at stake. Very often they are to receive watery graves in consequence of natural disasters and other allied calamities. But the government should take the responsibility of paying the necessary premia considering the ill-fated condition of the fishermen and their effective contributions to the national economy.

Sundarban mangrove ecosystem in its totality is, no doubt, highly prospective so far as its fish population is concerned. Owing to large-scale deforestation the balance between the vegetative and the animal world became disorganised day by day. The destruction of the mangrove plants caused a great deal in giving a death blow to the growth and development of fishes. Mangrove dominated regions are known as the ideal breeding ground of large varieties of fishes. Sundarban rivers as well as the parts of the Bay of Bengal have become the victims of industrialization of the country. Polluted water is one of the main causes of the marked decrease of fishes in Hugli river. There are more than 150 big factories on the both sides of the river Hugli. From these factories industrial effluents are discharged into the water of the Hugli without any pretreatment. The different pulp and paper, textile and petrochemical industrial complexes here affect the aquatic organisms by their regular discharge of rejected materials. Various chemicals like amonia, caustic soda resist the normal life of the fishes and thus their growth becomes retarded. These also bring adverse effect for the growth and development of fish food in the form of zooplankton, phytoplankton, fish spawns and larvae. The river Hugli at one time was specially famous for multitude of hilsa fish (*Hilsa ilisha*). The rapid process of silting of the Hugli at its mouth is on the increase due to less pressure of water from upward course. This situation is also backed by the pollution of water currents due to the presence of various chemicals. These factors have in recent years resisted the natural entry of the hilsa fishes to the sweet water of the Hugli. Thus the dwindling of the hilsa population is the direct result of ecological disaster.

Considering the high prospective background of the land, water, plants and animals of the Sundarban region and thereby to take a pledge for protecting the ecological balance, which has so beautifully been adjusted through the ages, attempts have already been made to restore the balance through a close-set development programme. During recent years the natural balance of the ecological domains developed through the interactions of many biological and non-biological factors is assessed and oriented with different bio-eco-cultural perspectives to maintain the Sundarban mangrove ecosystem in its vitality and grandeur. This has resulted in the formation of Sundarban Biosphere Reserve. Biosphere is a specific terminology which indicates the zone of the earth where living organisms exist in constant interaction with flora and fauna through energy and metabolism. As a supreme animal man used to live side by side with those flora and fauna and consumed those for his requirements maintaining a particular balance. But during the last two centuries growth of human consumption had greatly been increased and this situation had exerted acute pressure on the resources of the earth to such an alarming extent that it exerted a death blow to the very existence of man. In order to resist this ill-fated situation UNESCO, in 1970, introduced "The Man and Biosphere Programme (MAB)" relating to international scientific cooperation between man and his environment from polar to tropical regions and from sparsely populated regions to dense human settlements. It aims at filling up the gaps in the understanding of the structure and function of ecosystems and of the impact of different types of human interventions. The Sundarban Biosphere Reserve is characterized by the largest mangrove ecosystem of maximum biodiversity in India. It was established in 1989 through a notification by the Ministry of Environment and Forests, Govt. of India. It covers an area of 9630 sq km., and is intended to promote the overall well-being of the Sundarban residents while preserving plant and animal life and maintaining the ecology of the region for sustainable production of natural resources. In the interest of development of Sundarban region and upliftment of the economic conditions of the people, the mangrove forests together with the diverse wild life must be conserved with due care and importance. In this unique and fragile bioclimatic zone maintenance of ecological balance is of supreme need through the improvement of habitat, reduction of biotic interference and minimizing age-long man-animal conflict. Economic development of the Sundarban region can only be effected considerably through the proper conservation of the plant and animal resources of Sundarban which should be done through scientific mobilization of the natural resources, harmonizing the development with conservation.

The Sundarban Biosphere Reserve aims at significant planning and its effective implementation of the whole region. It is practically a multidisciplinary project meant for all-rounded development of the region. In the different processes of activities like eco-development, eco-restoration, soil-restoration against degradation, water-conservation, checking of the river erosion and coastal area protection as well as adoption of large scale mangrove afforestation the multifaceted amelioration of the Sundarban ecosystem has been brought under the systematic process of improvement.

It is to be noted, in this connection, that Sundarban Biosphere Reserve has been fighting incessantly to fulfil the three essential functions of the Biosphere Reserve like the following:

Firstly, the preservation of the mangrove ecosystem of Sundarban together with its species and genetic variations of multiple nature.

Secondly, sincere attempts for fostering the social, cultural and ecological sustainable of economic and human development through the efforts for improving the quality of life of the local people.

Thirdly, the specific provisions to be made for facilitating research, monitoring, education and training in relation to the indigenous and regional issues of conservation and sustainable development.

There should always be an active and relevant effort for establishing cooperative agreement between the various local communities through the principle of Joint Forest Management. There is specific pledge to achieve community support of fringe dwellers in the whole of the mangrove area for sustainable management. This Biosphere Reserve put special stress for taking the preventive measures against the deforestation of the mangrove groups of trees by the local people to save the ecosystem complex. Mangrove forest has the specific role in flourishing the nursery for different varieties of fish as well as crabs and related other aquatic species. This would very naturally promise the possibility of improved coastal fishing throughout the eastern India. Moreover, all sorts of endangered animals and plants would get the suitable and safe habitat as a result of implication of the idea of the Biosphere Reserve. The sustenance of the coastal fishing requires the conservation of mangrove forests, otherwise it will face the destruction for ever.

The work of Sundarban Biosphere Reserve has been designed in conformity with the "Seville Strategy for Biosphere Reserves" framed up during the 2nd World Conference on Biosphere Reserves held in Seville, Spain, during March 1995. Sundarban has been brought under the classification as sensitive zone of West Bengal in the Integrated Coastal Zone Management Plan with the addition of the specific significance in sustainable development of coastal resources.

Most of the items in this programme have been framed to improve the basic environment for growth and development of fishes. Taking of specific measures for minimising the overall pollution of the river water would, no doubt, be proved as an active step for the benefit of the fish crop. Artificial regeneration technique of mangrove plants tends to bring fruitful results to the almost broken down mangrove ecosystem. There is no doubt about the fact that if the environment of the Sundarban river system and that of the sea is improved properly and at the same time the people are instigated not to fish indiscriminately, there is every hope that the fish-based economy of Sundarban would face an overall improvement in the strict sense of the term. Sundarban Biosphere Reserve, if it acts categorically according to the programmes in relation to the restoration of the tradition-bound ecosystem, the lost glory of the Sundarban fishing community would certainly be reinstated.

Bagdamin Net–a Threat to the Ecosystem

Setting of the Net in Shallow Water–a Suicidal Venture

7

SUMMARY AND CONCLUSION

While enquiring into the life and work of the fishing community in a specific ecological setting in Sundarban region requisite emphasis has been laid on the human interactions with the immediate nature as well as with the aquatic species centering round which the fishermen's holistic life is intermingled. As the very intention of this book is to highlight the forces of reciprocal actions amongst the diversified traits in relation to the human-animal-natural-supernatural chain of activities, so in all the chapters a specific framework of such a pattern has been adopted to depict the fishing economic pursuit as the result of integrated modes of activities and mutual discernment. The fishermen who are the centre of focus of this study are the traditional workers in a distinctive ecological and environmental setting which markedly differ from other fishing-oriented regions of the country in many of its characters. It is because of this fact the project in question is characterized by certain patterns and perspectives of its own.

Fishing population groups all over the world have got their own ways and means of conduction of work of fishing in turbulent water, and these patterns of activities characteristically mould their life situation as well as philosophical understanding. This life-philosophy of these fishing-oriented groups of humanity would be highly discernible through the systematic analysis and deep-based evaluation of the various elements of their interactional processes with the surroundings. The present work is exclusively based on the fisherfolk in the Sundarban mangrove ecosystem which is the unique bio-climatic zone having various unparallel ecological characteristics which have moulded the total situational context. The data, exclusively based on empirical findings, have been systematically laid out in six different chapters centred on the specific intention of the life and work of the people concerned but these are not isolated whole. Special stress has been laid on the maintenance of close linkage amongst the chapters to help the readers understand the overall nature and extent of the work based on the attempt for explanation of basic process of interactions in the whole domain of fishing activities.

The study starts with the expounding of the characteristic ecosystem of Sundarban which is marked by the development of mangrove swamp forests. Being flourished in the whole of Lower Bengal this landmass is not only unique in the world perspective but also it provides innumerable sources for collecting information on the dual processes of land formation and human occupancy as well as on the depth-oriented interrelationship patterns on man and nature which has now become the basic requirements in ecological studies. At the very outset, the fishing pursuits developed in this landmass have been categorically explained and ample light has been thrown on the point that fishing activities are basically governed by a number of factors in which both fishing as well as non-fishing groups are involved directly. Fishing dimension in Sundarban mangrove ecosystem is characteristically shaped according to the ecological and bio-climatic surroundings and the fishermen, as a necessary consequence, have adapted themselves to fit with that circumstantial perspective.

The history of the development of the fishing activities and its spread through the ages reveals that the personnel attached with this specific economic sphere are all belong to migrant communities having both the fishing and non-fishing ways of life. The heterogeneous caste groups like Bagdi, Tiyor, Malo, Jele Kaibarta, Mahishya are all outsiders. After immigration to this landmass these caste groups adapted the profession of fishing and with those caste groups the people from tribal and Muslim communities joined their hands in fishing pursuits. From the different facets of behaviour it has been understood that through the making of joint efforts for continuous period the caste groups had been able to win over the unfavourable circumstances of danger-oriented Sundarban and thereby they could become part and parcel of the mangrove ecosystem. But in order to make the total endeavour effective they had to struggle through the untoward events in the different phases of the work of fishing. Thus the principal aim of study has centred round the finding out of the nature and extent of man-mangrove-fish interactional processes and to pin-point how the fisherfolk engage themselves in a continuous struggle right from the remote past period.

The caste-based fishing practices of this region have become the characteristic features which have been traversing through the ages without any interruption for a long time. These tradition-oriented fishermen have been following their indigenous methods in fishing and their modes of operations have highly been conditioned by social norms and cultural traditions. With the change of time there has developed a new group of fishermen with newer technologies influenced by the process of mechanization. It has been observed through close-set survey that the new entrants in the fishing domain of Sundarban are constituted by non-caste based fish workers. As because the later groups of fishermen are out and out business-oriented people they utilise the advantage of mechanization as far as they can. The study reveals that mechanization has opened up a lot of problems to the fish population as well as the mangrove ecosystem. Mechanization has aroused indiscriminate fishing in the Sundarban rivers and estuaries creating irreparable loss to the bio-climatic zone principally comprised of the fragile mangrove ecosystem.

In the understanding of the trends and perspectives as well as the severity of the age-old struggle of the fisherfolk against the different adverse situations specially the patterns of land forms and the nature of tidal waves of the rivers, creeks and estuaries have been brought under consideration. Sundarban region has always been under the process of change due to repeated occurrence of subsidence and earthquakes resulting in conspicuous disasters to the land and people. The eco-geography of the region is specifically dependent on the broad-based tidal effect of the drainage system. The exuberant growth of mangrove forest is the uniqueness of the region and there is a beautiful inter-relatedness amongst men, animals and different vegetative species. The day-to-day interactions of the fishermen with the different species of plants and animals have focused the idea that the fishermen alongwith other workers in the mangrove ecosystem always try to make adjustment with the different elements of the ecosystem. The disasters like cyclonic storms, tidal surges, ferocious animals in land and water are coped with through the application of their traditional knowledge, courageous attitudes, effective precautions together with some supernatural ways and means. Having been developed and processed through the direct impact of the world famous mangrove-based ecological setting the fisherfolk of Sundarban have drawn attention of the inquisitive scholars belonging to the different disciplines from lone time past to find out their patterns of survival and work in the midst of the lots of inimical forces. On this ground, the present study deserves the credit of exploring the way of life characterized by the struggling propensities of different patterns of the fisherfolk living in the rich but arduous eco-climatic zone. The broad-based discussions on the types and roles of the mangrove ecosystem as a whole that have been made systematically here help in highlighting the total situation.

The fishing villages in Sundarban depict the holistic life of the fisherfolk. These are of various nature–some are traditional multicaste villages, there are others where the fishing groups dominate, and a few others are very small and simple type developed instanteously. The micro study on the three types of villages present the patterns of interactions between the fishing and non-fishing caste groups centering round fish-based economy. In the traditional fishing village the fishing castes maintain social norms and cultural traditions in the sphere of their fishing activities and there is always a close-set understanding with the non-fishing caste groups and the Muslim community in the village as regards their assistance and cooperation. The service and remuneration patterns in the caste-based fishing village organisation are tradition-oriented. The patron-client relationship is governed by the age-old custom. But it is specifically absent in the non-traditional caste-oriented fishing village. Here the fishing groups of people may not all belong to the fishing castes. In such a type of village many transformed fishing groups may be seen. The process of transformation had been effected after migrating into this landmass. These people care very little for the caste-based traditional norms of the fishing activities. There is a broad-based mechanization of fishing gear here and these people need non-fishing technical personnel more than the traditional fish workers. It has been noted that in the non-traditional fishing village there is very little urge for the maintenance of the age-old norms and customary practices. These fishermen were out and out business-oriented persons who always conduct their activities in terms of monetary profit. Unlike fishing groups in the traditional village the fishermen in these villages try to put a broad-based control over the other caste groups–they like to make a command on them. It is due to this trend amongst the fishing people here a distinctive class formation has been noted. The leading class is represented by the fishermen having financial control over the total situation. The socio-economic pattern of the small and simple types of villages is centred round fishing and the overall interdependence of the people belonging to the different castes. Here non-fishing caste groups are seen to be less connected with their traditional non-fishing operation–they have without any hesitation accepted most of the fish-based activities though they have not lost their caste identification. In this type of fishing village the fishing caste group do not exert any sort of economic supremacy despite their controlling of the fishing operation. Maintenance of the traditional life patterns of the fishing communities are carefully done here and the village life is specially characterized by a number of ritualistic performances centering round various deities meant for the general well-being of the people engaged in fishing activities far away from their homes.

Unlike agricultural activities the fishing pursuits always require that the personnel engaged in direct fishing and other non-fish related activities should be in a cooperating state of affair to make the endeavour a success. The fishing group formation is the basic criterion for achieving that success. In this matter the group leader or the owner of the fishing unit is required to look into the experience-oriented qualifications of the unit members and at the very beginning it is his duty to see that there must be a mutual understanding, closeness of social relations and disciplinary attitudes amongst the members joining the fishing team. During their activities in the distant rivers and sea the fishermen and other members of the team are completely detached from their respective families and the villages. In order to compensate the mental agony there is always a tendency to form kin-oriented fishing groups, sometimes it may also be village-oriented.

Fishing operation is a long-term planning and its implementation requires broad-based financial support. The fisherfolk in Sundarban are characteristically poverty striken and they are to face a lot of troubles to satisfy this financial need. Thus they are to depend on some capitalist-rentier who invest money to the owners of units and as per convention they are to hypothecate the whole year's total catch to the capitalist-rentiers. In the same way the fishing personnel working under the owner of the unit take advance payment on the condition that they would work in the unit throughout the season without any break. Moreover these fishermen most often borrow money from the private money lenders with high rate of interest to meet the essential requirements of their families during their long absence from homes. It has been seen through the different happenings that the fisherfolk inspite of their tremendous labour and the taking of full risk of life they are always the victims of ill-fated conditions. The study reveals that almost all the fishermen including the group leaders and owners of the units are in a profound indebted situation. All are working under the rigid condition of *dadan i.e.* a system of moneylending in which the fishermen are obliged to hand over all the fruits of the labour to the moneylender concerned.

The fish trade embraces a large number of persons at the different places who are tied up in a chain organisation. The primary producers at the rivers and sea are always in a dilapidated condition–they are the most sufferers. The distance between the active fishermen and actual consumers of fish is so great that the direct participation of the middle men is inevitable to keep the producers-consumers relation in a continuous process. In the patterns of economic dealings the personnel in the middle stages draw most of the benefits. Four large fish markets in the region are fully controlled by the *aratdars*, *jaidars*, *kantadars*, *muhuri* and *paikars*. All these personnel demand various types of payments from the fishermen during their disposal of fishes. In order to satisfy these conventional demands the fishermen are to sacrifice a considerable portion of the catch. This is the case with the traditional fishermen but their counterparts having the advantage of working under the mechanized units organised by the non-traditional fishing personnel having financial affluence are not victimised in this way, so, there has developed a categorical dichotomy in the nature and condition of the fishermen in Sundarban.

The mechanization of the fishing gear has exerted a tremendous impact on the fishing behaviour in Sundarban. It is seen that the fishing groups with mechanized equipments and trawlers are very much effective in the line of fishing. These groups of fishermen are at liberty to traverse through the rivers and sea to search out the different corners of the fish-dominated areas. It is due to this reason they can cover a broad-based sphere and naturally their efforts do not totally fail; whereas in the case of the traditional fishermen equipped with indigenous fishing gear there are specific uncertainties in getting requisite catch as their fishing practice has got conspicuous limitations. In spite of the positive efforts taken up by the Govt. of West Bengal to provide financial assistance to the indigenous fishermen for the purpose of having mechanized trawlers under certain legal conditions the fishermen concerned could not fulfil those conditional matters. Owing to the lack of proper leadership in governing the net groups these became disorganised and the financial derailment became so acute that they could not repay the bank loan as per terms and conditions. The total situation disheartened them all.

Sundarban fishermen working incessantly in the world heritage setting are very much efficient in the analysis and evaluation of the different natural circumstances, that are directly and indirectly related to the fish behaviour. Their indigenous knowledge and understanding are highly effective for successful hauling of fish and at the same time for keeping their lives and properties out of danger. From their day to day work it is seen that all the aged fishermen have got the broad-based knowledge on the topography of the sea and river beds, their tidal waves, cross-currents and nature and pattern of fish movements in water. They can also correctly apprehend the presence of different varieties of fishes in observing the colour of water. Fishes can also be identified by analysing the smell emitting from their bodies, and also the fishermen are seen to be expert in recognising the type of fishes through the hearing of sound created by them in water. In addition to these indigenous methods to get themselves acquainted with the fish behaviour the fishermen feel that there exist so many factors in the line of effective fishing which are beyond human control. To bring these within the human capacity it is essential to appease various supernatural powers governing the diversified events and this particular belief pattern of these people have given rise to the development of a number of deities like Gangama, Bisalakshi, Manasa, Dakshin Roy, Kalu Roy, Banbibi, Makal Thakur and the like. These are all the presiding deities of different devastating natural forces, ferocious animals together with many untoward events that very often create problematic situations in getting fishes and in moving safely throughout the region of fishing. Thus supernaturalism in the life of the fisherfolk should not be considered as the result of anomalous thinking pattern but it is their specific tool for fighting with the unfavourable circumstances. Therefore, supernaturalism plays a tremendous role in their uncertain and struggling life. In this way, it would be seen that the fishermen fight continuously against the dichotomized situational context i.e. the realistic situations at the one hand as well as the condition, which is beyond any human control, on the other.

The society, economy and ecology of Sundarban not only differ conspicuously from those of the other regions of the country but also these constitute an integrated pattern of their own. Sundarban region with its bountiful natural resources have developed into a renowned fragile environmental zone characterizing an excellent balance between man and nature. So far as the efforts for fishing is concerned the region provides a prospective field of work in its network of rivers and creeks, deltaic estuaries, distinctive tidal waves, mangrove ecosystem having varieties of wild life. The Sundarban rivers in which the fishermen exert their utmost endeavour have tidal saline water with flushing of sweet water constituting a unique ecological niche for a rapid and large-scale fish propagation. But these unique resources for fishing have never been utilised properly and still today most of the resources could not be brought under the active programme of utilisation. It is nothing but an irony of fate. Being the traditional workers in the prosperous fishing zone the Sundarban fisherfolk have failed to reach the goal and still today they are passing their days with tremendous financial stringency inspite of their continuous and heavy pressure of work devoted to the cause of fishing. Thus there is an emergent necessity to conduct further research to highlight this specific situation in the light of the integrated activities of the different facets constituting the totalistic fishing domain of Sundarban.

The fisherfolk in Sundarban are the traditional workers in the interlaced situation of man-mangrove-fish line of understanding. The fisherfolk as per socio-cultural convention struggle continuously to maintain the equilibrium in the inter-connected ecological perspective. The present work has specifically focused discernible light on the patterns of adjustment to the different settings. The study has brought to light the diversified roles played by the fishermen to make themselves fitted to cope with the surroundings. These have been done through the following steps:

1. Socio-economic adjustments like kin-based group formation, organisation of fishing units, marketing of fish through well-integrated action orientation of different personnel, capital investment.
2. Technological adjustments like designing and preparation of diversified tools and implements for fishing, their techniques for effective manipulation, fish sorting, classification and preservation.
3. Environmental adjustment like the development and analysis of the ideas on the river and sea water, their various conditions during the different seasons of the year, their abnormalities and related problemetic situations.
4. Ecocultural adjustments like various adaptive measures to save themselves from the biotic as well as abiotic hazards in the different ecosystems, impact of supernaturalism and the development of various belief patterns in the day to day life as well as fishing pursuits.

It has already been noted that the traditional fisherfolk of Sundarban is caste based and it has been seen through different types of investigation that fishing caste oriented group considers it compulsory to follow the modes of restriction imposed on them through social legislation. Thus there was always very little or no attempt for the destruction of the ecosystem. Owing to the development of a new type of fishing groups which are principally non-caste based i.e. the personnel representing the group do not necessarily belong to the traditional fishing castes. The non-traditional fishing groups are specifically commercial in nature and most of these possess mechanized or semi-mechanized fishing boats, launches and trawlers as well as improved types of nets. With the help of these they conduct fishing activities throughout the region, both in shallow and deep waters, and thereby catch all types of fishes indiscriminately. After the successful catch they select the required varieties of commercial importance and the unwanted species are thrown over here and there. Alongwith these there are numerous non-fish aquatic species of various types which act as essential food materials of the fishes. The different types of indiscriminate fishing creates an acute type of natural imbalance in the Sundarban mangrove ecosystem–the world's richest and variegated type of mangrove-oriented atmospheric zone–and thereby causing abrupt destruction to the splendid natural wealth. It is really a matter of greatest shock not only to the nature lovers but also it puts a pertinent question on the human existence. These devastating activities of some groups of fishing personnel in the name of fishing should be looked into with specific emergency, and there is an immediate need to take effective measures on this hair-raising issue.

Besides these, an observer or traveller in the Sundarban river system would come across another event of indiscriminate fishing by the people as a whole which can easily be termed as the suicidal policy adopted by the common inhabitants towards their means of subsistence. The large-scale catching of *bagda* (*Penaens monodon*) spawns by the inhabitants of the region irrespective of age, sex and community has recently become an worried practice. The spawn collectors are depleting the natural resources of this region. They catch the spawns by nylon drag nets which entangle thousands of other frys alongwith the spawns. After picking up the spawns of *bagda* from amongst the numerous other frys everything are thrown away or are left at the place of selection. It simply means enormous wastage of aquatic species. It is true that getting no other alternative occupation the poor people of the region has been compelled to take up this practice of spawn collection finding its economic basis but at the same time it should be noted that if such malpractice goes on unabated, it would certainly exert a death-blow to the aquatic species as a whole. This immediate gain, in the long run, would bring irreparable loss to the land, water and people of Sundarban. In order to make an end to this mishap and at the same time to protect the people from economic hazards there must be a broad-based attempt to enquire into the total situation and thereby to make the people alert in conserving the ecological balance for their own benefit.

Sundarban region with its network of rivers, estuaries and creeks–their direct linkage with the Bay of Bengal is vastly resourceful in respect of fish crop of diversified nature but what is a matter of deep concern is that these are not being converted into resource base. In order to make it effectual there is an essential need of large-scale and integrated research work on the nature and extent of resources and the manner of utilisation considering the total layout and structural as well as functional attributes of the mangrove ecosystem and the behavioural pattern of human communities depending on fishing activities. In this programme of activities the direct participation of fishermen having age-old experience and profound love for the fish-oriented work is inevitably required and, therefore, microlevel studies on more and more fishing villages are essential. Owing to multiple adversities caused by various evil deeds and indiscriminate drawing of sustenance for day to day living the highly flourished and invaluable mangrove ecological settings of this region have faced a challenge in their very existence. To rear up the different varieties of fish and for the continuance of their effective and proper breeding patterns the mangrove ecosystem is an inevitable factor. The traditional fishermen equipped with practical knowledge and understanding of fish behaviour in the mangrove dominated background are expected to suggest different measures to develop the resource base and orient it according to the environmental situation, biological setting and cultural traditions of the region. In order to make this endeavour a success and fully effective an integrated investigation centering round the principal disciplines of human science putting requisite stress in the chain of activities participated by men, animals and nature is the basic and instanteous issue under the present circumstances.

In the sphere of Sundarban mangrove ecosystem there are, no doubt, large number and complicated type of problems, and the life of the fishermen working throughout the region in question is in a state of continuous hazards, anxieties and distress-oriented condition, but still there are lots of prospects which, if these can properly be utilised, would cause the overall flourishing of fish as well as the fishermen in the region under study. There is no denying of the fact that until and unless the fragile mangrove ecosystem of Sundarban is properly protected and thereby made it exclusively effective for the totalistic development of all sorts of plants and animals including human beings, the life and work of the fishermen cannot be improved to give them relief from ill-fated conditions of various nature. Fishing in Sundarban region, once highly productive, has recently faced complicated problems putting the fishermen in an atmosphere of dispair. What is needed most at the present moment is the immediate protection of ecological balance. Alongwith multitude of difficult situations the problems of fish and fishermen can best be solved to a considerable extent if the multiplex of biosphere is resisted from wanton and rapid destruction. The formation of Sundarban Biosphere

Reserve under the initiative of the Government and which has been formulated through the UNESCO's "The Man and Biosphere Programme" (MAB) certainly indicates a bold and positive step towards the inevitable act of rejuvenating the so far destructed mangrove ecosystem. But at the same time there is a specific need for the creation of consciousness in the minds of the people of all concerned living and drawing their sustenance within this ecological zone and thereby putting an end to the practice of wanton destruction of the valuable resources through people's participation. Besides the common problems of the region the fishermen pose their particular problematic situations which demand immediate solution considering the gravity of the situation. The basic problems, as stated below, must be dealt with the top priority for the cause of rejuvenation of the tradition-bound economic problems centering round fish and fishermen in Sundarban.

1. The prosperity of Sundarban in fish wealth is well-known, but it has been decreased, lately, to a considerable extent due to silting up of the rivers and estuaries as well as the havoc pollution of the Ganga.
2. Almost all the fishermen are over head and ears in debt and which in a gradual process has caused the transformance of the fishermen into the day labourers.
3. The fishermen are the victims of abject poverty. They get least opportunity to show their ingenious ways and means to explore new dimensions in fishing.
4. Despite various developments of natural science and their subsequent application to the diverse fields of human life the fishermen here are to work in the primitive way till today. They do not even get the timely cyclonic warning.
5. Uncertainty in catch, no doubt, results from various causes but the basic cause of failure in getting a good catch is the want of improved type of fishing

gear. The effort for mechanization in the fishing procedures is still in the hands of a few commercial fishing groups.

6. The matrix of fishing economy in Sundarban has recently been terrifically injured by indiscriminate fishing especially by the groups of commercially-oriented fish workers. This process of activities has caused a great deal in bringing an adverse effect to the ecological balance.
7. The large-scale catching of *bagda min* (seeds of tiger prawn) and the direct involvement of the local people, irrespective of age, sex and community, which is going on unabated is the indicative of a dreadful situation to appear very shortly in the sphere of Sundarban resource base formed in land and water.
8. In the overall trade pattern developed in the domain of fish markets through time and space there are many instances of exploitation of the actual producers. The middle men working as the linkage between the active producers and the final consumers most of the time go against the interests of the fishermen concerned.

The above are the principal types of problematic situations that are continuously faced by the fisherfolk. Mention may be made that these problems are multi-linked i.e. varied factors of different spheres are involved in these. Thus there is a profound need to evaluate these problems item by item and in the background of multiplex interaction between man and nature before suggesting any requisite solutions to these. The integrated study like the present one is expected to provide relevant data along with their analyses which would do a great deal not only in assessing the present conditions but also these would create a historical link between the past and the present dimensions facilitating the implementation of positive measures for the development of the fisherfolk so intimately associated with the mangrove ecosystem of Sundarban.

GLOSSARY OF LOCAL TERMS

Abad	–	Cultivated land
Arat	–	Godown
Aratdar	–	Godown owner
Amabasya	–	New moon
Ashram	–	Hermitage
Asvamedha Yagna	–	Horse sacrifice
Badaban	–	Mangrove forest
Badam	–	Sail of the boat
Bagdamin	–	Spawn of tiger prawn
Bahardar	–	Owner of the fishing unit
Barandala	–	Sacred winnowing fan containing articles for worship
Berajal	–	Siene net
Bhasan	–	Float-cum-signal made of bamboo
Bhata	–	Lowtide (ebb)
Bintijal	–	A type of bag net
Buno	–	Forest dweller
Bouley	–	Person versed with charm
Chandijal	–	Gill net
Char	–	Submerged sand bar
Charandar	–	Agents of wholesalers
Chutor	–	Carpenter
Dadan	–	Advance payment
Dala puja	–	Ceremonial tying of the first two pieces of nets
Danri	–	Oarsman
Dashahara	–	The sacred day of descending of the Ganga on earth
Dhal	–	Lowest land soil
Dhopa	–	Washerman
Dhrubatara	–	Polestar
Dhuti	–	Lion cloth, male garment
Doania	–	A canal connecting two large rivers
Dubochar	–	Submerged land during spring tide

Fakir	–	Muslim mendicant
Gab	–	Mangosteen
Gachtala	–	Underneath of a tree
Galui	–	Prow
Gamcha	–	Napkin
Gangama	–	Mother Ganges
Gazi Sahib	–	A Muslim pir
Ghat	–	Earthen pot
Ghaat	–	A particular spot from where water vehicles are anchored
Ghai	–	Spot where net is set
Goala	–	Milkman
Gunin	–	Witchdoctor
Hala	–	Depression
Hanria	–	Rice beer
Hatjali	–	Hand operated net
Hatkhola	–	Place where weekly market is held
Jaider	–	Boat owner
Jajman	–	Client
Jala	–	Big earthen pot
Jantal	–	Annual ceremony of Banbibi
Jatra	–	Dramatic entertainment
Jele	–	Fisherman
Jele dingi	–	Fishing boat
Joar	–	Spring tide
Jotedar	–	Tenure holder
Kumar	–	Blacksmith
Kantadar	–	Weighman
Kastha Devi	–	Goddess of wood
Khari	–	Maximum depth of water at the spot of net setting
Kheplajal	–	Cast net
Khuntejal	–	A special net for sele fishing
Khunti	–	Fishing camp; a piece of wooden log
Kirtan	–	Devotional song
Krishnapaksha	–	Darker half of the month
Kumar	–	Pot making caste
Mahajan	–	Moneylender
Majar	–	Sacred place where the mortal remains of the saints are buried
Majhi	–	Helmsman
Makar bahini	–	Carried by shark
Makar Sankranti	–	Last day of the Bengali month *Pous* (December-January)

Mangal ghat	–	Sacred earthen pot
Mantra	–	Incantations
Mela	–	Fair
Moyra	–	Confectioner caste
Muhuri	–	Commission agent
Muni	–	Sage
Napit	–	Barber
Nauka	–	Plank boat
Nishitara	–	Midnight star
Ojha	–	Magician
Oolu	–	A kind of holy sound created by the vibration of the tongue
Paikar	–	Wholesalers
Panchayat	–	Adhoc committee for administration
Para	–	Ward of the village
Patal	–	Infernal region or nether world
Patitpabani	–	Purifier of the defiled
Pir	–	Muslim saint
Pirsthan	–	Shrine of the Muslim saint
Pradip	–	Earthen lamp
Pous sankranti	–	Last day of the Bengali month *Pous*
Prasad	–	Ritual offering of food
Puja	–	Worship
Purnima	–	Full moon
Rasatal	–	Infernal region or nether world
Sagar	–	Sea
Sal	–	A kind of plant, Shorea robusta
Sandhyatara	–	Evening star
Sankhadhawani	–	A sound created by blowing of couch shell
Satamukhi	–	Having hundred mouths
Satjali	–	Name of a star
Sattara	–	Group of seven stars
Selejal	–	Stationary net used for sele fishing
Shabar	–	Fishing unit
Sukhlapaksha	–	Brighter half of the month
Suktara	–	Pole star
Sunri	–	Wine distilling caste
Tanti	–	Weaver
Telsindur	–	Vermilion mixed with oil
Than	–	Spot, shrine
Tithi	–	Luner position
Tulsi	–	A sacred plant, Ocimum sanctum
Urs	–	Birthday ceremony
Vesal	–	Sacred fire
Zamindar	–	Landlord

BIBLIOGRAPHY

Ahmed, M. (1996), "A Monograph on village Nuagolabandh, Village Survey Series No. 5", *Census of India*, Vol. 12, Part, 6 Orissa Govt. Press, Cuttack.

Bagchi, K. (1944), "*The Ganges Delta*", Calcutta, Calcutta University Press.

Banerjee, Anuradha (1998), "*Environment, Population and Human Settlements of Sundarban Delta*", New Delhi, Concept Publishing Company.

Basu, M.N. (1946), "Economic adjustment and suggestions for improvement of fish, fishing and fishermen in a Bengal village", *Calcutta Reviews,* March.

Bhattacharya, A. (1947), "The Tiger Cult and its literature in Lower Bengal", *Man in India,* Vol. 27(2), Ranchi.

Bhattacharya, R. (1975), "Settlement Pattern in Deltaic West Bengal", *Geographical Review of India,* Vol. 37(4), Calcutta.

Blake, B.A. (1970), "*Technological change among the coastal marine fishermen of Madras State*", Wisconsin, University of Wisconsin Press.

Bonnerjea, Biren (1938), "Ugrian Fishing Implements and Some Indian Parallels", *Man in India,* Vol. 18(4), Ranchi.

Bose, A.N. (1989), "Fisheries Development in Coastal West Bengal: Socio-economic Implications", *Coastal Zone Management of West Bengal,* Sea Explorer's Institute, Calcutta.

Census of India, (1981), "Series 23, West Bengal Part XIIIB", *District Census Handbook,* 24-Parganas.

Chakraborti, Kalyan (1989), "Development Perspective of Coastal Eco-system of Sundarban Forest", *Coastal zone Management of West Bengal,* Sea Explorer's Institute, Calcutta.

Chakravorty, Sujit and Irani Sen (1999), "In Troubled Waters", in *The Sunday Statesman*, 26th April, Calcutta.

Chattopadhyay, Haraprasad (1999), *"The Mystery of the Sundarbans"*, Calcutta, A. Mukherjee & Co. Pvt. Ltd.

Chattopadhyay, Kumar (1990), "Social Ecology of a Forest Delta", *Man in India,* Vol. 70(3), Ranchi.

Chattopadhyay, Kumar (1995), *"The Desperate Delta"*, Social Ecology of Sundarban, New Delhi, Gyan Publishing House.

Chandhuri, A.B. and K. Chakraborti (1974), "Wild life biology of Sundarban Forests–Bioecological Study on Fish and Fish Researches", *Science and Culture,* Vol. 40(3), University of Calcutta, Calcutta.

Chaudhuri, M.K. and others (1987), "Impact of Coastal and Marine Fishery Schemes in the Districts of Midnapur and 24-Parganas", *Bulletin of the Cultural Research Institute,* Vol. 17(3-4), Calcutta.

Couper, A.B. (Ed.) (1989), *"Development and Social Change in the Pacific Islands"*, London, Routledge and Kegan Paul.

Das, Amal Kumar and others, (1981), *"A Focus on Sundarban"*, Calcutta, Editions India.

Dalton, E.T. (1872), "Descriptive Ethnology of Bengal", Calcutta, Bengal Government Press.

Das, Tarak Chandra (2000), "The Cultural Significance of Fish in Bengal", in *Through the Vistas of Life and Lore,* ed. by R.M. Sarkar, Calcutta, Punthi Pustak. (First pub. in 1931 & 1932).

Datta, J.M. (1959), "Some Practices of usages amongst the fishermen of Panihati-Sukchar, 24-Parganas", *Man in India,* Vol. 39(2), Ranchi.

De, Barun (ed.) (1994), *"West Bengal District Gazetteers"*, 24-Parganas, Govt. of West Bengal, Calcutta.

De, Rathindranath (1990), *"The Sundarbans"*, Calcutta, Oxford University Press.

Dwivedi, S.N. (1980), *"Socio-economic Problems of Fishermen"*, Bombay, Central Institute of Fisheries Education.

Dyson, J. (1977), *"Business in Great Water–the Story of British Fishermen,"* London, Angus and Robertson.

Fergussan, J. (1963), "Delta of the Ganga", Quarterly Journal of the *Geological Society of India,* Vol. 13, Part I, Calcutta.

Firth, R. (1966), *"Malay Fishermen–their Peasant Economy"*, (Revised and enlarged), London, Routledge and Kegal Paul.

Frasher, T.M. (Jr.) (1966), *"Fishermen of South Thailand: The Malay Villagers"*, New York, Holt, Rinehart and Winston, Inc.

Ghosh, Basudebdatta and Bakul Rani Ghosh (1989), "Geography of Sundarban–A unique part of the Biggest Delta in the World", *Applied Geography,* S.P. Chatterjee Commemorative volume, MAMTO, Monograph No. 9, Calcutta.

Goswami, M.C. and C.H. Singh (1973), "Cooperatives of the Fishermen of Thonga village in Manipur", *Man in India*, Vol. 53(1), Ranchi.

Guljari, M. and Chhedilal Sahani (1958), *"Fishermen's Profession and the Problems of their Cooperatives"*, Lucknow, Kandhri Bazar.

Gupta, A.C. (1957), "The Sundarbans–its problems and possibilities", *Indian Forester,* Vol. 83.

Gupta, K.G. (1908), "Report on the results of enquiry into the fishery matters in Europe and America, Calcutta", *The Bengal Secretariat Book Depot.*

Gupta, R.K. (1979), *"Essays in Economic Anthropology"*, Calcutta, Institute of Social Research and Applied Anthropology.

Gulati, L. (1980), *"The Role of Women from Fishing Households, Case Study of Kerala Fishing Village"*, Centre for Development Studies, working paper No. 144, Trivandrum.

Gulati, L. (1981), *"Fishing Technology and Women"*, Part I, Centre for Development Studies, working paper no. 155, Trivandrum

Gulati, L. (1984), "Technological Change and Women's Work participation and demographic behaviour" A case study of three fishing villages", *Economic and Political Weekly,* Vol. 19(49)

Hardesty, D.L. (1977), *"Ecological Anthropology"*, New York, Johan, Willy and Sons.

Hawley, A.H. (1950), *"Human Ecology, New York"*, Ronald Ross.

Hazra, D. (1967), "Marine Fisherfolk of Gujarat: Preliminary exploration", Seminar on *Research Programme in Cultural Anthropology and Related Discipline,* ed. by S.C. Sinha, Anthropological Survey of India, Calcutta.

Hora, S.L. (1940), "Life History and Wandering of Hilsa in Bengal Waters", *Journal of the Royal Asiatic Society of Bengal,* Vol. 6(2).

Hora, S.L. (1948), "Knowledge of the Ancient Hindu concerning fish and fisheries of India", *Journal of the Royal Asiatic Society of Bengal,* Vol. 14(1).

Hora, S.L. (1952), "Fish in the Ramayana", *Journal of the Asiatic Society of Bengal,* Vol. 18(2).

Hora, S.L. (1953), "Knowledge of the Ancient Hindu concerning fish and fisheries of India", *Journal of the Royal Asiatic Society of Bengal,* Vol. 19(8).

Hora, S.L. (1954), "Proverbs and popular sayings concerning the Hilsa fish current in Bengal", *Journal of the Asiatic Society of Bengal,* Vol. 20(1).

Hunter, W.W. (1875), *"A Statistical Account of Bengal",* Vol. I, District of 24-Parganas and Sundarban, London, Trubner and Co.

Hutton, J.H. (1963), *"Caste in India",* 4th Edition, Bombay, Oxford University Press (First edition in 1931).

Jhingran, V.G. (1982), *"Fish and Fisheries of India,* Delhi, Hindustan Publishing Corporation.

Kannan, R. and others (2001), "Socio-economic Status of Coral Reef Resource users of Pamban Region, Gulf of Manner, South India", *Man in India,* vol. 81(1+2), Ranchi.

Klausen, A.M. (1968), *"Kerala Fishermen and Indo-Norwegian Pilot Project",* Bombay, Asia Publishing House.

Lal, K.B. (1961), *"An Introduction to Fishing Gear Technology",* Delhi, Metropolitan Book.

Mathur, P.R.G. (1978), *"The Mappila Fisherfolk of Kerala",* A Study in the interrelationship between Habitat, Technology, Economy, Society and Culture, Trivandrum, Kerala Historical Society.

Mathur, P.R.G. (1983), "Religion and Society among the Mappila Fishermen of Kerala", *Man in India,* Vol. 63(2), Ranchi.

Mitra, S.N. (1945), "A note on the estuarine and foreshore fisheries in the Sundarban Forest Division" Calcutta, Govt. of West Bengal.

Mondal, A.K. and R.K. Ghosh (1989), *"Sundarban: A Socio-bioecological Study",* Calcutta, Book Land Pvt. Ltd.

Moses, T.S. (1929), "The Valayans of Pamban," *Man in India,* Vol. 9(1), Ranchi.

Mukherjee, B. (1969), "The Noliyas of Puri and their sea fishing organisation", *Bulletin of the Anthropological Survey of India,* Vol. 17(3) Calcutta.

Mukherjee, B. (1979), "Comparative Study of the Fisherfolk: Coastal West Bengal and Orissa", in *Research Programmes in Cultural Anthropology and Allied Disciplines,* ed. by S.C. Sinha, Anthropological Survey of India, Calcutta.

Mukhopadhyay, A. (1968), "Fishermen of the Sundarbans, *Frontier,* August 24, 1(20).

Naskar, Kumudranjan and Apurba Ghosal (1989), "Mangrove Forest of Sundarban, its Impact on estuarine fisheries", *Coastal Zone Management of West Bengal,* Sea Explorer's Institute, Calcutta.

Nayak, N. (1996), "Women's participation in fisheries", *The Unique Struggle of the Fisherworkers,* vol. 2(7+8).

Neogi, Tushar K. (1966), *"Tiger Cult of the Sundarvans",* Calcutta, Anthropological Survey of India.

Neogi, Tushar K. (1987), *"Aspect of Flokcults in South Bengal,"* Calcutta, Anthropological Survey of India.

Noble, Alexander (1980), *"The Scottish inshore fishing vessel design, construction and repair",* Ed. by Eric Makee, Greenwich, National Maritime Museum.

Norr, K.L. (1975), "The Organisation of Coastal Fishing in Tamil Nadu", *Ethnology,* Vol. 14 (3+4).

O' Malley, L.S.S. (1914), *"Bengal District Gazetteers",* 24-Parganas, Calcutta, The Bengal Secretariat Book Depot.

Pal, Ashis Kr. (1996), "Land and Environment of the Sundarban", *Samaj-Tattva* Vol. 2 (1), Calcutta.

Panda, S.N. (1971), "Economy and Society among the Fishermen of Coastal Orissa," *Man in India,* Vol. 51(2), Ranchi.

Pargiter, F.F. (1989), "The Sundarbans", *Calcutta Review,* Vol. 89.

Pramanik, S.K. (1993), *"Fishermen Community of Coastal Villages of West Bengal",* Jaipur, Rawat Publications.

Pramanik, S.K. (1994), "Work participation of fisherwomen: A case study of two fishing villages in West Bengal", *Man in India,* vol. 74(1), Ranchi.

Pramanik, S.K. (1996), "Women Dryfish Workers in Sundarban– A look into their working spirit and levels of involvement, *Man in India,* vol. 76(2), Ranchi.

Pramanik, S.K. (1992), "The Effect of Mechanization on Fishermen of Hara and Sultanpur", *Socialist Perspective,* Vol. 20(4), Calcutta.

Punekar, V.B. (1959), *"The Son Kolis of Bombay",* Bombay, Popular Book Depot.

Razaq, K.A. (1970), "Marine Fisherfolk of Andhra: A preliminary exploration", *Research Programme in Cultural Anthropology and Allied Disciplines,* ed. by S.C. Sinha, Calcutta, Anthropological Survey of India.

Roychaudhuri, B. (1969), "Some fishing communities of West Bengal", *Man in India,* Vol. 49(3), Ranchi.

Roychaudhuri, B. (1980), *"The Moon and the Net",* A Study of a Transient Community of Fishermen at Jambudwip, Calcutta, Anthropological Survey of India.

Saha, K.C. (1970), *"Fisheries of West Bengal",* Calcutta, West Bengal Government Press.

Samuel, C.T. (1968), *"Marine Fisheries in India, Oceanographic Laboratory",* Cochin, University of Kerala.

Sarkar, R.M. (1999), "Patterns and Perspective of a Fishing village in Deltaic Bengal", *Man in India,* Vol. 79 (3+4), Ranchi.

Sarkar, R.M. (2001), "Work and Understanding in Dasherchwak– A fishing village in Mangrove Ecosystem, *Man in India,* Vol. 81 (1+2), Ranchi.

Selvaraj, C. (1975) *"Small Fishermen in Tamil Nadu",* Madras, Sangam Publishers.

Sen, Aparajita (1992), "Mangrove Ecosystem in India with special reference to the Sundarban, *The Observer,* Vol. 32, Calcutta.

Srivastava, U.K. and S. Vattasale (Ed.) (1987), *"Brackish Water Aquaculture Development in India: Status and task ahead",* New Delhi, Concept Publishing Company.

Stirrat, R.L. (1988), *"On the Beach: Fishermen, Fishwives and Fish Traders in post colonial Lanka",* Delhi, Hindustan Publishing Corporation.

Subha Rao, N. (1988), *"Mechanization and Marine Fishermen",* A Case Study of Visakhapatnam, New Delhi, Northern Book Centre.

Suryanarayana, M. (1977), *"Marine Fisherfolk of North-East Coastal Andhra Pradesh"*, Calcutta, Anthropological Survey of India.

Thompson, P. (1985), "Women in fishing: the roots of power between the sexes", *Comparative Studies in Society and History,* Vol. 27.

Trivedi, R.K. (1967), "Sutrapada Fishing Hamlet", *Village Survey Monograph,* 1961 Census, Publications Divisions, Vol. 5, Delhi, Manager of Publications.

INDEX

N

O